TWO-MINUTE NOODLE

A Backpacker's Tale
by

Howie Cobb

*

Hambledon Press, Hambledon

Hambledon Press, Woodlands Rd, Hambledon,
Surrey GU8 4HW

Published by Hambledon Press, Hambledon 1996

Made and printed in UK by
Biddles Ltd, Guildford, Surrey.

Many thanks to the following people for their invaluable help
before, during and after this trip:
Steve Blackman
Andy & Martin at Clarion
Desiree Werner
Brian Harding and family
Andrew Calvert and family
My family

I held Chantal close, kissed her one more time, before she jumped in and was obscured by the smoked glass windows of the minibus. I was standing in the middle of the Khao San Road waving, as the bus disappeared round the corner, and it wobbled slightly through my unshed tears. I wasn't to know then that I would never see her again. Nor would her family or friends

This book is dedicated to the memory of

Chantal Geets
Neerweg, Belgium
(11/3/68 - 31/3/95)

with whom I had the privilege of travelling
through Thailand, and falling in love.
Returning home after a year backpacking, her
last flight,from Bangkok, crashed over Romania.
Two hours from home.

Sleep well my little Flem.

CONTENTS

DEPARTURE

THE 747 banked right: hard: it's wingtip neatly picking a Guns & Roses T shirt, washed that morning, from a line in Jardine Street before jiggling down amongst the buildings to bellyflop into Hong Kong.

Along Tsimsatsui, gargantuan signs snarled and spat neon across at each other using the wet roads as a palette. Raindrops the size of grapes hurtled down at an angle of 37 degrees, bouncing back up to knee height. Like eggs carried by unseen ants, umbrellas scurried up and down to find their nest.

Lying prone beneath a ceiling fan that whirled *chuck-a-chuck-a chuck*, pressing me into the mattress, I looked back over my first day in Hong Kong and then further back to Gatwick on a chill January day.

"...last call for the Aids trust ski party!" rattled from the loudspeaker. embarrassed giggles, stifled chuckles and barefaced laughter rippled round the departure lounge as the irony of the statement sank in. But it made me think deep, for the rest of the week, while the shiny Alpine air blew through my head like an enema. How long do we have? I should go: go on the trip of a lifetime, before the lifetime runs out.

So that's why I'm here about to tell of first day at school, new pals, rules and games. Tears and laughter.

*

CHUNGKING MANSIONS, HONG KONG

As THE sliding doors of the air terminal opened, the heat wrapped round me like a poultice and dragged me silently screaming towards hundreds of oriental faces. None of which were waiting for me.

The rivulets of sweat from my face gathered momentum, joining the streams from my armpits, and raced to the pool at my feet. Splashing onward, I found the bus terminal, the correct fare and destination, and my first hostel tout. I feigned indifference as I slipped my backpack to the ground and effected a thousand yard stare.

"You wan' hostel?"

"No" I said guiltily, as I lied to the first oriental I'd met. While he tackled a Jap, I tried to slip past him onto the bus.

"How much you pay?" he rounded on me.

"Single room with bath?" I asked, destroying my alibi.

"200 dollar!" he snapped. Virgin back-packer I was, but not that stupid.

"100 dollars!" I offered in his general direction, my glasses being steamed up.

"Dormitory!" he spat at me.."only dormitory for 100 dollars."

I sneered as he turned back to his Japanese 'kill' to help him on the bus. As we headed towards Tsimsatsui I stared out the window past the back of his Beatle-wig haircut. He turned and wrote behind a veiled hand "150". I wasn't going to lose my first barter so I whispered "120" as quiet as Tom Jones singing 'Delilah'. He winced, put a finger to his lips and signalled OK. "Yesss!" I'd done it.

Then, behind the ever present hiding hand, he whispered properly,

"Kee quiet! I charge him 180 dollar" gesturing at the Jap.

We tumbled from the bus at Nathan Rd into the sort of deluge that flattens crops and whole acres of Bangladeshis. The tout disappeared into the storm with his Jap, shouting back, "You go with her!" Looking round I could see no 'her' but noticing a movement below I saw my backpack crawling onto the back of a woman the height of cricket stumps. Like a tortoise on speed it scurried into the building, pushing through the melee, bowled aside two huge Africans and nestled in the corner of the lift, while I watched the illuminated numbers above me climb to fourteen.

The accommodation in Hong Kong was multi-layered. At the top end the international hotels and top class hostels sat smugly on Hong

Kong island. Some quality hotels flirted around Kowloon which also contained the majority of the travellers' hostels. The epicentre of this phenomenon centred on Tsimsatsui and here, slumming along Nathan Road, lay my first night's destination.

Nathan Road. A six lane neon disaster with a weather system of it's own making. When dodging along the pavement the condensed waste from thousands of air-conditioning units descended like a summer shower. Even at 95 degrees the refreshment value was diminished by possible disease content. Along with the tailors' touts and the icy blasts from A/C shops turning you hot & cold, the pavement competed with the road as the most unpleasant place to walk. I took my chances with the traffic.

Midway along this lunatic thoroughfare, under it's very own brown cloud, smouldered Chunking Mansions. Sixteen stories of fire hazard and filth that housed the escapees of Europe, Africa and Australasia in any nook and cranny left between the sweat shops, Indian messes and knocking shops. The accommodation prices lowered as the floors rose, due to the lift queues and reduced chances of escaping a fire whilst racing the rats to the ground floor.

So it was with some trepidation that I followed my backpack into a cupboard in 'The Garden Hostel', fourteenth floor. The room was 3m x 2m, including the bed and the bathroom, and the ceiling fan threatened to trim my flat-top if I stood on tiptoes. I felt as though I'd taken a swig from the bottle marked 'Drink me'. The shower and basin were above the toilet and allowed the possibility of having a shit, shower and shave at the same time. It was a haven though. It was privacy and although I knew I would have to move to cheaper dormitory rooms the next day I was going to sleep well this night.

So, laying there, looking back over my first day, I wondered at my own audacity. I was ill-equipped for such an adventure. Well above the average age for backpackers, I was carrying with me the mental scars of divorce, bankruptcy and a parcel of broken hearts in a spotty hanky on a stick. I had no idea of how backpacking worked, what hostels were like, how to get around, and I was going to do it on my own!

A fresh film of sweat washed over me at the thought of it. But then the reason I left came back to me. Things could only get better. Couldn't they? And I wasn't running away, I was running *to* something. I just didn't know what it was yet. I turned onto my right side to sleep. I turned to the left, then right, face down, onto my back, sat up. Thoughts of home had crept back into my head like Pol Pot re-entering Cambodia. You'd like to ignore it but you can't. But they were good.

So good they hurt, and lying back down it wasn't the salt from the sweat that stung my eyes. Sleep crept in.

Refreshed, the next morning, I apologised to the owner for being unable to carry on accepting his luxurious hospitality, loaded up my backpack and with glasses steaming trudged one block north through the shower of Legionnaire's disease and cut price tailors' leaflets to Mirador Mansions. Sixteen stories of fire hazard and filth, 'The Garden Hostel' was only on the third floor. I was going down in the world.

It was here I made my first breakthrough. Mirroring my thinking, Phil had spent his first night in a shoebox in Chungking, whilst I was in my cupboard, and was now moving to the dorms. As I arrived at the reception a myopic Indian was processing Phil, who looked the epitome of calm, whilst I slipped my backpack to the floor with ease due to gravity and sweat. Mohammed's eyes seemed fixed on a cockroach to the left of the shower, or an insect stuck behind his glasses, I couldn't tell which. He dismissed Phil with a grunt and a key and I stepped up to sign in. His eyes didn't move. despite the fact that my hand was shaking fit to turn milk into butter. His aide stared just as hard, but at the spidery line I was producing. Having bartered the price down by absolutely nothing, and pulling out my wallet, I chaotically sprayed the reception with small change. A coin with a crinkly edge like a mince pie rolled across the room and jumped the threshold of the shower room indicating the point of Mohammed's long hard stare.

There, peeking out from below a towel, whilst it's owner bent forward clipping her nails, was a freshly laundered twat, puffy and fluffy from it's shower. Mohammed wasn't as myopic as I thought. Whilst their attention was diverted I shoved the offending kleg back into my sweat-limp wallet with fingers that felt the size of bratwurst. I left the crinkly coin in the shower room.

Almost bigger than my ensuite room at the previous 'Garden Hostel', this room had no toilet and four bunks, not so you could shower sitting or shit standing, but change clothes simultaneously if more than two left their bed at the same time and stepped into the communal area. Phil, shuffling as far as possible into the room, looked relieved to have another 'new boy' in the camp and climbed onto the top left bunk to leave me room to 'move in'. Beneath him sat a sparsely thatched man, collars up around his chin as he struggled to tie a knot. The white shirt was translucent with sweat by the time his black patent shoes were laced, and with a thick suit jacket, he cloaked the misery from the public eye.

Jumping up with a..."How do I look?" he took in our puzzled expressions. "Ah! I'm a film extra tonight, must dash chaps, Giles is the name, ta-ta." Squeezing his formidable head back round the door as he departed, he announced, "The other bod's name is Keith."

Keith wasn't actually present in the other lower bunk but, like a murder victim's chalk outline, his body area was marked with clothes, yellowing newspapers, old takeaway menus, educational aids, sex aids and probably, Aids. I saw later that Keith did indeed fit very snugly into the jelly mould he'd created. It was one of the very rare occasions that his activities coincided with the rest of the world's time frame. Keith slept all day and at ten to four, ten minutes before his alarm rang, would rise from his pit, fully clothed, clean his teeth and leave to teach Japanese kids English, leaving us to turn off his alarm. After work he would go onto nightschool to teach locals English, and then to the cinema complex at 1am to watch two films: onto a couple of bars and back to his hole by about 8am. What worried Phil and I more than his timescale was his choice of teaching material. There, piled amongst the cinema tickets, bar receipts and food wrappers were photocopied pages from 'Viz' magazine, starring 'Cockney Wankah!', 'Buster Gonad and his unfeasibly large testicles!' and 'The Fat slags'; Each copy with the pupil's name at the head of the page. I was going to ask him, but we were never awake at the same time.

I took the remaining bunk next to the window. Was this good? Why hadn't Phil taken the window bed? Why was I here? I hiked my backpack up onto the bed; my brand new backpack which I had cunningly dragged around the garden before leaving home to indicate how experienced a traveller I was. It looked like a new backpack that had been dragged around a garden.

The mattress was the thickness of a Jacob's Cream Cracker and the consistency of a cracker soaked in sweat and piss. This was in-effectively masked by the thousand micron sheet which was clean on arrival but soaked with your own sweat and body tissue within 30 seconds. Lying down, the sheet attached itself to your body and the moisture aroused the mattress into life like a desert orchid blooming after an unexpected shower. Four of such outputs created a cloud that hovered midway between upper and lower bunk. Thankfully at high altitude, and next to the window, I could escape this smog until either a fart or rapid turnover from a body below would elevate it level with my nostrils. With the backpack taking up half the bed and the sheet wrapping itself around, sleep resembled Chinese acrobatics, where one false move would disturb the hovering cloud. It seemed that Phil's first night had been sleepless so he was going to try and catch up by going to bed early. I had already formed a deep dislike of my bed and I needed food, beer, experience. I decided to go out.

Pausing a while in the common room, a very beat room with a motley collection of vinyl chairs gathered round an old telly, a girl leant over my shoulder and exclaimed, laughing from the depths of Adelaide,

"Jeezus mayt, y'wife's a bit of a mongrel!!" I'd been told by other travellers at home to carry photos of family, friends, house...anything to show to villagers, locals, other travellers so I'd packed fondly into my wallet - my family, my Volkswagen camper; and foremost on my mind and in the clear window at the front, 'Bumble'... my Border-Collie, as handsome as any star of 'One man & his Dog'. With a smile on his face, head turned to the camera I wasn't to realise how appealing he was to others and eventually came to regard it as my second passport.. Bumble was normally 18 inches from my legs on an invisible wire or lying with his head on my feet, so at the end of every check.; backpack, passport, tickets, wallet, cameras, I would halt. God, what have I forgotten?...I know, it's Bumble, he's not here. Which was why I was staring into the wallet missing the wee boy a tad.

"Aagh Jeez, that's a choice dog mayt! What y'doin?. M'name's Catherine. Not Cathy. I'm goin t'work, comin? Get y'a cupple a beers free. I'll introduce ya t'the girls. C'mon then, move y'arse!"

Well you would, wouldn't you?

We hoofed it along, Catherine shoulderbarging the tailors' touts aside. "Y'bin travelling long?..one day? shit yer a virgin ...bet y'not a real one... y'look like y've been around...get y'leaflet out m'face mayt!!" We hopped on a number something bus.

"I hate Hong Kong business men with their bloody mobile phones" said Catherine with venom, "Look at this drongo over here with two!"

The Armani suited Hong Kong trendy had a mobile slung on each hip like a gunslinger and as I looked he reached for one, tapped *bip, bip, bip, beep, bip, beep*, and put it to his ear. At this moment the other, still in it's holster, rang, and he looked at the two of them in turn. Catherine was off. Pushing her face to within inches of his she bellowed..."Y've rung y'self y'dumbfuck!"

When I left the bar, hours and many free beers later, I needed food. I'd needed food for hours. I wasn't going to succumb to the Big Mac with it's universally nauseating dill pickle. I picked a Chinese joint, menu in Chinese, full of Chinese, and sat at the round table in the centre of the room, alone. The menu had subtitles, the tea was free and bottomless and I sucked, slurped and chopsticked with the best of them. Old friend, beer, had taken me by the hand and led me through the streets of Hong Kong, depositing me in probably one of the best eateries around. Returning to the hostel common room, the other inmates were gathered round the TV noshing McDonalds out of styrofoam trays or two minute noodles from mugs. Phil, awake but groggy asked... "Where did you eat Howie?"

"At some Chinese restaurant on Cameron Rd,"

"No, I was the only Westerner in there"

"No, it was bloody good"

"15 dollars..about one pound sterling"

Several pairs of eyes looked into their soggy, tasteless meals and back at me. Someone muttered..."I can't eat that foreign shit, you don't know what you're eating," and others just stared into the void in the corner called TV..

"Well, I'm off to bed" I said with a smug smile, "I've got a busy day tomorrow" and thought...if I was a virgin, I've just lost my cherry. I know it was only Hong Kong, but perhaps I could do this thing yet.

*

It was a bull-terrier of a day with a hot, steamy wind buffeting the harbour, causing the khaki waves to snap at the ferries and sampans.

Victoria peak was being strangled by mist.

A quick phone call home, to confirm I'd arrived, brought bad news. No, everybody was well, but Bumble wasn't eating. They'd had to take him back from my friends who were looking after him, until they could get him better. I panicked, and then thought - 'he's a dog, I can't let him rule my life'. Well I'd be here a few days yet; if I had to, I could fly home.

Phil and I were out sightseeing and seeing more than we'd bargained for. Before we'd even left Nathan Rd. we realised that, scattered like jewels on a stable floor, were dozens of flawless Chinese girls with skin of honeyed porcelain and clothes that revealed nothing; but shouted of the beauty below. The latest fashion was a skintight black skirt that ended just two inches below the plimsoll line and black stockings that failed to meet it by three inches. The resulting area of bare flesh had two effects. One...to produce a new layer of sweat due to increased metabolism and second...a tendency to bump into lamposts, small Chinese, or any other sights we should have been looking for.

But these were 'bought' girls, bought flats, bought clothes, bought with big money, and the pitiful amount in *my* pocket would never have caught their eye. The two most beautiful that I'd seen yet, sprang from

11

an ice-cold store that screamed - 'Gold cards only!' and sashayed down Nathan, seemingly a few inches above the ground. I followed slowly for a couple of hundred yards, feasting my eyes, then before I got too greedy, speeded up to come abreast of them. Steady. As I edged up to them, the nearest oriental beauty let loose,

"It's not my forlt ees got the fuckin 'ump, ees bin like it orl day, wot am I meant ter do ay?"

I'd cleverly arrived on the Friday of a holiday weekend, so I had to wait till Tuesday to pick up my Chinese visa. But it gave me time to acclimatise to the noise, heat, humidity; to being away.

Phil and I spent the weekend wandering the island, on foot, bus and tram, funicular up the mountain, ferries round the harbour. And though the water lapped lazily, invitingly, onto some half decent beaches, the pollution warning boards showed 'high' so we stayed dry. Leaving the cross harbour ferry, heading north, a strange sound grew. A twittering. Turning a corner the sound became a noise, a clamour. As we entered the square it was a deafening screeching, like a huge aviary in panic.

The square and surrounding streets were barely visible under a host of women, sat in circles, groups, clusters, all picnicking. As we wove our way through, they flirted with us, shouted things that made their friends giggle, invited us to sit with them and eat. We stopped several times to talk and took small tidbits out of politeness. They were all Fillipino maids. Sunday afternoon was their only time off. They worked constantly and lived in at their employer's, alone. All the money that they earnt was sent back home to their family, where they had children and husbands who they may not have seen for years. So this afternoon was their's, where they could talk of home, enjoy the company of each other; every single one of them.... 'Maid in HongKong'.

On the Monday we visited the mammoth floating restaurant in Stanley harbour, catching the Dragon races. Then, taking a water taxi, we checked out the new Airport site where Phil would be working, the very next morning. Later, at the arse-end of yet another fine Chinese meal and many Linquan beers, we toasted each other.

"Here's to you old mate!"

"Yes, it seems like it, doesn't it?... Cheers."

*

I LAY, hands behind head, pondering the useless air/con unit, and registered that Bumble was at last eating at home, and I could pick up my visa to China the next morning. Time to move.

12

"Do you have to pay to get it working", I asked, to nobody in particular.

"No," replied Giles, seeing the object of my gaze... "I think it's just knackered". Whilst I twiddled the knobs in vain, Phil hit the switch by the door that wasn't for the light, the fan or room service, and the unit vrroooomed into life.

"Bugger me!" said Giles. He'd been in this sweatbox a month.

"Keith told me it didn't work!!". Keith had been in this sweatbox three months.

Giles resembled Mister Potato-head, a toy we loved and often found in our Christmas stockings. When his head appeared at birth, the midwife had stuck the oversize ears haphazardly on the sides, selected the larger of the two noses from the box and put it roughly in the middle, between the eyes, leaving hair to be supplied by the potato sprouting at a later date. This one however, failed to sprout at all over the top, at any stage in it's life. Fortunately for Giles the midwive had lacked a sense of humour and neglected to use the Groucho Marx glasses and moustache. As with all potato men, the whole head ensemble overshadowed the body and hunched forward. To balance this caricature though, Giles had been blessed with intelligence, a bubbly sense of humour, honesty, and an infectious grin; even if they'd used a giant parsnip or water melon, instead of a potato, I would still have liked him very much indeed. Which is why, when Giles asked me to help him, I jumped at the chance.

"Howie; didn't you say that you worked in advertising?"

"Yep...in my old life I had my own agency."

"Well, I can't just go on being a film extra, I need a proper job. At last night's filming, two priests grabbed a woman thief, who was being chased, and beat her up. One had her in a headlock between his legs while the other punched her."

"Was this a martial arts film or something?" I asked, puzzled.

"Good God no!" laughed Giles, "these were just spectators!... I've applied for a marketing job and you've got to help me get it. Help me rewrite my CV. Give me some of those whatsits, you know, thingamee phrases."

"You mean........."

"Exactly old chap. You spout 'em, I'll write 'em down, chuck a few of 'em around at the interview eh!, pretend I know what I'm going on about." Giles scribbled like a maniac, almost dribbling with delight and exclaiming to each new one I dragged up.

"OPT's-opportunities to see" ...."Excellent!"

"Publication frequency"........."Brilliant!!"

13

"Bullet points".................."Oh yes!!!"

"Demographic distribution"........"Bloody marvellous!!!!" And then I finished him off with.

. "Full page, full colour bleed, first right hand page opposite letters" ....and I swear he almost swooned.

"Now, what do they mean old chap?"

We re-shaped and re-wrote the CV, bought a new printout from a girl in a hostel one floor up, and Giles rushed out to present it by hand to the company. Returning, breathless, sweatsoaked, he asked.

"Thanks a million old chap, how can I ever return the favour?"

"You can give *me* some advice. You've been up to Yangshuo before, have you any tips or advice?"

"Oh yes!" said Giles, "I certainly have!" and fell silent.

"Well?" I asked after a long pause.

"Avoid Canton station by any means possible."

*

CANTON - GUANGZHUO

PHIL started work that morning, labouring on the new airport site, leaving at 6.00 am. I'd enjoyed my time in Hong Kong, but it was my day to leave. Scattering the cockroaches to the four corners of the shitty room, I slipped a cold beer into Phil's plastic bag, which huddled noisily amongst the others in the smelly fridge. I knew how welcome it would be when he returned in the evening. A defiant roach stood it's ground in a puddle, lit by the light from the open fridge door, and I asked myself; 'Would I ever see Phil again...my first travelling companion?' and the answer that came back was pessimistic.

I'd worked out that two easy trains, a boat ride and a short bus connection, would see me to Yangshuo; to the peace and quiet of rural China. This was never meant to be intrepid exploration, and I had no intentions of hacking all the way around one of the largest countries in the world. I might drift further on to Dali or even Lijiang, if time permitted, but I thought, 'let's see what I can learn on the way.'

The morning was blunt as lead; greyer, heavier; as I stood with my back to Chungking Mansions. My journey started twenty yards across Nathan Road on the underground and went downhill from there. Down on the platform, an extremely tidy queue of roughly ten people, were formed at every ten feet along the platform, their feet each side of a yellow line, noses pressed against the back of the person in front. I joined one, curious, and saw as the train arrived that this was where the doors opened. Simple. It was the last 'order' I was to see for a long time. Arriving at Shensheng to change stations and trains, I walked from the building and into a storm. I stepped aside from the throng to try and make sure they were going the right way for me. It was then I realised that everything was in Chinese, the characters like exploded boxes, the people were *all* Chinese, and I was in China. People were talking at me, I didn't know why. The language was full of spitting and gulping and galumphing as if the words were broken in the teeth. My self-esteem collapsed like a biscuit in hot tea. I held off a panic attack with a Silk Cut. I could do this. I couldn't. Spotting a blond head in the crowd, I rushed after, not caring if it was German, Swedish, or Danish, as long as it wasn't a Chinese in a wig.

"Can you speak English?" I asked desperately. 'Yes', she could, but didn't know where the train went from; but she knew a man that did. She was being met by a courier who shook my hand and went with me halfway. Taking my pack off for a rest, I didn't notice my watch come off, but on setting off with the masses, it wasn't there. I expected to see it on turning, having only lost it for about four seconds, but no; it was gone. I noticed a young Chinese at the edge of the road, and had the feeling he'd seen something. Tapping my wrist I asked,

"Did you see my watch?" He discreetly nodded at a man nearby with a red shirt; his back to me.

"He has my watch?" He shrugged his shoulders; looked the other way. I marched over to the huddle, in the middle of which was my watch. Now this was not a Rolex, merely a five pound Casio from a garage, but it was useful. Breaking through, I pointed to the white mark on my wrist and took the watch from his outstretched hand, which stayed hovering in the air like a swan with it's beak open. They looked at me, mouths agape, as I said thank you, and smiling, walked away. Yes, it probably *would* have fed his family for a month, but I needed a watch *DIDN'T I?* All the signs at the ticket office were in Cantonese, but after studying the Lonely Planet and seeing that every booth had the same characters (Guangzhou-Canton), deduced that I couldn't buy a wrong ticket if I tried. Clutching this, I joined a queue and spotted two backpacks ahead, and they'd spotted me. It was love at first sight. I needed them and they needed me. They were Doron and Sharon, an Israeli couple who spoke good English. We chatted all the way to Canton and enjoying our mutual support, left the station terminal, confident; me to catch a sleeper bus to Yangshuo, them to stay in a hostel in the city.

We had entered the gates of hell, and damnation came down upon us. It was like being a lone Celtic fan at a Ranger's match, a ping-pong ball in raging rapids, a piece of meat. They hassled and pushed, pulled and poked, whilst we tried to watch each other's backs. Hands were pulling at our straps, our arms and Sharon's blond hair. They seemed to know we were virgins. We put Sharon between us and pushed and slapped back until a space formed around us. There was no refuge in sight and I realised that the only safe thing was to get out of the station. Dodgy characters were thrusting Chinese characters in our faces. We bartered a taxi driver down from a terrible price to a bad one, and were being led away; a crowd following us like gulls about a trawler, shrieking and laughing. To our horror, they led us to a dank corner at the back of the station, to a car without a taxi sign. We were completely surrounded and things were looking nasty as the driver insisted we put the packs in the boot which, as we knew, was when they got stolen. We refused, and putting them inside, got in and locked the doors. We urged the driver to go, but he kept getting out of the

16

car. Sharon had real fear on her face now, as the car resembled a pop group arriving at an awards ceremony, people beating on the roof.

"Go, go, go!" Doron shouted, two inches from the driver's face.

"NOW!" I joined in, holding the handle the driver was reaching for.

We rattled off through the crowd, Sharon crying in the back.

In hindsight, away from the panic, the scenario probably ran more like this:

"If you want to go to this hotel it will cost $20."

"You can't charge them that Lee." "I can try."

"No, see, they are very angry at your affrontery."

"Did the big nose with glasses say $15!?"

"Yes! he sweats so much he has a puddle at his feet."

"Take them before they change their mind."

"This couple sound as though they are clearing their throat when they talk, but they don't spit it out like us."

"Hey everybody! these bignoses are paying $15 to ride in Lee's car, what a laugh, let's go and watch."

"They're looking very worried."

"So they should be, getting in that heap of shit."

"One of them shouted 'Go, go, before the wheels fall off'."

"Ha, ha, ho, ho."

The hotel that the Israelis had written down turned out to be one of the plushest in Canton, and a room for the night would have kept me in Chungking Mansions for a week. We trudged over to the youth hostel and booked in, though it was three times the price quoted in the Lonely Planet. The place was luxury, sanctuary; it had other travellers who spoke English, bucketloads of English, albeit tinged with Israeli, French, and South African. After introductions we were told that we'd have been wasting time trying to get any tickets. The Wouzhou region, through which we had to travel, was in the middle of it's biggest flood for a hundred years; many people had died. There were no buses or boats today; perhaps tomorrow.

I took a walk off the island to the infamous market, where I'd heard that dogs hung, skinned, from hooks. I didn't really want to see this, but thought that I should. At first I walked through mounds of fruits, foodstuffs, silks, porcelains, and a dozen other commodities; the air was heavy with the pungent reek of salted fish and spices. And then I saw it, like something from a horror movie, unmistakably a dog; it's muscles, sinews and ligaments exposed to the world, shining scarlet, a cruel hook impaling it's eye.

17

The floor was slippery with blood and guts, claws, eyes, hearts and livers, and all things that crawl or hop or slither were here to be dispatched and eaten. A litter of kittens, their necks tied together like a posy of summer daisies, meeowed and cried. Two fish, the size of a small boy, wriggled in an inch of water, their tails flapping faster than the tongues of the locals. Picked out by a shopper, one was laid on the slab. The cleaver sliced into it's side, just behind the gills and in front of the tail. Holding the blade flat, she ran it up the fish, then took the steak and wrapped it in newspaper. As she dropped the coins in her pocket, she hung the fish by a hook to the roof, where it's organs, yellow and purple, open to the air, carried on their beating and throbbing.

Each time I stopped a crowd would gather like flies round a fresh turd, and call over other flies they didn't even know; to take a look at you. And when you moved off, some would follow, hoping you would stop again. Writing this, I had a spectator across the table, the hostel guard, in uniform. He was genuinely fascinated at the marks and squiggles coming from my pen. With a big smile he accepted a cigarette, and when other Cantonese moved to occupy the spare seat next to me, he shooed them away. An Australian girl walked into the lobby, the majority of an ample breast clearly visible through the armholes of her vest. He was embarrassed and looked to me for help. I shook my head with disgust.

Keron was asleep in the bed by the window when I moved into my room, a Kiwi - I presumed her boyfriend, between us. I felt a bit of a gooseberry sharing their room, but meeting her in the lobby, introduced her to Doron and Sharon and they immediately fell to jibberjabber and talk of home, but were kind enough to include me every now and then. Keron had already bought a ticket to Guilin for the next day, so we decided to join her. I asked where her boyfriend had got to, and she told me that she didn't know the Kiwi, hadn't actually spoken to him yet. It was my first mixed room, you see.

The next day we again entered the maelstrom of Guangzhou station and with the time running out before the 5.30 train, tried to buy some tickets. We were tossed around like straw dolls in a whirlwind; went from black marketeer to crook; crook to beggar. Tickets were offered but were they real? where did they go to? We held hands to try and stay together but eventually, chasing after a man who spoke some English, Keron was swept off into the swirling crowd.

A baby-faced man said "I can get you tickets to Guilin" and led us off into a shopping arcade. They blocked off an aisle, two men at each

18

end, whilst we exchanged money. They only had two tickets. They went. Keron had already gone.

On the way back to the hostel I thought that I wouldn't be displeased to see her again. But I was going my way. They told me later, in Yangshuo, that their tickets had been useless. They'd been taken off the train at some godawful station, Sharon crying, Doron verging on violence, and made to pay again. The full tourist price.

Back on the island, I went with an Australian-South African-Pole to a ticket agency.

Trevor's accent made it impossible for him to pronounce Chinese names, they were much too soft. Despite endless different phonetics, Xho, Chu, Shuo, Ju, Tsu, Trevor reduced them all to 'shoe', so as we sat in front of the agent he asked:

"Ken you git us a train ticket to Yangshoe?"..."No."

"How about a bus tickit to Xangshoe?"..."No."

"Boat to Woushoe?"..."No."

"Any tickit to Goushoe...or Gangshoe?"..."No."

"Have you something in a brown comfortable walking shoe?"

I got a sleeper bus ticket to Yangshuo for the next day. I stood with a German woman at the place we were told the bus would pick us up; an Irish couple catching it too. A bus pulled to a halt fifty yards further up the road and quickly filled with Chinese. We had the feeling it was ours, so rushed up the road. The doorman looked at my ticket, blankly, as though I'd tried to board a 747 to Los Angeles with a Blackpool tram ticket.

"Guilin? Guilin? Yangshuo?" I asked. The passengers near the door were nodding, the doorman pointing down the road. The bus was pulling away, doors closing on the German girl behind me, the Irish outside fighting to get on. The bus stopped and we wrenched the doors open and pulled them in. We were in this together. We roared off, being shouted at to sit down. We sped off a hundred yards to a bus depot and parked. We stayed parked. The 4.30 was now the 5.30. At 6.00 we moved; forward into the next parking space. After a furious row with a passenger, which lasted fifteen minutes, the driver reversed into a sort of garage. 6.20. 6.40. 7.00 and then we were off. But the seats were quite comfortable; half-length bunk beds, with a tilting back, three rows along the bus, so we looked like a busload of pensioners in bathchairs watching a Gloria Swanson movie ahead.

We drove into the deepening night, and further up the route, reached the flood area. The rain had caused landslides that had all but closed the roads. At these points, the buses; of which there were many, and lorries; many, many more, battled with the diggers and bulldozers trying to clear the road, to reach their destination. I stayed awake, watching the confrontations, and several times saw labourers leaping for their lives out of the path of our bus; the driver, trumpeting his cigarette, seeming to ignore their very existence. At one narrow point, the left side of the road was a solid line of buses and lorries, the right, a rat-run for those chancing their arm through a dip where the road was slurry and the edge dropped forty foot into a flooded paddy. Our driver didn't even break wind; he bowled some watchers aside and flew into the dip, the bus sliding sideways. We straightened up, slid, straightened up, and then I felt the rear end going over the side. My heart skipped, I reached for a handhold and heard *"SShhhiiiiiitttt!!"* in five languages down the bus. He gunned the engine at the front and the rear followed on behind, up the hill and onto firm ground. Where the road wasn't mud, it was potholes and when not potholes...crevasses and we went across them whompity whompity, bang into China. Whilst the rest of the bus slept, I saw things, I heard things, I'm telling.

I saw glow-worms twinkling beside the road; a wobbly moon jitterbugging on a flooded plain, brighter than it's twin in the sky, as though it was fed by the water. Old men and children rode on bicycles with no lights, like ghosts on two wheels, with wicker baskets in which to carry their troubles. And sometimes lovers on scooters - the girl, flimsy dress flapping; late home or escaping for a secret tryst.

I saw a meteorite blaze an arc across a black sky, like a sparkler tied to a cat's tail, and disappear behind even blacker hills. And to this I could only say...Wow! But nobody heard me.

I heard the bus engine straining and spluttering, wheezing and gasping, but like a racehorse, determined to run to the last for it's rider. Great creaks and groans came from it's body as he coaxed it over humps, through trenches and ravines, thrashing the engine and murdering the clutch. Then a landslide brought the convoy to a halt. A dead stop; engines off. All was dark but I could hear frogs barking and bats whispering sweet nothings. The sounds illuminated the night, competing against the noise of the passengers. They snoozed and snored, talked volumes to worlds unknown. Whistles and whoops were interspersed with coughs and galoops. Farts marked the quiet gaps, some arriving wrapped with ribbons wrapped around. Chuckling, I said "Wheeeee!" as the bus moved off to new trials, bubbling and backfiring into the dark over the corrugated road.

20

HOLIDAY INN, YANGSHUO

THEN it was morning, and in the weak light, trees, mountains and bullocks were waking, brushing themselves down and listing their chores for the day. The mountains were strange, unjoined, like a giant's discarded toys or a fleet of sailing ships. The morning wore on, as we tacked through the peaks. I'd been on the bus eighteen hours when we entered Yangshuo itself, a harbour of huge limestone schooners and frigates, and further out, cutting through an emerald sea of rice and vegetables, men-of-war and brigands sailed south to pillage Hong-Kong.

Yangshuo was a small town set on the banks of the Li river, which had the serenity of a silkworm but could grow into a roaring dragon with heavy rain, submerging the island in the middle under thirty feet of water and washing the stilts away from villages built too near the bank. The mountain that rose up almost from the back of my hostel was called Telegraph Hill, the least romantically named of the peaks that the town wrapped itself around, and shaded itself under. Man Hill bowed to Lady Hill, Swan and Crab hill swam below Dragon peak; there was even one that was 'Green frog watching the Moon dance.'

They were all there to be gawped at and then climbed, stopping at altars and pagoda'd galleries for a rest. The second morning, with the night still wearing it's silk pyjamas, I slipped out of the hostel, and walked over to the public park. Here at sunrise, the locals came, and as the light shafted through the trees at angles and shuffled through the leaves, they mirrored it with their Tai Chi; even the bodies of the old crones looking supple as saplings. I watched until the heat grew and sent them scuffling and pedalling off to work, leaving me alone with the butterflies that crashed through the sunrays; silently.

YANGSHUO was certainly geared for backpackers, which suited me fine for the moment. It meant people to meet, balmy evenings, few difficulties. At the same time it took very little effort to take a bike and ride off into the countryside to see things the way they'd always been.

I took a boat trip up river to Xing Ping, still unspoilt, down to Fuli; walked straight out of the town on any old path that came my way, stumbling upon and into small villages; circled lakes, their own pet mountains reflected on their shiny faces. I followed the opposite bank of the river and conversed in sign language with swimming children, too bashful to come out of the water and show their nakedness. I found my own Banyan tree, not the tourist one where Mao was meant to have spoken, but in a clearing by a rushing waterfall. I sat with my toes in the chill water as tumbledown women fanned ochre chaff onto the surface of the pond, from their hand threshing, a step away. And in the town itself I only had to go to the station yard to sit on midget stools and eat with the locals, or stroll through the market at night to savour dubious delicacies, sift through the geegaws on tables in front of the flaky shops. I could sit outside the dentist with it's open front, and watch a performance of human emotions. Rows of hairdressers shared whole streets, the girls at the door, enticing you in. They were prostitutes, all instant charm and lies, but you could have your hair cut first if you wanted.

I was helping Huang, who worked in the Green Lotus, with his English.

"Is it safe to swim in the river Huang?"..."Yes." he said.

"But why don't I see anybody in it?"..."Many people." he said.

"No, Huang I've never seen anybody in the river."

"Many people. 7.00 o'clock." I went to the river. A full moon hung from the sky, brightly smiling, dipping it's wick into the river to draw up more light. The Chinese, hordes of them, for as far as I could see from left to right, stood up to their waists in the daytime brown water ...moonbathing. For, wherever you stood, the moon's reflection beat a wobbly path right to your stomach, where it imparted some of it's power and you could reach out, cup a handful and let it slip through your fingers...slivers of moonbeam. I joined them, the current tugging at my trousers. Well I'd had a few beers.

A crowd was gathering by the station, around a domestic dispute. A young woman was being chastised by her husband under the scrutiny of an old lady, halfway between them, head swivelling left and right. He raged at the girl, then stepping up pinched her cheeks painfully. Her eyes watered with the pain. He ranted, then rushing forward, poked her in the eyes with two fingers. The old lady nodded in approval, and he carried on his shouting, as the girl sobbed quietly. The onlookers were unperturbed, or perhaps it was their duty to watch to ensure she was properly humiliated, but as he snapped her head back by the hair, viciously, I had to leave; it was too painful.

The view from Moon Hill, nearby, was considered the most beautiful in all of China, and here, we were offered babies to take back to England...free, as they were too poor to feed them. And these were the loveliest of poppets, learning their alphabet in a sing-song that made your heart skip tra-la-la. On the river, boats waited for darkness,

22

cormorants tied to the front, lanterns primed, waiting for the night fishing. So, when people said to me, "Yangshuo is not the real China", I said, "take your blinkers off." Or words to that effect.

I 'D MADE a very difficult decision before I left - to travel alone. The reaction to this was split between, "You must be mad, I couldn't do that." and "It's the best way, you'll meet more people." The latter, though the more frightening, proved true, whilst the former only strengthened my resolve. In only two weeks I'd met a menagerie, a pot-pourri of people from all places and I wondered how long I would remember their faces and places. The bog-standard conversation of the backpackers revolved round places been, or going to, how to get there, what to do; picking up pieces of information like magpies stealing shiny objects. Though this led to a well-trod path, and hardly intrepid, it was still an exciting road with surprises, and was sociable. The ease with which you could start a conversation, still surprised me, and it became second nature to share living space with complete strangers. In my little room, like the tide, I'd seen them come and go: An American boy studying Chinese, excited to be going home, who told me to be glad I couldn't understand what they were saying - it wasn't pleasant; A chattering Frenchwoman, whose incessant babble seemed to increase the output from her stinking feet; An Englishman who slept the whole 36 hours he was there. He woke briefly while I was reading, looked at his watch and said....

"Oh shit, it's gone twelve, I might as well stay tonight as well." rolled onto his back, and in seconds rattled off snores that could cut down trees. When the other bed was empty, the room seemed smaller through lack of conversation, as though it was necessary to push out the walls with a cloud of words all chopped and jumbled by the ceiling fan. It was exciting waiting to see if the next occupant would be a fat, sweaty Turk or a vision of beauty.

BACKPACKERS could be split into three groups. The hardened one's had a major aim in life - to see as many places as possible by the cheapest means, resulting in perhaps three days sleeping on a spit-carpetted floor with other people's feet as pillows. Arriving at their destination there were things to be 'done' before moving on. If these could be 'done' in the shortest possible time, more information gathered about the next, honour was satisfied and you could go direct to Lahsa, without passing go, or collecting your wits about you. Shell-shocked scarecrows with a self-satisfied smirk, usually induced by dope, were often seen entering town looking for the ultimate low, the weed being necessary to dull the wits and avoid boring each other shitless about how they slept on a piece of toast for a week, used it as an umbrella on the bus that had no roof, and finally ate it for six days as the fungus growing on it induced a magic mushroom effect. Whilst in a place, there was no need or time to actually look at the countryside, feel it's warmth or drink in it's presence. The locals were obstacles who made it difficult to move around and always wanted too much money, even though the small amount extra they were trying to extract, could save them from giving away their children.

The second category rode in possees, backpacks slung casually like bandoleers, and their aim was to stay among their own, sing their own songs, breathe their own air. The undisputed champions of these were the Israelis, with the Dutch and Swedes fighting for a close second. We had a theory that it was instilled by national service and that they rang home at night to receive orders for the next day. An advantage of their technique was that they could sweep through streets and stations in a wedge, parting beggars and hawkers and whole dynasties like a combine-harvester in a field of wheat. Another was that you could absolutely perfect your Israeli, Dutch or Swedish with each other, over a long trip, as long as you didn't tag onto the wrong squad in a station melee. The English were never in this category as, in any number over three, they would fight amongst themself or would want to fight another 'gang'.

And then there was the sector I think I belonged to. I liked to call us the Romantics. Or Fools. We could be seen wandering around, normally alone, eyes wide in wonderment and confusion, completely ill-equipped, bumping into situations and lamposts. Though alone, we craved company and had no qualms about approaching another traveller, not due to a sudden change in personality since leaving home (or perhaps it was) but a survival instinct; a need to know the answers to the problems gathered along the way. We could often be seen unsuccessfully talking to locals, to their amusement (and ours at times), paying over-the-top prices, knowingly, for peace of mind or a piece of melon. We knew you see, how far the money went compared to at home, and appreciated it enough not to wring it's neck or suck it's bones dry.

Regardless of category though, I was proud of them all, proud to be one. Somebody asked me to define the difference between a real traveller and a tourist and I told them:

"The tourist interferes, spoils, whereas the traveller tries to move through the country without disturbing, so that smells and sights and sounds cling to his clothes and hair like dandelion seeds, and drift through his head like a senseless children's rhyme."

"Pardon?" he said.

"They're different." I said.

I lay semi-naked on my bed, the one next to me empty. It was so hot out, that droning insects sported sunhats, water-buffalo were living up to their name and Chinese eyes were rounding with disbelief. Refuge was my room; cool concrete floor, mosquito-net dancing mambo under the fan. Through my earphones blasted The Cure... Robert Smith crooning interminable woes with a style that made you go *'yaaassss!'* Organs grind, trumpets coo, and flute dances merrily round the melancholy. I ventured out for a beer and as I met the road, the heat picked me up and slapped me, daring me to carry on. I made it to the shade of the Green Lotus Cafe, on the corner, the best viewing point in town; little was moving but the lorries that thundered through, air-horns blasting, day and night.

"Too hot" I said to Huang.

"No problem" he slung back. Liar. It was 95 degrees. Through a heat-shimmer above the dusty road, three figures appeared, Doron, Sharon and Keren. It was like the arrival of long lost friends and it'd been less than a week. Whilst Doron and Sharon went for a siesta, Keron and I trotted on down to the market. It ran along a single road parallel to the river, stalls each side, and stretched for a mile. On the left side every stall sold jade eggs, bracelets, or figures, all the same colour, all the same. On the right the choice was bountiful. The stalls alternated between selling a fruit like a giant pear, and dried ginger. Scaled up, this would be a road the length of the M40, with Boots the Chemists up one side, and pears and ginger down the other. How you were meant to make a choice was beyond me, and at the end of the day they packed it all away, possibly minus a large pear.

A strange species arrived in the market. I was starting to consider myself a traveller now, and the sight of overdressed, overfed Yanks wearing coolie hats, sunglasses, brash jewellery, and Nikons, jagged a nerve.

"What are they Howie?" asked Keren. I told her they were American tourists. "What are they doing here? ask them please...for me." They were on a package tour. They were doing China in two weeks. It seems that they were shipped by bus from a market full of crap to another similar.

"Do you like it here?" I asked one.

"Where?" he replied.

"Yangshuo, it's a very beautiful town, don't you think?."

"Hell, I don't know, is this Yangshuo?, well we're only here over-night aren't we honey? It's Guilin tomorrow, I hear they've got a great market."

I stared at him the way that the Chinese had been staring at us. I was thousands of miles from home but a million miles apart from this man.

SINCE I'd introduced them in Canton the three Israelis had taken to each other like a duck to orange. Keron was their mother, sister, clos-est friend. Doron was dark, lantern-jawed with a gaze that still scanned the Golan heights for danger. He tended and joyed in Sharon; small, fair, with eyes that cuddled you and ate up babies and peasants with honest sympathy.

Keron explained that they were Kibutzniks, used to sharing their lives, bodies and feelings and were very innocent. Doron, unashamed and unconcerned, explained to the Chinese maid in the corridor where he'd been that day, arms and genitals flying, naked and fresh from the shower. Unable to look down, the maid ran off shouting, leaving Doron confused in the corridor.

They didn't agree with national service and resented meeting so many Israelis when they were trying to be away from home. Sadly for them, Keron had been an instructor in the army and we were constantly being approached by her past recruits who ignored the Kibutzniks and watched me, strangely. I would find out why later.

" Howie", Doron would say, nodding at an approaching squad,

"Look what's coming into town."

"Israelis" I would reply.

"Yes," he'd say, eyebrows knitting, "more bloody Israelis!"

The heat broke the sky that evening and the four of us sat as the rain sheeted and sluiced through the cafe and under the tables. The fish that normally lived in the red bowl on the toilet floor swam past in a bid for freedom, Huang in close pursuit, trousers rolled up to his knees. The sultry air had forced a group from Hong Kong to shed their shirts, behind me. Doron's gaze was fixed on them.

"Don't stare, it's rude Doron" chided Sharon.

After a long silence he remarked...

"When you see something so ugly, it's hard not to stare." And as I turned, what appeared to be a sea-lion, with thick black glasses and sagging breasts, shovelled rice into his gob. His friend had a face like a smacked bum and looked like he'd been eating cushions. He slicked back his oily hair with his hand then wiped his mouth with it.

"I'm sorry Sharon," I said, "I have to agree." Doron winked.

The next day, the sky a washed-out blue, we cycled and walked in the park; talked and talked. We stood atop Moon Hill, in a film of sweat from the hard climb, and below us lay a patchwork quilt spread with stones, silk ribbons winding between them as rivers. It was as beautiful as the Chinese said. It was then I realised I'd been studying Keron all day. Small, with soft brown hair, her glasses failed to hide her smiling doe eyes. She shone. She couldn't sweat in a monsoon in China and that's just where we were. We left the other two and cycled out of town.

Despite slaloming between other cycles, people and bullocks and being beat by the airhorns, we managed to tune in to each other. She was attracting me more by the minute. I shook myself, knowing that I could easily fall in love with her.

Several golden days later, I'm sitting, writing, with the usual Chinese scrutineer. A worn old woman walks by, basket in one gnarled hand, a squawking duck in the other twisted fist. Behind in ragged formation, six ducklings race to keep up with their doomed mother, and such is the value of a duck in China, lorries swerve or stop if one of the brood skips into the road. My tablemate watches and talks whenever she gets the chance. She's a kitchengirl, and a new word picked up like a scrap, from the table, is stored for the future like a precious coin. You see, in Yangshuo, the riotous life of colour juxtaposes with ground in poverty and filth. The western style cafes are a stageact, a window dressing. Check out the lovelies in the back of The Minnie Mao cafe, daytime smiling. On a late night stumble to the toilet from the front of the stage, you cut across the kitchen, all preparations done on the piss- stinking floor, cockies whirring around clockwork-like. Tiptoe around the bed where three girls are sleeping, into the toilet with no door, and try to relieve your bladder of a full load which, minutes earlier was bursting to get out. It's not possible now, as the three girls, their raven hair faded to grey by the mosquito net, are barely two feet from your dick, and a pair of almond eyes are flickering open and shut. So you retire to a dark alley for relief, where again, almond eyes stare, but this time at the opposite end to a thick hairy tail.

I met Keron in the park. It was raining hot water. We kissed under the umbrella of a banyan tree, ignoring the statues of good Chinese workers, their arm muscles exaggerated by the teachings of Chairman Mao. We kissed like schoolchildren, hungry, wayward, then clung to each other, waiting for the ship to go down. I didn't want to sleep with her, as I knew that if we climbed inside each other's bodies we would break our hearts.

She had a betrothed to go home to. We were exhausting each other with guilt and longing. She had to go on alone. I had to go somewhere else. But I did love her. She was the cat's meeoow.

I bought her a jade butterfly, wrapped it up in park tickets, hostel cards and receipts, reminders of a fine time, and wrote a farewell letter full of angst and tears. I knew the piece was good as, when I offered the old crone a price, she ranted as if I'd called her son a halfwit, and her family - dung. I only got it by hitting her round the head with a small boy, and handing over a shoeboxful of money. It was my penance for falling in love with a girl who couldn't be mine and I paid it gladly. The three had a jade namestamp made for me, which I packed away with feeling into my backpack.

So they set off for Dali, and Keron, further into China before returning home; me to stay and watch roomates come and go with the moon, and struggle back to HongKong with the pieces of my heart wrapped in a Chinese Newspaper.

Returning from the station I saw, strolling towards me, a large potato dressed in conservative shirt, shorts and sandals, waving stick-on-hands and waggling it's ears. Giles had arrived in town. It seemed the new CV had worked and he had two days grace before starting his new job, so he'd come to find and thank me. He'd been relieved of his cassettes on the bus, but not his sense of humour, and his company carried me through my gloom until he left for work.

Then, having just seen three Israelis off at the front door, three more crept in through the back. After a timid knock at my door that woke me, I saw a woolly head appear in the dawn light.

"I must move in here." it said; and with such conviction, who was I to disagree. Issel, short, stocky and ironically Arabic, like the enemy he despised. Again, the room had grown with conversation and sunlight crept up the walls and into the corners. With him, as a package, came Guy. He was handsome, full of games and tricks, mischievous, and charm hung all over his riotous garb. Guy was very careful to dress carelessly. And the inevitable - Shirley, those same brown, doe eyes,

28

fair, with golden skin. So I joined them on the ferris wheel of life, and it spun oh! so fast. We lurched over and over for three days, it's lights twinkling and dancing. Whilst recounting happenings one evening, Guy and Issel looked at each other delightedly, clapped their hands and said, "You're the one, we heard about you in Kunming, the Englishman that was having an affair with Keron Ran!!" They were delighted, as they didn't like the four who'd told them, and slapped my back with glee. I hoped it wouldn't pass down the way, as I wanted Keren to be happy.

Their intrigue at the photo of Bumble in my wallet, and my explanation of his skills, led to the strangest episode of 'One man and his dog' ever seen. Out of town on bicycles, in a vast area of rice fields and crops, they demanded a demonstration. So, telling this invisible dog to stop barking, I whistled him away about half a mile, to the base of a mountain, then dropped him down.

"What's he doing Howie?" asked Guy.

"He's lying down." The whistling was very loud now, as he was so far away and peasants in the field and on bikes were stopped dead, as though also responding. I sent him slowly, then quickly, across the valley to the west, and the three followed him with their eyes. He swam through paddies, vaulted coolies and tore across the plain like a wonderdog. They looked at me in unison to see if he'd got there, and I whistled him down.

"Well he did that alright," I said. Unaware of the ridiculous situation they'd conjured up, Shirley asked, sweet and hopeful,

"Could you bring him over here now?" as if she was going to be able to stroke his ears and ruffle his chest.

"No," I said, "when you weren't looking, he ran off and he's fallen down a well." They realised what they were doing and grinned... sheepishly.

On a final turn by the riverwall; it was their last evening; Guy said,

"I want to do you a favour Howie," and held out a small string bag containing the biggest lumps of hash I'd ever seen.

"You can have these for twenty dollars, I can't take them home with me." It was about a thousand dollars worth at home.

"Guy, thank you, but in three days I fly into Vietnam, do you really think I want to take that with me?" He pondered a moment and replied,

"No, you're right," and swinging them around above his head, flung them into the Li river: and giggled.

"I'll see you at Minnie Mao's, I have a phonecall to make."

Whilst waiting for them, a trio of extremely well-dressed backpackers approached, and in a mid-American drawl asked...

"Could you tell us where there's a hotel with western-style toilets?"

"Not here I'm afraid, that's the most expensive hotel in town." I pointed it out; "...and they don't have them."

"Really?" he said, shocked. I nodded. "What are we going to do?" they said in unison and despair.

"You're in the middle of China, I suggest you go back to Hong-Kong." and they stumbled away just as Guy, Issel and Shirley arrived, a screaming Chinaman chasing behind them waving his bony arms.

"6 dollar, you owe me 6 dollar!!" They sat down with me, ignoring him, as he fluttered and batted around their heads, a ninja moth.

"GO AWAY!!" Guy shouted.

"What the hell's up with him?" I asked.

"He's trying to rip us off for a telephone call. We agreed a price and now he's trying to double it." A crowd was gathering at a discreet distance. We tried to ignore him and his noise until he made a grab for Shirley's waist bag. Issel had hold of his wrist before he could blink, his other cocked fist held back by Guy. "Leave him Issel, sit down, drink."

"You give me 6 dollar or I bring the police!" and made another grab for the bag, now on the table. I got there before him and Issell, who was coming round the table.

"Look, fuck off!" I said, in a friendly tone, "..or I think you might die." nodding towards the approaching Israeli. He took the hint and jumped away to his bicycle. "I get the police!"

"Yes please do, we'll be here waiting." They explained the problem after he had gone, and showed me the piece of paper they'd written the agreed price on. It dawned on me as we spoke that the spectators had melted away. Instead the cafe had acquired some new customers. Pan-faced men had moved into the bar, and contrary to normal behaviour, wouldn't look at us. From the corner of my eye I saw the seat next to me fill. I looked at my neighbour, whose thigh was touching mine.

"Hi mate, have you had a nice day?" I said to his ear.

He turned his head and I saw a strange and frightening thing. I saw nothing in his eyes. No fear, no anger; a cold dark pit.

"I think it might be a good idea to pay the money Guy," I said as two more ferreted into a dim corner, "...he didn't go to get the police."

"No, fuck him, I'm not paying!" and I realised that they didn't know what was going on. Marcus, a Swiss football fanatic who'd been watching every World Cup match in Chinese, joined our ranks, but we still weren't enough. The gangsters were still arriving, and then, a policeman on a motorbike, 'at last...the cavalry' I thought.

"I am the foreign liaison officer," said the bullet-headed, pig featured millicent, "pay this man his money!" 'Good liaison' I thought, my heart sinking. Guy explained the problem while the phone-man and his friends whispered in the officer's ear and fed him cigarettes.

Shirley explained it while he supped free beer. Issell explained that if they didn't stop giving him cigarettes he'd shove them down their throats. They carried on whispering to him, as he carried on drinking.

"You pay him his money."

"We will not pay him." said Guy quietly and calmly, and I tensed ...ready. The policeman went off on one. He ranted, screamed...

"You fucking foreigners, come here, everything is wrong, you don't want to pay for anything!!" and flicked his fag butt in Guy's face.

"PAY HIM!!!" "NO!" He stomped off to his bike, and I waited for the gun to come out. But no, he shouted something back in Chinese and rode away. There was a deathly silence, in which I quickly worked out what he'd said. Half out of my seat, the adrenalin pumping, I saw the gangsters fidgeting, hands reaching in pockets,

"Guy, pay him the money NOW!"

"Yes, I think that would be a good idea." added Marcus who, like myself had probably learned some savvy from the football terraces. Outnumbered by knife wielding hoods is not the time to get heroic.

"Oh shit! here is the money we don't owe you" Guy spat at the phoneman, peeling off six notes and ramming them in his shirt pocket.

"Now go away!" He did, cursing, and looking round, the hoods had already gone; melted away into the dark, and I wondered if they'd ever been there. The sweat trickling down my face told me that they had. The bar owner appeared sheepishly and I forced him to tell us what the policeman had said. "I not frightened of policeman, frightened of men, they not care if they go to jail, kill people. The policeman was scared he said that he could do nothing and they would have to fight you when he had left." "Would they have fought us?" I asked.

"I don't know because they are frightened of Israeli and English, maybe not, but probably as they had knives."

"They had knives?" said Guy.

Dumbfuck.

Outside the Green Lotus the next day, the lorry horns hitting me like a soldier beating his drum, I saw an English couple that I'd met, led from the back of a van by a policeman, into the post office. The girl was crying. I slipped over the road and followed them in. The man was on the telephone, guarded on both sides, the girl leaning against a wall, bottom lip trembling.

"What's going on, who's he phoning?" I asked. She told me.

"Dave and I were out cycling towards Fuli. We came up to a village and a man stopped us. He said we couldn't come through without paying twenty dollars. Dave told him that it wasn't a closed village and we didn't have to pay, and we went to cycle on. This bloke smacked Dave round the ear so of course Dave lays him out." Dave had now handed the phone to the officer. "Well," she carried on, "this bloke gets up from the floor, pulls out a gun and shows us his police ID. We're now under arrest and the policeman's demanding compensation as he reckons he's gone deaf! What's happening Dave?" she asked as Dave joined us. "I got the consulate. He's demanded that we're kept out of the jail until a doctor's examined the policeman, and then he'll discuss compensation."

"You're joking Dave, yeah?"

"No; we're under house arrest at the hotel and he's demanding five thousand dollars. The consulate say's we'll probably have to pay it."

"Look, I've got to go now" I said, as I watched the foreign liaison officer approaching the post office, "I know it's not much help but, good luck." and as I reached the door he shoulder-barged me aside to get in.

Returning to the cafe I asked the owner, a ticket broker, "What time does the sleeper bus leave today?" "4 o'clock?, well I want to be on it." And I was.

*

I WAS happy to be on the bus and on the way back to Hong Kong. I wasn't so happy though with my neighbour, one level below. A policeman. To add to my discomfort he'd removed all his clothes bar his boxer shorts. Six hours later the whole bus slept, apart from the two of us, him sitting bolt upright, me watching out the corner of my eye. Was he queer? Insane?. No, he was travel-sick. He rushed to the doors, and with the conductor hanging onto the waistband of his briefs, leant out into the dark to throw up. He was out there so long I began to wonder if the conductor was just holding a pair of pants in the breeze, but eventually he swung him back in. Almost as soon as he regained his upright position on the seat, the bus slammed to a halt, bags, bottles and bodies flying down the bus. Ahead, a white van had blocked us in a narrow lane, and in the stark headlights I saw what appeared to be the cast of Hawaii-Five O leap from all it's doors; loud shirts, white trousers, barracuda faces. I was in the front seat, streetlit through the windscreen, in full view, as they formed a semicircle round the front of the bus, not to sing Christmas Carols. I was the only

32

westerner on the bus, and I tried to screw my eyes up Oriental style, but I wasn't fooling anybody. I was the target.

The conductor was holding the doors shut with his back, as the driver spoke to them through his barely open window.

Holding grimly onto my bag, I looked down to the left, straight down the barrel of a Smith and Wesson revolver. The policeman was smiling manically at me with one finger to his lips...*sssshhhh!*. The driver must have had an ace-card up his sleeve as they moved off back to the van; apart from three, who remained dead centre between the windscreen wipers, staring straight at me. I stared back, mesmerised like a rabbit in a stoat's gaze. The middle of the three pointed a loaded finger at me and I knew it had been my lucky day. My dick was like an acorn in a brillo pad, with fright. I looked down at my guardian angel. He smiled as he buttoned up his holster and resumed the lotus position; smiled a sickly grin.

At a food stop, in those heinous hours that are neither night nor day, I found that there'd been another westerner on the bus, tucked way down on the bottom tier at the very back, and he looked like Jesus, but more ginger; Aaron from Wales. We were both too weary to brave the circus inside and sat out in the air. Attracted by his hair and colour, a toddler stood in front of Aaron, expertly smoking a cigarette and giggling. He was joined by his brother who could just walk. A call from inside pulled the older boy away, but hesitating, he gave the fag to the little brother to look after. The baby smoked it, and stared at Jesus.

Once again, Guangzhou station had me in it's grasp, and try as hard as we could, we couldn't get a train ticket, and took a bus. Hard seat. The two hour train journey was five hours on the bus, sandwiched between Chinese women spitting on the floor or throwing up out the windows. Apparently we were a contributing factor to this due to our body odour and at one stage the rest of the bus were triple seated until two rows from the back, where we sat in glorious isolation, grinning at our revenge; until the conductor forced them to sit next to us with a bottle above his head. He pulled unwilling people from bus stops onto the bus, and working up and down, fleeced the passengers one by one, the bottle raised to any objectors. Each time he came to the back he told us that we had to pay double.

"Fuck off" we told him

"If you don't pay double there will be men to take care of you at station."

"Fuck off" we told him, and I think our red-rimmed wild eyes and crappy clothes, persuaded him.

He accused a university student, between us, of not paying; took his bag, emptied it on the floor, stole some postcards from an album, body searched him for money, slit open the collar of his spare shirt to find a dollar. At this point he raised the bottle but, seeing us glaring, went back to the front. The boy was gulping air with fright and made to jump out of the window next to me. I told him the driver would see him and he should stick with us. The gangsters were there as the bus rolled to a halt, waiting for the doors to open, and deal with any offenders. We took the boy out with us and put our packs on the ground, waiting for the trouble. But the conductor said nothing and shrugged at us as if to say, "Well you have to try it on, don't you."

We went round and round this town, on buses, looking for the train to HongKong. Each time they set us down, they said, "Yes, station, over there." It never was. Only a demonstration of a steam engine by Aaron, arms pumping, choo-chooing through a huge crowd got us the right directions. We were both demented by then, with tiredness and anger, and battled the rest of the way into the city, begging Hong Kong dollars from anybody to get the last underground ride to Nathan road. Aaron was ten pounds short of his airfare home, and rather than see him have to get a job, I lent it to him, giving my brother's address. He never sent it back.

On the way out of Hong Kong, the aeroplane neatly pegged the 'Guns & Roses' T shirt back on the line in Jardine St, next to a pair of Levis and rose into the cloud obscuring the peak.

*

34

BI-BI HOSTEL, OLD QUARTER, HANOI.

WE PLANED across a green patchwork quilt and touched down on Hanoi bowling green after a small leapfrog over a particularly wet patch. There were no bomb craters in sight, napalm absent in the morning dew. Nor were gunships buzzing around spitting fire and damnation at peasants and soldiers, only bullocks wading through the paddies, their coolies waterskiing behind, failing to mix the different shades of green together. The family working the last paddy had taken advantage of the runway and spread their clothes and cooking pots on the end of the concrete.

Still stressed from China, and reading warnings in the Lonely Planet of police and customs hassles at Noi Bai airport, I was at boiling point. I realised that I'd had no time in the previous month to even try and imagine what to expect. I just arrived.

I'd found my visit to the consul in London quite odd, but then a small piece of Vietnam tucked away behind Kensington High St staffed by "Charlie" is hardly everyday. I was given one piece of paper with my details and photo attached and a replica, both of which I signed. *They* kept one copy, I was to present *my* half on arrival at Hanoi. I assumed it was a sort of 'Snap', if mine matched theirs I could come in. But that was in London.

I had visions of child-size men in drab-olive fatigues pointing machine guns at my chest, and spending the night in a bamboo cage up to my neck in water while they questioned me about the photo of a dog! in my wallet and his teethmarks through my passport. Thus began the most trouble free arrival I'd ever had the privilege to experience.

The terminal handled one plane-load at a time. No comment from immigration on my 'half', no hassles from customs, no waiting for baggage, all smiles and politeness and "Here's a seat for you, sit!, we find person share taxi with you; make cheaper! We can go if you like but more money. Please wait. Want cigarette?"

They couldn't find another body but promised, "We will take you to as many hotels as you wish until you are satisfied." They did. I was. It was cheaper than the Lonely Planet had said. True, they did get me into a relative's hostel, at the south of the lake when I'd asked to go to the north; but I didn't find that out 'til I ventured into the evening. I walked north, shy but excited, buzzing to be there.

35

HANOI had a smile hanging over it, moonlike and grinning through it's streets like a cheshire cat on patrol. Here, youth sneaked to the lake in the evening and dug each other under dark tree umbrellas, kissing, necking and loving, to fuel their daytime smiles. And when you're in love with a girl, your country and life itself, who's worried about foreigners traipsing around?. They smiled at me, calling out greetings I couldn't understand but could tell were friendly.

Ho Hoan Kiem..The Lake of the Restored Sword held the fairy lights of the city on it's surface and as I reached the Island of the Turtle at it's head, realised that I'd been duped and was staying at the wrong end of town. I'd wanted to stay in the Old Quarter. But the hotel was good, though empty, and I was tired, too tired to be annoyed. In China I was racked with stress, dehydration, diahorrea and stupidity. I had carried on supping beer by the sampan full whilst writing, and though this opened the doors to creativity, it shut the windows on my health. I was mentally and physically as healthy as gorgonzola left in a hot place. I had to take myself in hand. And that's no dirty joke missus!. I already felt that in Vietnam I could do it, I could go on to better things and with this in mind headed for the Old Quarter and The Old Dahling Cafe where I knew I would find other backpackers.

Carrying my muddy coffee, still filtering in it's pot, to their table, I asked the two lads, "Excuse me, could you recommend a good hostel in this area?".

"For sure" said the Australian lad, the first of a thousands times I would hear him utter this.

"Ours is OK, d'ya wanna go an' hev a look?, we'll take ya, eh Harry?" turning to the other.

"Four shore" said Harry with a Swedish accent. It was obviously catching. It was at the top end of the town, and we walked through the streetlife... noisy, smelly and chaotic. The people were cooking, eating, sleeping, bathing, doing...in the street. Small hillocks of rubbish, the jetsom of the day, punctuated the pavement. Later, as the people moved indoors, these were removed by ladies with handcarts and facemasks and the street washed, like a table preparing for it's next cover. It seemed that every Honda 50, 70 and 90 had emigrated to Hanoi and happily played amongst themselves and the bicycles and the people, in streets not big enough to accomodate Hondas, bicycles and people. In China where Hondas don't go to live, the bicycles often crashed into each other, into kerbs, posts and man size cockroaches. But walking across or along Hanoi streets you could be in a flock of bats. They seemed unable to hit each other or you through some silent sonar device. If, when crossing a wide road, a red light winked green, a phalanx of Hondas and cycles, forks and pedals linked, came for you;, but walking or standing nonchalantly with camera raised, or picking your nose, they would pass on all sides perhaps tugging faintly at a shirt sleeve or leg hair. The average number of riders on a Honda was three. Not possible? it certainly was. Whole families of five and six sardined past on their trusty steeds on the way to who knows where.

The proudest of the scooters always bore two girls, with their 'ao dai'- dress pressed even closer to their bodies by the rush, waistlength chestnut hair waving gossamer in the breeze behind. Their beauty was unmatchable and their giggling heartbreaking, as they sneaked you a look with almond eyes and let you know they were unattainable. The ao dai contrived to be both modest and provocative at the same time. Fitted tight from neck to hip, it accentuated every curve of their slender, willowy bodies, the curve of the back, the budding swell of breasts and buttocks. The top was slit up to the waist and below this loose silk trousers cloaked the thighs and calves in secrecy. Walking on the evening breeze they seemed like butterflies, flitting under the tamarind trees, from cafe to pavement, friend to lover.

Reaching the Bi-Bi guest house with Nick and Harry I was dizzy with desire and noise and smells and booked in for the next night, tripping up the stairs for a quick look at the room. The bunks grappled with each other for space but at least the room was being cooled by a wall fan, and a white-tiled bathroom sat cleanly in the corner. I went onto the balcony and, looking out in the demi-light of the city, saw that we were surrounded by humped red roofs, like a cluster of crabs.

Between these were the living lanes of the city, narrow lanes stuffed with people, vehicles and dogs, washing back and forth like a tide of flotsam, all held down by garlands of thick telegraph wires strung between the crumbling walls; and the noise was a cacophony that jumped up at me from below like a pack of mad-dogs. I just wanted to be here amongst it all; and knowing I would be the next day, shambled back past the lake, content, to my hotel and slept the sleep of a dead thing.

*

Bi-Bi was on Hang Chai St, which translated meant 'Ladies' Hat street'. All the streets in the Old Quarter were named after the trade which they plied exclusively. We came to navigate by the trade or craft and would direct people with...

"You need to go up Tin street (which was a hurricane of hammers beating tin), turn right into Shoe street, along Jewellery, cross over Red Street (where all manner of furniture had been hit by the reddle stick) and you'll find the market".

Hang Chai however, had said goodbye to it's hats and was now a backwater where a few families lived to the left and right of the hostel and where, we were told, the kids were the worst robbers in the city.

So picture me, sitting in front of the hostel, soft, buttery morning light floating around. With me are winsome Dwim, her brother Nay Ahn and their friends. Dwim is eleven and looks eight, with a whisper that wouldn't disturb the air. Her first pair of earrings swing proudly from her pretty little ears. She pushes my nose, (for we are long noses to them) tickles my chin, (as it is hairy) and as a reward for putting up with this I get a big cuddle. I don't know what to think about this as I can only see her in five years time, flying through Hanoi on a Honda with her flawless girlfriend behind, or trotting down to the lake with her boyfriend, sitting holding the moon between them as it bobbles across the water. Remembering that she's a street urchin and this won't happen for her, I wish that she could be the daughter I can't ever have. And this piece of delight and most innocence seeing my eyes fill with pain, reaches behind my glasses and catches a tear on her tiny shell fingernail. It hangs there like a transparent ladybird and as though she could and does carry the woes of Vietnam and the world on her tiny shoulders, her great and helpless eyes fill for me, and her little head drops onto my shoulder. I was gone.

If I'd been offered this one, like the many in China, I would have packed her in cotton wool, stroked her into my backpack with my Walkman and asked Robert Smith, Julie London, Slim Gaillard and the rest to sing to her and care for her till I got home, because to look at her would still my feet and set them in concrete in Hanoi, there to remain with a marble Lenin and a stuffed Ho Chi Min.

Swimming through Cha-Ca street then arcing round the walled city, I entered a new world to the west. This was 1930. I was in France, rolling down broad leafy boulevards. Colonial minipalaces ticked off the route. The Indian Embassy, the Chinese Embassy, the Algerian, French, Finnish, Australian, and as though transported from a film set, a tall, balconied, weatherbeaten Romanian Embassy with perpetual thunderstorm above.

Amongst these tidy and thoroughly beautiful thoroughfares lay Ho Chi Min's mausoleum. A marble block guarded by soldiers wrapped in the crispest white tableclothes the Savoy Hotel could spare. Barred from entering the mausoleum through a lack of sleeves, I wandered the paradeground. The guard was leaning at an angle of 89 degrees against the cold marble and seemingly holding up the whole building,; bored. As I approached he snapped to attention with a steely grimace, but realising that I was going to speak, his face cracked, a huge grin that bridged continents. After some small talk, very small talk, I asked "Do you enjoy serving here, the resting place ofi Ho Chi Min?".

"No" he replied, looking worriedly to each side to see if he could be heard, and explained haltingly but quite clearly... "I'm bored shitless. I have to stand here all day like an imbecile; it's 105 degrees and I guard a lump of marble and a stuffed body. It's so good when somebody comes and talks; they all think I will arrest them or shoot. See this parade ground, it is made to hold a quarter of a million people. I never see more than a few hundred at a time and where you stay in the Old Quarter people have to live on top of each other and in the road."

He gestured his partner over for a chat but he declined with a worried look and shakes of his head.

"He is frightened," my soldier said "living in the past...me I don't care about the army, I like Guns & Roses, America number one!"

I shook his hand and photographed the two of them in front of the field-size flag, gold star rippling over red, and at last the other soldier beamed. I strolled happily back into town, though the Vietnam sun shrivelled on. Huang had been right in Yangshuo, Vietnam was hotter even than August in China.

I passed the nondescript but emotive 'Hanoi Hilton' prison. A triangular windowless structure, ochre-yellow, the colour of the American pilots' skin when they emerged from here. The small door set in the large studded gates was open and I moved to poke my nose in. The guard anticipated my move and barred the way.

"Can I come in?" He shook his head and smiled.

"No, I didn't think so".

Cutting crabwise on a whim, back towards home, Madrid suddenly appeared on the left, a slap round the face with a gothic cathedral. It stood alone, a white giant amongst mulatto midgets. After circling the building, I found a side entrance and slipped into a cool silence. Green arched paths walked all around the cathedral touching it's buttresses and caressing the walls. The hum and buzz of the city passed over the top of this haven or waited outside the squiggle-iron gates, sulking and squawking. Not built for pomp or show, but worship, this vessel was never filled with the roar of organ pipes, only a Hammond organ to one side. The priests were not elevated skywards in a demi-god position but preached along the floor, nose to nose with the people who filled the cathedral with a deafening noise of feet, shuffling in obeyance as they entered. The windows were the only compromise to excess with colours dancing around and through St Theresa and St Joseph and Saint anybody else you can think of, and falling like petals on the cold floor. And when the sun played hide and seek with the puffball clouds the colours glimmered cooly, waiting to be fired back to life with a booh! and spattered round the gloom.

Confession boxes waited hungrily in line for their evening meal for between 5.00 and 7.00 the locals came in earnest, in taxis, in cyclos, to confess perhaps their trips to the lake or thoughts of Chairman Mao.

Then as dark darkened outside and confession boxes swayed, the massed band of Catholic cicadas paraded, unmoving round, and round the cathedral, each and every one a 'Johnny One Note'. I went home.

It was in love again that I was and this time it was a city. Morning, afternoon, evening and night were the best times and I tried to wrap them all around me, snug. Once again I couldn't see past the place I was at and I didn't care and I shared all this with Harry.

First appearances had let me down. Or rather, I'd let myself down by judging on first appearances. When I'd approached them in The Old Dahling cafe it was Nick who'd spoke and Harry, tall, skinny, looking sullen with ice blue Mongolian eyes, stayed quiet all evening. I had him down for miserable son of a Swede but four days later we were walking and talking and thinking on the exact same wavelength. We would spot things that the other had already noticed and laugh and sigh at the same beauties.

And when silence and distance were needed they reigned supreme until, like two clockwork toys wound to the same tension, we would click into action, banging drums and whirring lights and knocking into new things.

Harry had something hidden in his backpack. I flung down my earphones with..."I can't listen to that!" and explained to Harry that it was a taboo record, to be taken in small doses and never after a broken heart.

"I have one also" he said, as he put my earphones on and raised the volume. His eyes widened..."Oh faaark!...it's the same one, Robert Smith - Pictures of You!" The bassline pumps sorrow into each ear with a rocksteady beat pounding at your quavering heart. Then Smith injects the sadness deep into your veins where it strolls nonchalantly around and escapes from the corner of your eyes..."I picture you...

40

standing silent in the rain..." *oh, oh, oh!* But knowing that this tune caused pain to more than just me made it easier to bare, and I played it.

And now, seeing her standing silent in the rain, I walked towards her stronger, with Harry beside me for support, who was picturing faces of his own. I wasn't to know at the time that the picture I was to hold one day would make it impossible to listen to the tune again.

We spent our halcyon days in Hanoi wandering her streets, watching and waiting for the next happening; crawling sluggishly through the alleys, loathe to miss a thing. And when out on solo missions, we knew of each other's position through the network.

Familiar now to the postcard sellers, we each had our own favourite. Thuy, my own little poppet, would wrinkle her nose at me (a Vietnamese insult) each morning, as I refused to buy a card, though she knew that I'd succumb eventually during the day, perhaps paying for a photo of her and a friend, or a glass of coke. On a circuit of the lake, the Chinese lanterns from a cafe wavering on the water, or leaning through a temple door to gather inscence fumes, I would be turned by a...

"Hello Howie, what are you doing?..you want postcard?"

"No Thuy, I'm just walking, then I'm going to have a cold beer."

"Harry is in the Old Dahling Cafe, he said he has bought you one"

And that's where I would go with my escort, to spend the rest of the afternoon just watching, talking and trying to wring the truth out of Thuy about her life. She would frequently cut me to the quick with a casual... "Will you be my father...take me to England?" I wish.

Walking south one morning, on the look-out for a barber, I saw Thuy approaching, her piece of folded cardboard pressed to her chest holding postcards and guide books.

"Where you go? Harry at the fire." she said.

"What fire?" I asked, and she pointed behind me. I turned to see a column of angry grey smoke climbing into the sky above Old Quarter, and it registered then that I'd smelt an acrid burning; tasted it on my tongue... caustic.

"The old market is burning, let's go watch" and taking my hand led me round the eastern shore of the lake. The whole of Hanoiì seemed to be heading there, but Thuy pulled me past the stream hurling insults here there and everywhere, the people's shocked faces bearing testimony to the degree of vulgarity, and through a phalanx of police who had closed the whole block. By now the greasy black cloud was a pall across the sky; had spread across the width of the city, and was still growing in menace; sooty filaments spiralling down onto the crowd. Harry appeared with *his* band of followers, face spotted and streaked with black and, agreeing that we'd seen enough, agreed to a beer. The crowd stayed virtually unmoving for three days until the last flickers of flame were doused and the smoke-pallid sky turned back to blue.

*

As with all lovers, Hanoi and I had a tiff one day, a quarrel, a misunderstanding. Balmy evening beckoning with crooked finger, Harry and I steamed down to Cha-Ca restaurant and weighed anchor in the corner of this beat but lifeful fishdish fooderie. Expecting a shoal of choices and service we looked hungrily around and about, and at each other, and at the ceiling and floor and other face-eeding customers. An hour had passed but no menu seemed on offer. Just when hope was a great pretender, a meal arrived - with a bill.

"What is this?" we asked.

"40,000 dong each person" was the reply.

"But we haven't ordered yet!".

"This is meal at Cha Ca".

Not taking to the meal formally or otherwise we said... "No want".

Shrugging, he took the meal away and the Vietnamese at the next table, thinking we were broke, offered us their leftovers. We thanked them and left, headed straight for the Western style joint by the lake and ordered two simple meals in the hope they might arrive the same day. To eat up the time before the food arrived, I told Harry of two incidents that had shaped my day.

As I ambled along Le Loi St, locks of freshly cut dark hair spun around the pavement in whirlwinds whipped up by the passing traffic. With a speckled gilt mirror hung on the brick wall at every ten paces accompanied by a stool, the pavement was a mile-long salon, and this was 'barber' street. The owner of each and every empty stool plied for my trade with giant smiles, simpering grins or outright camp posturing. I wanted a haircut, but which one to choose? I realised that I was being closely accompanied by a youth on a bicycle who stopped me with a

"Hello...where from?"

"Anh," I replied "England."

"I speak England," he said, his skinny chest puffed with pride, and carried on "You very big."

"No; I'm quite tall..." I said, indicating a point way above his head, which he looked at; "but not very strong," flexing my biceps which looked huge beside his puny arms.

"No!" he said pointing straight at my crotch, "English have bigger dicks than Vietnamese?" and I realised it was a question. Flustered, and remembering China and 'saving face' I replied...

"Yes I believe that is normally true...but I am an exception to the rule." But he still wanted to hold my hand and accompany me home. I managed eventually to persuade him that I wasn't interested in boys or men and he pedalled off on his oversized lady's bike with a smile and a wave. I was still grinning at the encounter when I realised I'd strayed into a back-alley where the words 'shanty' and 'slum' were fighting it out. I was being watched by every window and dozens of shaded eyes. Three bemo drivers sat cross legged ahead of me, sharing a pipe, still wearing their Vietcong fatigues and helmets. Coming abreast, I looked for an expression on their faces. The nearest stretched a hand out to his side, where it rounded and closed on a rock. It cracked into my hip-bone, but not wanting to show alarm, carried on walking, searching their faces for signs of their mood. I could see none and puzzled and hurt, turned back.

"Thank you," I said smiling; again...in Vietnamese "Cam onh," and smiled even more. They looked blankly at each other as I walked off whistling.

"And then what happened?" asked Harry.

"I went to The Old Dahling Cafe for a beer!"

"Aaaaarrrgh, you English, so bloody charming, somebody throws a rock at you and you say thank you; charming!, I will put this in my book." and shook his head. I took it as a compliment.

The food started to arrive, piecemeal. 8.00 a plate of chips. 8.30 a beefsteak. 8.45 my pork chop. 9.00 a salad. 9.45 spring rolls and as we were about to leave at 10.00 along came, lonely on a plate with no butter...a piece of bread. By now we were fagged and fashed and bushed, still hungry and tired, so it was off to a bar to fill the holes with beer alongside two huge Norwegians. On the tiny TV in the corner the world cup was being played out, Bulgaria 2 - Germany 1. And as is the wont of the world today, in the depths of Hanoi in a small bar, in a corner, there was an English football hooligan. He'd dropped his trousers standing on the table, to treat everybody to a look at 'his weddin' tackle' and spotty arse. Jumping down from the table he'd decided that we were Germans and strutted over.

"Alright Krauts, y'wanna know, outside...now!"

"Well cum on then, outside!" spluttered his mate, the one that hard lads always have to egg them on, or hold them back when they don't really want to fight. The Norwegians were looking at each other and Harry, baffled. Even Harry, with his brilliant English, was at a loss.

"Cum onnn!

" I decided that a little diplomacy and translation were needed...

"What's your problem mate?" I asked in my best Millwall FC, "Why y'takin a pot at us?".

"You're fuckin' Inglish!...fort you was Krarts, fuckin look like 'em"

"Give it a rest then, eh?"

"Yeah, no 'ard feelings chief, eh?" They returned to the other end of the bar and, explaining to my companions that they'd been challenged, the two Norges laughed like barrels and looking at them I figured I'd done the Brits a big favour. And wished I hadn't.

The blade of the new moon hung sharp and keen overhead, as we rounded the corner into Hang-Chai and slap bang into the middle of a game of football. Though way past a bedtime, here were all our daytime buddies, none higher than our waists, chasing an old, grey leather football up and down the alley. And there was Dwim and her friends getting in the way and annoying their brothers. The steel shutters were closed on the hostel and our hammering brought no response so we took off our shirts for goal posts and joined the game.

Choosing Dwim's brother as my first team-mate I said to him,

"We'll be England!"

"No," he said "USA number one!, always number one."

"England number two then?" I said confidently.

"No, Sweden number two."

"Why" I asked.

"Sweden help us in the war," he replied, and I remembered then that a large area of the Embassy quarter *was* the Swedish Embassy.

"England must be number three then," hopefully.

"No, Brazil number three, best football players!."

"OK then; USA can't play football, *they've* got a Swede playing for them, so we'll be Brazil!"

"Yeeesss!!" he shouted and gave me a high five, with a slap.

We had an audience of mangy men, ranged along a bench, who smoked, and heckled the kids, and cheered the foreigners' every kick. By the time the alleydust was running down our torsos in rivulets of sweat, the night had been rescued and a blush of peach was creeping into the early morning sky.

44

This Hanoi of surprises and gladness. These people of guile and depths unfathomable. I wasn't surprised that the American GI's so shallow and stupid in their military way had never set foot in Hanoi. For an early Christmas present they once dropped more bombs in two weeks on Hanoi than fell on Berlin in the whole of World War Two. Further south, one of the underground towns, where 18,000 people had burrowed down by hand, was hit by three specially designed penetration bombs which failed to explode. The people dismantled the bombs and used them to make cooking utensils, and the three entry holes were used gratefully as chimneys to ventilate the town. I heard the clinking and clanking of those pots and pans as I drifted off to sleep.

WE SAT in the fresh-cool of the Bi-Bi foyer, hiding from the wicked, wicked sun, where even mad-dogs were under umbrellas. The burly security guard, naked to the waist, handed me a cassette. He was listening to Harry's Nirvarna tape and Harry was reading my Jack Kerouac. What a lackaday place.

And through the earphones MC Solaar, Senser, Cookie Crew and the baddest-mutha sounds from deepest dark Chicago, LA, Brooklyn and Brixton, poured forth. Quel joy. Into this wonderful cacophony of squealing children, adults winking smiles at us sharing music and food, came the lazy, balding, Australian slob who acted as overlord and he swept them all out into the street, leaving Harry and I alone. Once again a room shrank with lack of humanity. The light faded. Outside, mouthing through the window "Howie", was little Dwim and just to annoy I went to the door, crouched on the step, and gathered a clutch of gigglers around me. They stroked my amber pendant, my arms and my heart.

"They're all thieves you know." said the slob. *Don't care.* I hear you and Harry are going to Halong bay; you don't want to go there...the water's freezing."

*

So, I rolled onto my back and swam lazily backwards in the waters of Halong Bay, which were tepid. I swam through an archway, stalactites dripping, and into an auditorium. The mountains rose sheer above and this natural bowl was flooded with sun that bounced around and plunged in and out of the water like a dolphin. Still paddling backwards, ears under the water registering unmentionable clicks and pings, the sky above was an indigo plate, and there, stencilled just off

45

centre was a hawk, each dorsal feather clearly defined. Blinking the salt from my eyes, the plate was wiped clean again.

Harry and I had decided we needed to see the sea and had taken a tour. This was a proper resort where the visitors were wealthy Vietnamese from Hanoi; engineers, doctors and their offspring, sporting baseball caps, American football shirts and the inevitable Marlboro dangling from their lips. And being on an organised tour with a guide, we felt like tourists. I felt as lost as the day I'd walked into Asia, clueless. It was like taking a holiday away from a holiday, but we enjoyed the break, the fresh air floating above the sea; playing about on boats, playing in the sea, playing tourists.

We tried to relieve the torment of the trip home, lengthened by breakdowns, by standing, squirming; anything to gain some room for our screaming legs, and sticking heads out the window to gulp air. It wasn't a long trip compared with the buses I'd taken in China, it wasn't even 'hard seat', but it *was* the most painful; a modern minibus designed too small for Europeans, and I suspect, Vietnamese too. As we rolled to a stop in front of The Old Dahling Cafe, I embraced my beloved Hanoi with a sigh and looked fondly on the Cyclos scuttling past, all leg room, and spinning spokes and open to the damson sky.

Sitting around in a post trip piss-up, the talk turned to the subject of the Embassy parties, to which the English amongst us went "Eh?"

Apparently the Australians had a gathering at their Embassy every Friday, which by all accounts wasn't quite a wine & cheese party, but was still fairly convivial. The French entertained their countrymen with their own country cheeses, saucisson and Bordeaux by the crystal glassfull. The Swedes who had the largest Embassy, encompassing furniture shops, saunas and a swimming pool, laid on a smorgasbord as big as Malmo. Considering that the British Embassy wasn't even on the map, we speculated as to the nature of our 'soiree'. We decided that we would have to take a carrier bag of takeaway Special Brews so we could get 'lashed' before arrival. This would be necessary to dull the disappointment of limp cheese sandwiches served with Courage Pale Ale in plastic beakers by staff with fags hanging from their mouths. hs. After twenty minutes we would stagger out into the street, where a Kebab van would have been laid on to make us feel 'at home'. After throwing up, we could crawl home across Hanoi leaving a trail of salad and pitta bread along the road and chili sauce down our clothes.

But having read many a Graham Greene novel, and also a genuine query concerning the X-Ray machine at the airport, I set out next day to find the 'little corner of England in this foreign land'. It wasn't difficult to find; I just followed the trail of salad and pitta bread across Hanoi. Arriving at Sunday lunchtime, they were of course - shut. In fact they were shut for Sunday, and Saturday...and half day closing on Wednesdays. I almost reached for my ration book. By luck, as I hung my arms through the wrought iron gate and pushed my forehead against the rails in an effort to read the tiny plaque on the door, a Range Rover pulled up behind me. The occupant slid out in standard issue tropical Embassy attire; white short sleeved shirt - pen in pocket, shorts and socks; and brown sandals. The whole outfit blended with the pink-white skin to suggest an ice cream sundae. I 'hulloed' him omitting the 'old chap' as I thought it would sound facetious.

"Hullo old chap" he retorted, "I'm afraid we're closed...Sunday lunch you know, but what seems to be the problem?" I explained that I may have inadvertently put my films through the ancient X-Ray machines at Hoi-Ban airport, which could detect bombs bigger than a doodlebug, create cancer and possibly explode your films. He 'mmmmm'd for a long time whilst pulling the beard he didn't have.

"Come in and park your behind a moment, I'll think of the right man to have a natter with." The right person was 'Terry' at the South China Post, who he phoned.

"Terry old boy, got a small problem...rather, have a chappy here with a problem. Rather nervous that he's put his films through dodgy X-Ray machine...any clues?..mmm...mmmmmh" and all the time he nodded at me with reassuring smiles. "mmm, yaaass, champion!!, Oh well done, thank you, thank you," and dropping the phone back in the hook, exclaimed..."piiingg!" as though, twenty years earlier his last English phone had one and this one should have too. Swivelling sideways and leaning back at 30 degrees, hands locked behind head, brown sandal crossing brown sandal, he addressed the ceiling fan.

"Well young man, we can allay your fears, Terry has pronounced the Hanoi..X-Ray..OK! Haw, haw, haw." I slipped away with...

"Many thanks for your time."

" Not at all" he said, pulling the cork from a brandy bottle with a squeak, "it's my job you see," and the sunlight dashed through the facets of the crystal glass cherry brown, as the brandy tumbled in. I like to think that after I left he lit a cigar to complete his Sunday lunch.

*

ELBOWS leant on the rusty rail of our dormitory balcony, I looked down through the spider's web of telegraph wires that radiated from a point below and to my left, watching the two little girls below argue;

their voices shrill and staccato like moorhens bickering. A 'slap' echoed along the alley, bouncing off the walls of Hang-Chai street and one of the girl's faces snapped skywards with the blow.

"Oyyy!!" I shouted down, the sound of it stopping the bout. They stuck their tongues out at me, wriggling their behinds, then laughing, ran off up the alley arms around each other's shoulders; friends.

Leaning against the wall opposite was a motorbike, a 'for sale' sign round it's neck, like a slave. As in lovely Yangshuo, I was growing tired of being in the same place. It was time to move on. With sudden interest, I skipped down to the bar and, grabbing a chill glass of lemon, stood in the doorway, all but my toes in the shade. It had recently arrived; ridden the 1500 miles up from Saigon by Ian -an Irishman, and I had an irresistible urge to turn it around and take it back to, or away from it's home. Perhaps I was turning into a traveller at last! I was going to spend 300 dollars on an old Russian bike, ride through Vietnam alone and hopefully sell it for the same amount in Saigon before my plane left the ground, me chasing after it down the runway, the bike parked forlorn and ownerless at 'Departure' crying two-stroke tears.

She was a Minsk 250, Russian, I called her Minx. The Vietnamese called her 'shit', and as I was to find out...she was.

Harry, looking forlorn, hissed like a pressure cooker "Shhiiiitt!!...I want to cancel my Laos flight. *I* should be doing that; riding across Vietnam on a motorbike. Goddam I envy you!" Others in the Bi-Bi bar nodded agreement in French and Belgian and sympathy.

"What an adventure you will have, on your own, going the opposite way to everybody else." My stomach turned over and I smiled weakly. I wanted Harry's ticket to Laos very badly at that moment.

*

MINX, HIGHWAY ONE

THE NIGHTGUARD crept into our room at 7am, wearing only his Mickey Mouse boxer shorts, and cooed "Howie, Harry!" Our seperate trips were about to begin and though still half-bathed in sleep, panic swept over me.

Whilst packing, I had two cold showers and still reached the ground floor soaked in sweat. I tried to force some food down but it forced me to the toilet, sick, where I sat head in hands, gagging and sweating. I didn't have the courage to set off and even my team-talk failed.

"Come on!, you're a big boy now; pull yourself together, you can't stay here for ever, you've bought the motorbike!"

But I was a quivering jelly, almost crying like a baby. Harry jumped into his air-conditioned taxi for the airport and I managed to slaughter a goodbye. "I'll let you know how I get on Harry".

"Goodbye...you lucky bastard" said Harry as he closed his door with a 'thunkk'. I sat for another hour in the bar greeting the fellow inmates as they crept down from sleep to daytime Hanoi. "Not gone yet?"

"No, I thought I'd take it easy first day" Eventually, after several false starts, I stood up, plastic chair stuck to my arse, and strapping my bags to Minx enraptured a growing crowd of Hang-Chai dwellers with a performance of melting into a puddle in front of their very eyes. They almost applauded. Flinging out goodbyes and sweat at everybody, I started Minx, who obligingly roared into life, surprising me and the small boy sitting next to the exhaust and out of my sight. I wobbled the 50 metres down to the road, and realised that the wobble was Minx, not me. The front suspension was lethal, so turning gingerly I scurried back to the hostel, sweat drying by the second. Saved by the suspension. Later that day, Ian and I stood, embarrassed, as a minge of mechanics laughed a new pair of front struts into Minx and giggled as they pointed out other features that they had found.

But I had another night to steel my elastic nerves and the next morning the sweat that darkened my shirt was due to the temperature and not rising panic. I cockily ate a fruit salad and saying goodbye to the one traveller in the bar, rode out of Hang-Chai. I made it to the lake, half a mile away, where Minx flopped to a halt. Tinkering with every unnecessary bit I could find, in order to look knowledgable, I was joined by an old man who looked young, or a young man who looked old; I just couldn't tell which. He was a bicycle repairman and had a large, oilskin pouch containing dull steel tools which he laid out on the pavement in a fan.

We cleaned the sparkplug, checked the wiring, screwed in the mixture screw, screwed it out again. The postcard sellers, who'd been steadily gathering, had lost interest in selling cards by now and were also tinkering. The old/young man flew at them when they started to use his tools and as he wielded the largest spanner above his head they scattered. They returned though, like carrion to a road-kill, and he gestured to me to push the bike. We wheeled the little bitch round the corner into a lagoon of quiet, and a proper mechanic. My man and his man huddled over the engine and eventually, calling me over, indicated that Russian petrol taps worked the opposite way to the rest of the world. I slapped their backs, shook their smiling hands and shared a smoke with them as they poked and pointed at Minx, looking at me with obvious concern.

I smacked Minx out of Hanoi on Highway One with Hondas all round me sneering, and set to my task, weaving in and out needlepoint fashion...1800 miles to go. I bucketed along, trucks bowling by and hitting me with a wind like the blow of a fist.

I HAD cleverly chosen the hottest part of the Vietnamese summer in which to ride. Huang, the young Chinese waiter in Yangshuo, had predicted it graphically to me. "Huang...is it always this hot in June in China?" I'd asked, sitting under the jacaranda tree, where a dappling of shade fell onto me like a cold compress. He nodded, stony-faced.

"And July?"

"Hotter!" "August *much* hotter", and knowing my travel plans well he added... *"Vietnam hotter than August!!"*

As I left the outer limits of Hanoi, the surrounding crowds thinned in proportion to the increase of potholes. Most of these were avoidable but in particularly bad patches, or lapses in concentration I would slam into holes big enough to bathe a baby. With the weight of the backpack strapped to the petrol tank, the suspension would hammer into the frame and both the pack and myself would be momentarily airborne, the shock having travelled up my spine. At times I resembled a Rodeo rider, as Minx bucked and bolted across the road, the engine whinnying when the wheels were off the ground.

All traffic now seemed to be lorries or buses, the latter travelling at the same speed as me. Following close behind, I would be in a maelstrom of dust and flying grit which would force me to overtake.

Travelling at only a few miles per hour faster, I would crawl alongside the bus, turning the heads of the passengers. I'd now be in a desperate race as the rest of the bus would be called over to my side to look, unbalancing the bus and veering it towards me. Many times, with Minx on the grubby verge of the ditch and the bus inches from my right handgrip, I would wring the life out of the throttle to gain a last morsel of power and pop out into clear space like a cork from a bottle.

I managed to sneak glances at the passing countryside between traumas, though at this stage my goal was to put miles between Hanoi and myself, and keep the gap between Minx and I minimal. The region was featureless, spreading out tableflat with only a faint grey smudge on the horizon to suggest a landscape. The route was ticked off by telegraph poles, none of which were upright. At rare points the road ran through small groves that hung over to meet above the road and cast cool, green shade. These flashed past in a blink of the eye.

The paddies ran right up to the edge of the road, brown stalks sticking up from brown water, held in by brown banks; the odd shooting crop, an emerald flash like a diving Kingfisher.

Stood, fifty metres apart on their own island, were shacks,or houses; each one linked to the road by a dirt causeway or a bridge of railway sleepers. Each one was a family. Each one was a business. At the front of the shack by the road would be a small display cabinet, the top half glass, the bottom - wood-effect formica with stickers from worldwide manufacturers. In each cabinet could be seen several cans of soft drink; Panda, Fanta, Coca-Cola, their splendid liveries faded to pastel from being left on the the shelf. These normally shared their shelf with a roundel of processed cheese triangles, the cow on the front leaping and shaking it's bell across long forgotten Alpine pastures. Once I stopped and turned back, as alongside the usual victuals was a pot-noodle. Someone had anticipated the backpackers. The cabinets puncuated the whole length of Highway One. The longest convenience store in the world. Each shack was the same.

As I pass by, the smell of dry stones and sunburnt bushes fills my nose, a mother stirs greens in her wok with a SSSSHHHH!! and acrid smoke rises from the burning oil, drawing a veil across her face. A child, from head to toe the colour of the road dust, lifts his T shirt and scratches his round and stretched belly. The man bends over a wheel, stretching a rubber tube on, using spoons as tyre levers. The Dansette transistor radio sits on a shelf with a rusty oilcan, talking mumbo-jumbo and spitting out songs. Gravel from my wheel peppers a chicken, which flaps into the sullen air, beating it into life with

flapping wings. Inside, shaded from the world, an old man lays dying.
In the sales cabinet by the road the carton of cheese slices weeps.

For hour after hour I rode on, leap-frogging with lorries and buses;
the slowest of the buses on their side in the ditches; one aflame - it's
passengers seated in a row along the verge watching the show. My
arms and thighs were burning despite the total sunblock I'd applied, my
shoulders popped at the sockets with the strain of hanging on and my
arse was nowhere to be felt. I had to stop.

Along a deserted stretch of road I spied a bamboo-shelter and
slowing, drove straight through the opening and into the shade. I cut
the engine and through red-rimmed and dustcaked eyes, as the gloom
lightened, saw a boy lying inches from my front wheel, legs tucked up
to his stomach, hands curled around his head. As cheerily as I could, I
called..."Chao em!..Anh!" to which one frightened eye appeared from
behind the hands and blinked. But as I busied myself wiping off the
grimy sweat, applying more cream, bashing the dust from my hat and
neckerchief against the bamboo wall, he stood and watched me, hands
twisting together behind his back. Unfolding my decrepit map (free
with the bike!) I asked him if I was going in the right direction. My
sudden appearance had struck him dumb, as did the map of Vietnam
which he'd probably never seen before. He stayed silent. Taking down
my shorts he, rather gentlemanly I thought, looked the other way and I
pulled on my trousers to cover the tomato coloured thighs. This left
only the beetroot arms to stare at, but perhaps it was his favourite
colour as he suddenly pointed in the direction I was going, and after
fingerjabbing at the floor and me and Minx and the map, he showed me
that I'd covered one inch of a map that could have been used for a
tablecloth.

I was beat. The boy was an idiot. Surely.

I fished my bottle of water (sterilised with a tablet the night before)
from my backpack and drank. It was hot and tasted of plastic and
chemicals. I held it out to the boy who drank without complaint or
grimace. I sat propped against the wobbly wall, and lighting up a
cigarette offered him a drag. His face broke into a smile and he
dropped down to sit next to me, taking the cigarette between dirty
fingers and blowing blue smoke into the chinks of light that wriggled
through the bamboo. We spread the map over our laps, pointed to
names, reading them to each other pointlessly then, using the little
yellow book, we carried on a phrasebook conversation. He mimed
eating and pointed at me, and I thought 'that would be handy' and read
'Yes please' from the book. 'No' he indicated and pointed at my pack;

52

he wanted food. Seeing that I had none, he rose and shaking my hand set off towards Hanoi. I noticed that as he turned the bend he was a diminishing silhouette against a crimson flecked sky and to my right the sky was a charcoal juggernaut rolling in for the night. It was too late to try to reach Sam Son. I decided to stay put. I watched the sunset until dark swallowed up the hut, listening to my walkman and smoking. I pulled Minx across one of the corners and curled up behind it on the dirt floor, backpack for a pillow. The thunder of lorries passing thinned, but each one woke me from a half-sleep with a start. In-between each, the only sound was of reeds brushing up against each other, hissing at the warm night breeze.

I woke with a start, sweating, banging my head on a footpedal; and knocking Minx over ran out to the road cursing and stamping. The sky, almost a false blue, stretched to receive the heat of the day. It was already hot, and after applying suncream, wheeling Minx out, strapping my pack on and starting her up, I was already panting like a dog in the road.

I set off, doubtful of my position, hopeful, but after stopping at several hanky-sized shadows and asking passing cyclists to look at the map, it was confirmed. The boy had been right. I stuck to my task, basted my arms and rode on with swarms of bees raging inside my fingers. Approaching a rare bend in the road I found with horror that the handlebars were no longer attached to the bike. I stood on the brake, the back end snaking in the loose gravel, and leaning as gently as possible to the left, hit the footbridge to the next shack, missing the ditch. Minx flick-flacked left and right and throwing me to the floor, ground a tricycle into the dust. I sat up and seeing the cogs and wheels, inner tubes and spokes hung on the outside wall realised that I'd crashed right outside a bicycle repairman's.

He must have dreamt of this day; he was laughing as he pulled Minx, wheels still spinning from the floor. He almost hugged the crushed tricycle and held it up with glee to show the children, who had now gathered in a row outside the shack. The neighbours had arrived now, laughing and shouting and dusting me down; holding up the handlebars like the head of a guillotine victim, the sinews and tendons still attached. My host bore a striking resemblance to Elvis Presley and wore a snow-white T shirt, but he set to straightway with the help of his friends, to fix Minx. She was stripped of her outer clothes, her undies, and then she was poked and prodded with steel. I hoped it hurt. I tried to help but they waved me away, made me sit in the shade, brought tepid tea. I decided to entertain the crowd of women and children. I pulled faces, tweaked little ears, sweated profusely for them.

Elvis showed me the retaining washer that had sheared off and then a bicycle equivalent that he proposed to alter to fit. I gave him the thumbs up, relieved.

As they hammered and sawed and cursed and spat, the afternoon wore on. I stood, sat, tinkered with the engine, drank tea, and tea, and tea, and translated words from the phrasebook. In this way I managed to explain who I was, where from, how old, what I did for a job, to the procession of spectators that filed past on their way through life. The day dwindled down and with it my hopes of getting to Som San, a resort where I could eat, drink and sleep. Flicking through the book I had a sudden inspiration and under 'illnesses' I found what I was looking for. Getting to my feet, I announced to the remnants of the crowd and the mechanics that this bike was 'behn ia chay' (diahorrea) and mimed kicking her to death. It was the best joke I'd told in my life. The crowd were in hysterics; I thought they would harm themselves. I suddenly felt a little better. Perhaps this was the way to help myself through the difficult times.

Dusk darkened down and they put Minx's clothes back on under a ten watt lightbulb. They'd fixed the handlebars but as revenge for her treatment, Minx wouldn't start. They threw spanners and hammers around in frustration but carried on tinkering as I sat, head against bamboo, falling into slumber brought on by hunger and the ride. Elvis shook me gently awake some time later, defeat in his eyes, quiff flat, 'T' shirt blackened, and indicated that Minx was still dead by pulling a finger across his throat. I shook his hand, and then motioned 'sleep here?' pointing at the floor of the workshop. He shook his head. I found 'cheap hotel' in the phrase book. He shook his head. He strapped my pack on the back of his Honda, motioned me onto the pillion, and off we went, South. We rode for half an hour under a cloud-shagged moon; lamps twinkling off to each side in the paddies, like fireflies, the only things visible in the dark. As we approached the feeble glow of a small town, Elvis pulled off to the left and up to a set of closed gates that barred the drive of a large hotel. It looked like a communist worker's holiday camp and there was no other entrance. A chink of light grew into a flood that blinded us as the door to a small office next to the gate swung open. From behind the light I heard a gruff request, and gesturing me to stay where I was, Elvis disappeared into the light. After a short, but lonely time, he reappeared and taking me firmly by the elbow, led me into the office. Although bright in the outside gloom the room was dimly lit by a single bulb. The shade had a piece missing as if chomped out by something that ate glass. I took in the bars on the window, the solid wooden bed, the uniform of my interrogator behind the bare desk; and Elvis shrinking into the corner, face agog with fear or awe. The guard asked for my passport and called in a colleague to look at it. They scrutinised each page and indicated for me to open my daypack. The guard shifted through the contents, expressionless, whilst his friend leafed through the phrase- book, and became engrossed with my Walkman. I decided it would be worth losing if I was in trouble. *"I would like to pay the bill"* read the second, haltingly. The first had the earphones on and was mumbling to a tune. *"Where is the shoeshop?"* said the linguist.

I looked to Elvis who, holding up three fingers, pointed up the road. *"Is it an express train?"* I hoped he meant that there was a hotel three miles up the road or a guesthouse for three dollars. It occurred to me that I may be about to get three years. *"Do you have cheese?"* and with this he smiled broadly and handed back the book. He pulled the plug from the Walkman, and taking it from the sulking guard, repacked my pack. He led me to the door and pointing into the darkness said "LOTOBA".

Elvis had already started his bike and was moving. I hopped on whether he liked it or not and we sped on further into town, a clutter of cafes, shacks, and tyre dumps lit by strings of white lights; and near the centre we stopped outside what resembled a communist worker's holiday camp. Elvis came in with me and explained the situation, and though they were shocked by the small amount of money I wanted to pay, allowed me to stay. The owner explained that it was a trucker's hostel, and looking round the motley collection of grimy men seated around on steel chairs and plastic sofas, all looking at me, I was pessimistic of reaching the morning with my arse intact, or any belongings.

It was a gem though, a haven, a palace. It was a family suite with a fridge, air-con and fans, bed linen and a wood panelled ceiling a long way above the Princess mosquito net which wafted away any strays that had chanced the Arctic temperature. I could have fitted twelve backpackers in here, comfortably. I hadn't eaten for two days now and had no appetite but I knew that I had to get something inside if I was to survive the journey, besides, I needed beer so I could at least stay sane. I hid my cameras in the mosquito net cabinet and checking the door-lock several times, tripped across the strip to the row of indistinguishable cafes. They saw me coming. Each proprietor was at his or her doorway, leaning like dominoes, eager, smiling, hopeful. I had to choose one and quick as I'd run out of road to cross. Providence lent a hand, and delivered a small pothole into which I could stumble. Falling forward, hands outstretched, I was caught by a dominoe which had rushed from it's doorway. Thanking her, I sat down on one of the small stools and ordered a beer to gain some time to work out the food. I smiled at the neighbouring proprietors, whose faces were set in stone, and took a little bet with myself that the pothole would be filled in tomorrow. Before I could shout "No!!...beeeeer", the old crone was shovelling things into a tall glass. I leapt across in the semi-darkness and saw the glass filling with cod's roe, olives, raspberry jam, eyes, and a topping of grated Gouda. She handed it to me smiling and the two police officers at the next table fixed me with a deathly stare, their mouths still chewing. I saw that the bottom portion was ice so, plunging the spoon through all the shit, scooped some out and rammed it into my mouth with a *"mmmm!!!"* waiting to gag or retch. It was a fruit cocktail; with coconut topping: but it was like no fruit I'd ever seen or tasted. I got my beer, and so managed to make the meal look enjoyable. One of the policemen reached over and without word or gesture, handed me a cigarette. Was this a reward? or payment for another performance. My usual audience had now gathered around and above and below me as Vietnamese stools are four inches high. This put my knees up beside my ears whilst my forearms were on the floor: a Barbary ape with glasses. The crowd always gathered in the same order: an eight year old boy would sit next to me (They always had some English) and find out where I was from, going to, and how old.

His friends, initially shy, would move in and sit, and growing bolder, stroke my leg. An adult would then approach and having got the details from the boy, shake my hand or squat down on his haunches to smile at me and listen. This would be the signal for any other grown-ups to join in the circle.

At this point, (adding more as I travelled down the country) I would do the coin trick that Guy, the Israeli taught me in Yangshuo. It was a simple sleight of hand trick that never failed to amaze. The men, being great gamblers, would then elbow the kids aside shouting "Get thee behind!!". I would do the trick until one of them saw the secret and then, estatic, he would either let on or clam-up. Either way, the pressure was then off me.

The routine carried on as normal. The initial boy, holding my hand, asked "You like her?" pointing to the person now seated to my left who I hadn't seen yet seen, "You want her?...five dollars."

I turned sideways to look at the beauty I knew would be there. She was gorgeous; stunning, with head held coy. "She work your hotel." Her hair shone even in the dark. "Four dollars." She looked the most innocent girl in the world. Tearing my eyes from her I asked him,

"I suppose she's your sister?"

"Yes" he said, "three dollars." At a quick reckoning she was about the one hundred and fiftieth 'sister' I'd been offered since I left home and I'd refused them all. Would this be the first? After two days of fighting Minx and the weather I was filthy and beat. The cockroaches would pack their bags when I took my boots off. I had nappy rash, hadn't eaten much, and had to get up early. But the main persuader was the thought of being the only foreigner in a hostel full of Truckers, shagging one of their girls. I said no. I retired gracelessly but slept like Valium in anticipation of Elvis turning up at noon.

HE meant nine. Sitting outside honking on Minx's horn, he had me scurrying around at five past, trying to clean my teeth, pack my back-pack and put on my stinking clothes. It was a scumbag that walked out that midsummer morning, all burnt and scrawny and raggedy-rawny. The faces of the men with Elvis told the story. Minx had been fixed, alledgedly, so I thanked Elvis and pulled ten dollars from my pocket, asking *'is that enough?'* with my face. From the look he gave me and the gathered truckers, it was more than enough. I roared away up the road, back on track again, the 9.20am air whistling freshly past my ears: for two miles. Minx hated me. I hated her. We rolled to a halt on a bare strip of road, the exhaust ticking as it cooled, and the day warming. I sat on the pillion smoking angrily as the caravan that was Highway One passed by. A man stopped, said hello, then passed out of my life for ever. The fields, which here at least were green as a Somerset pasture, gave off a whiff of clover and the bitter tang of dandelion; but there wasn't a moo-cow in sight. I pushed Minx the half-mile and rested. I was beginning to learn the nature of the heat, dashing from shade to shade like a Red Indian creeping up in ambush; standing still, waiting for nothing. Cyclists trundled by, shouting encouragements or insults back at me, and the honking of bus and lorry horns alerted the next bicycle repair shop who came down the road to meet me. They pushed Minx into the workshop, and me into a chair under the fan in the 'bar' next door. Bringing lemon water, they quizzed me as usual and I spent the next two hours being laughed at or with, while I worked through my expanding repertoire. Looking on at the gang repairing Minx I pointed out the largest of the men and asked him to hold the back of the bike. I took the arm of the fiercest looking and pulling him to the front, put his hands on the handlebars. The crowd looked puzzled as I mimed picking it up. The two men did.

"Now," I mimicked swinging it, "Mot.... Hai....Ba!...throw it in the paddy!!", pointing at it. "It's Russian, it's shit!" They suddenly saw the joke, hooted and hollered, took turns pretending to do it.

"Right," I said, as Minx eventually fired into life, "It's been a lovely Sunday lunchtime but I must go, how much do I owe you?" and unfolding my wallet, the photo of Bumble kept me there for another twenty minutes. "Five dollar" said the lemon juice boy. "Two dollar" said the mechanic. My patience was beginning to wear thin.

"No sunshine, you've got it round the wrong way, He gets the five, you get two, and that's over the top." His face flushed with temper but the mechanic's friends rounded on him for trying to rip me off. The mechanics were happy. I couldn't give a shite. As I rode off up the road I began to realise why Minx was such a mess. In her trips up and down Vietnam, she'd been raped and pillaged repeatedly and just wanted to lay down and die. I may have to let her do that at some point, but in the meantime, coax her like a sick foal as far as we could go.

*

SAM-SON

Minx managed to keep going for another few hours, but arriving at Sam-Son, our destination, she coughed and spluttered down the beach road and rolled to a halt with a final wheeze outside a cafe. Lounging in a deckchair to my right, mirrored sunglasses glaring, Hawaiian shirt shouting, was a man gesturing me to sit down.

"Can I sleep here?" I asked, miming sleep and pointing above the bar, "giuong?" (bed?) He gestured me to sit down, called the owner over and offered me a drink. Putting Minx on her stand I answered,

"Beer...I'll have a beer...big one." I offered him a cigarette, and then passed them out to his friends who'd been eyeing the Silk Cut packet hungrily. I lounged back in the deckchair and let out a long *"aaaaagggghhhh"*. He smiled, but was still silent. An anger suddenly shot through me, not a rage, but a cool, deliberate, dull feeling.

"Excuse me," I said to my companion, putting my beer down on the olive green oilcloth, "I have to do something." I walked from the shade to the burning pavement, which rankled me further. I kicked Minx over Kung-Fu style into the middle of the road and put the boot in: one for each tyre. Leaving her there and ignoring the open mouths, I returned to my deckchair and friend, who I noticed had a larger smile now. We sat silent together for a long time watching the holiday makers parade, his eyes cool and shaded, mine red-rimmed, sore, gritty and if I could have seen them - a certain mad glare had crept in. Periodically he flicked a casual finger to point out a girl, and once to see off a group of James Dean clad youths who stopped to stare. The finger told two of his cohorts to go and bring in Minx from the dust, petrol trickling from her tank. Another climbed aboard his new Honda, motioning me to join him. Looking at 'The Godfather', he nodded assent.

"Food" the driver threw back at me, as we spun through the town.

And then I was sitting alone in a restaurant with his family and their dog watching me, head cocked to one side. They brought a dish of rubbery chicken, yellow, tight skin, and sticky rice wrapped in leaves. It was good food and I tried to force it into my shrunken stomach. I tried hard. I really did, but I could only manage a little. Taken back to the bar, and staggering with exhaustion, I asked again if the place had rooms. The sunglasses flashed and the finger pointed to the hotel opposite that rose five storeys above the street-stalls. It looked like a refugee from Beirut. Nearly finished, or semi-demolished, (difficult to tell which), it had been built by the Russians and was damned ugly. But, it was a hotel and obviously upmarket, in a resort where two storeys left the occupants giddy. Sam-Son was a holiday haunt for office workers and families with money from Hanoi, so I replied to 'the Godfather' that I couldn't afford it; eight dollars was my top price for accommodation (more than I'd paid anywhere). He smiled, thinking perhaps that I was joking, and signalled two of his men to take me over there, one pushing Minx. I thanked him and offered him the rest of the Silk Cut. Shaking his head, he took a packet of Marlborough from his pocket and showed them to me. Of course; America number one! Marlborough country. I took my packet back, and pointing to his, said in Vietnamese, "Shit!." He smiled so wide I thought his gold filling would fall out.

The reception was huge, it's keeper tiny, with a shock of black curls. He was filling in the register which was a vast blackboard with the hotel drawn in plan. The occupant's names were chalked into each box with different colours. Stopping in his task, as my minders explained the situation, he let out a "Baaaggh!" and turned back to it. I shouldered my backpack and shrugging at my friends, headed for the door. One of them tugged at my sleeve... "twelve dollars".

"No" I said, "eight dollars only." Half way down the mezzanine steps I heard..."nine dollars." His face was spread with concern and I didn't want to make trouble for him and 'the Godfather' so I said... "OK."

He took Minx and I to the security guard's hut and explained that he would fix it for me, then we were off on the long climb to the top floor, and my room. I expected to be sharing it with the Munsters or The Adams family, but no; I had another family suite to myself albeit devoid of any trimmings apart from the solid board bed. I stepped out onto the balcony, legs quivering, head spinning and reached for the rusty railing for support. Below was a checkerboard of simple roofs; clay tiled, tin sheeted, flat concrete, and scattered amongst them like coolies were straw-hatted huts and shacks - the kitchens, food stalls and bars of the resort, blue smoke seeping through their thatch. From these arose a clamour of a hundred karaoke machines, all blasting their own tune, each one out of tune. The buildings crept up to the concrete promenade where pony and traps clip-clopped along between the holiday-makers, walking back and for, up and down, left, right. Then came the strip of yellow, scattered with bodies that lay still in the sun, or moving around like Mexican Jumping beans. In the water, which heaved sluggishly, the bobbing heads put up a great shriek, as if they were a flock of seabirds, and this clamour mingled with the karaoke that hit me like a soldier beating his drum.

I lay down on the hard boards of the bed and watched the ceiling spin and when I closed my eyes the bed whirled round and round. I fell unconscious; sounds of Brighton and Littlehampton drifting through the window.

I woke with a start. Where were my cameras? They weren't in the room anywhere, nor in my backpack. I looked in my head and there they were; in the mosquito net cabinet at the trucker's hostel, crying. I was almost crying. I raced down the stairs, two storeys at a time, trying to get my head straight. Would Minx make it back? What if I broke down in the dark? the lights didn't work. Were the cameras still there? Who spoke any English?

Lahn, the girl at the bar, apparently spoke a little. I sat with her in the deep sofas by the bar and using the little phrasebook explained what had happened. I had left 1000 dollars worth of cameras under a bed, while chasing round after a 200 dollar heap of Russian shit. It took an hour, throughout which other staff and guests tried to help, some by just standing and staring, puzzled. Lahn pointed in the book to 'Doctor' and I assumed this was because of the condition I was in.

"No" I don't want a Doctor, "I want my cameras back" I almost wailed. The Doctor was on holiday and they fetched him back from the beach still wearing his trunks under a towelling beach robe. He spoke English. "What was the name of the Hotel?"

"I don't know."

"What town was it in?" I didn't know. It was clear they thought I was a complete idiot. I was.

"It may have been Tha Trung, Hong Trung, Nam Dihn, Tam Dinh."

"You must sit quiet and try to remember the town and when you have, Lahn will ring the police there. They *will* go to the hostel and find the cameras as they know they can make you pay to get them back." And leaving for the beach, he added "You don't look very well."

I sat in the sofa trying to think, beating myself mentally with fist and boots and whips for being so stupid, while Lahn and a friend sat with me offering gentle comforts. "Will find camera. Police will find. Calm." And unfortunately their tenderness led me to the brink of tears which upset them and they held my hands, one each.

I went up to my room to give them a break from their vigil. A straggle of kids shouted over and over at me through the slatted door, their bright eyes shining through the gaps at different levels. I was in a dangerous condition. Each time I chased them away they returned like flies disturbed from a corpse. The last time I almost caught them, but a shout from the woman next door saved them from plummeting six floors to the ground from the end of my boot. The whole hotel was trying to help but I couldn't help myself. Everybody had an idea, I was a frigging celebrity. I went outside to sit on the Hotel steps for air, whilst the holidaymakers filed in from the beach with towels and rubber rings and even buckets and spades. I went back to sit in the sofa as twilight slipped into bed to sleep. Sitting facing Lahn again, a vision flashed through my mind. I was sitting on a stool, staring at the beautiful 'sister' who worked my hotel, and there behind her and next to it, was a ridiculous clocktower; it's huge Art Deco letters stood proud and lit in the sky: Perfectly round O and the front stroke of the A's curved. LOTABA; the B a small arc sitting on it's Father's shoulders. I looked into Lahn's eyes, so hopeful and sad and whispered 'Lotaba'. From the biggest grin in Indo-China she squealed...

'LOTABA HOTEL...HA TRUNG!!' and the words floated over and around and through the whole hotel, and the people passed them down to the beach where they were wrapped up in towels and brought back to the Hotel.

Lahn phoned the police who were going to ring back at 9.00. I wouldn't be able to return 'til the morning, even if they were there, so I consoled myself with a beer. Sitting there it dawned on me that if I'd lost my cameras my pictures of China and my first friends, Hanoi and Thuy, Dwim and Harry had gone with them. I groaned inwardly, and achingly sad, went out into the night to try and eat a last supper before sentence was passed on me. Down on the promenade I picked the emptiest cafe and a seat in the semi-darkness to avoid attention, found 'Chicken' and 'Rice' in the book and ordered. By the time the two fried eggs arrived alone on a plate I had calmed down and thanking the owner, tucked in with my chopsticks. My stomach had other ideas though, and only allowed me one. The owner looked disappointed when he collected the plate, but returned seconds later with a dish of nuts. I ate them singly and slowly as I watched the passers-by and wrote, head down to hide my face, until 9 o'clock came round. I left, complimenting him on the meal and paying double. I wondered if, when more travellers came this way, fried eggs with peanuts would be on the menu.

Reaching the hotel, I climbed the two miles of steps to where Lahn stood waiting, expressionless. Facing her eventually at the top, she said

"You look happy Howie." "No, Lahn, not happy."

"Yes" she said, and it came - a dashing twinkling starlight from out of the gloom..."Camera under bed in Lotoba!"

LOTOBA. I loved that word. I loved it in English, in French, Vietnamese or in Art Deco. I was going to have it tattooed on my dick for luck.

Whole families waved me off early in the morning, and I promised myself to come back later and thank everybody properly. Minx took me the whole way: almost. She coughed a final gasp; with that magic word visible above the huddle of Ha Trung. Pushing Minx into the car park, I went in to claim my cameras. The police hadn't bothered to get involved and left it to the manageress to give them to me. She seemed delighted for me and handed them over, beaming. The swarthy truckers seated around the reception on vinyl clad furniture were also beaming.

As I fiddled with the bike outside a group of them joined in, took over, and two hours later had found the problem. The key didn't work properly and was turning itself continually. I thank-thank-thanked them and we rode back to Sam-Son as happy as two deadbeats could be, and displayed the errant ones to the masses. They were all beaming. I owed these people something, if only showing my face around. I took off for the beach, a swim and food. Changing into my trunks, sarong wrapped tightly round, I was being watched by several hundred pairs of eyes, and as I swam around in the tepid sea a vast shoal of little black heads surrounded and followed me like pilot fish. Dried off by the sun, I walked amongst the lovely boys and even lovelier girls that paraded up and down the beach all day. Being an oddity I was pro-positioned by each and every one. Now I knew what it was like to be a film star, celebrity, public property: on call to all that pass by de-manding a 'hullo' or smile. It was damn tiring being a freak and 'giving' thousands of times a day; but at the same time, it could be lovely. But this night I reached megastar status.

I informed the mop-headed receptionist that I would be leaving in the morning and, packing my bag, slipped out for a meal. As I left the hotel I glanced back and the evening dusk made mirrors of the plate glass doors in which I could be seen looking forlorn and skinny.

I returned to the 'fried egg' cafe and placing myself at a prominent table, returned all the greetings sent my way. The owner's family had priority and so, joined my table. They brought me grilled fish, it's dead-eye round, despite the fact it came from the China Sea; with rice and a finger bowl of chili sauce which they warned me was ..."Hot..hot!".

"Good..good," I said. The hotel guard had arrived and joined the table, silent, and as I bought beers for the owner and myself, included him as well. After an hour or so, he started to look agitated, and rising, put his hand on my shoulder gently and hooked his thumb back up the road. The guard and the owner had a discussion which became heated, their arms and hands flying at each other, like two Sicilians arguing over the price of olives. "He arrest you. You must go to hotel. Pay the bill." I laughed and looking at the guard he shrugged his shoulders with a very weak grin.

"Okay, " I said, nonplussed, "Take me in Deputy, I'll go quietly." He'd ridden down on Minx, now fixed, and putting on my Walkman, used my arrest as an excuse to cruise the town. Having paraded me to the town, he stopped at his favourite cafe and surrounded by his peers, hammed it up. I helped him. We sat at a small table, legs outstretched, lounging like hoods. I put my cigarettes and lighter on the table so he could help himself without having to ask. As girls passed or stopped to gawk, we played 'that one's for you' and 'I want that one'. He'd ordered iced coffees, and to my delight as I sipped it, realised it was coffee-plus. The sting of a rough brandy cut through the creamy texture and mingled with the bitter tang of the beans. It hit the spot. Several of these arrived while we hung out and on leaving I reached for my wallet. He shook his head. They were on the house. We cruised a few more bars, increasing his kudos and I realised, as we wobbled down a fortunately quiet lane, also his drunkeness. Passing the hotel for the eighth time, I tapped his shoulder, indicating to pull over to the left.

I'd seen a flash of colour, and there sitting in his usual chair, was 'The Godfather', mouth smiling but eyes still hidden by his shades. I sat down next to him and noticed that the guard kept a distance. I offered him a Silk Cut, he offered a Marlborough. We smoked one of each other's and as the waiter arrived he motioned two drinks.

"Three!" I said holding up the fingers, "One for him," pointing at the guard. Three glasses of coffee-plus arrived. The guard stayed standing and gulped his down; I figured he was in a hurry. Tipping mine back I said, "Thank you, I must go now."

"What are you doing riding around the town with this idiot?"he said. Shocked though I was I answered, "I'm under arrest."

"What the hell for?"

"I'm not sure." I replied. He barked at the guard, growled low in the throat then savaged him with a stream of sharp language...*"Bac dang fa fang cho mot an thuc thuc baaaahhh!"*...or something like that. He calmed down as the guard explained, hanging his head and muttering to the floor. "He says, they thought you'd left the hotel without paying and he was meant to take you straight back when he found you."

"But my bags are in the room, how could I be leaving?"

"They don't have a spare key so they couldn't check. You had better go back now or this fool will get in trouble. I will tell the manager how stupid he is tomorrow. I hope you have a good trip, though with that heap of Russian shit you probably won't. Stop at Hoi An, you won't be disappointed." I shook his hand. He smiled, and although I had never seen them, I knew that the eyes behind the mirrored shades were kind. We crossed the road, the guard wheeled Minx into his bedroom, pretending to tuck her in for fun, and walked into the hotel with me.

Entering the lobby, I saw that half the hotel were gathered around the old TV, watching a black and white, dubbed English film, the light flickering off their flat faces. They turned, and to a man, woman and child, applauded. I bowed.

*

THE RAILWAY HOTEL, VINH

AN INNOCENT light radiated over the beach that morning and, as though affected by it, Minx pulled away from Sam-Son cheerfully and we set to the 150 kms to Vinh. She was eating them up for breakfast and humming a happy tune. But, as the day wore on, her smile slipped.

I was riding whole sections standing, to ease the pain in my back and my bruised arse, to the amusement of my fellow travellers. And once a whole paddy of workers raised their noses from the water as I passed, bellowing the longest string of curses I could put together. It was my third breakdown when I rolled into the village.

They streamed out to meet me and push the bike to the menders. It was the biggest crowd yet and something was wrong. They crowded round the bike and I had to push to get through. The children, usually timid, pushed back at me and I saw my tools disappearing. I shouted for their return and at once had men each side of me, shouting into my face from four inches, spit flying. I saw then that their eyes were red-rimmed and vacant and I was being baited. Turning to the phrasebook to explain, a woman, eyes mad, and Edward scissor-hands swishing through the balmy air, snatched it away. The mechanic jumped up and grabbed it from her, passing it back to me. She stood, hands on hips, and spat at his feet. She launched a tirade at him and me, worrying at the words like a terrier. Something hit me on the back; not hard.

The crowd were laughing, and with frightened eyes he indicated that I had to get away. He bent down to the engine, me with him, and screwed in the plug cap. He motioned - 'get out' with his thumb and kicked the engine over. She fired. He sensibly kept the throttle open with one hand while I took out my wallet. As they stepped back to make room, I put it between my teeth and grabbed the throttle. I shot through the stalls and spat gravel over the dress circle, praying Minx wouldn't stall. It must have frightened her too, as she ran all the way to Vinh without stopping. And the mechanic? I hope he lives to be a thousand and people the earth with his offspring.

We arrived in Vinh a couple of hours before dark. The people didn't seem to know their way around their own town. Using the Lonely Planet I searched for the recommended hostels. I was sent here and there, there and back, and with Vinh having absolutely no distinguishing features, covered the city several times. I decided that I wouldn't be putting any roots down here. Then, as the dark grew with my temper, I remembered the Station. They had to know where that was. They didn't: I stumbled on the tracks in the middle of a night market, rode along them to the station and through the waiting room into the forecourt. As there were a few shouts being hurled at me I stopped the bike behind a bush and, walking quickly away, headed straight for the hotel I could see glowing in the corner. After a few sad attempts to ask for a room in Vietnamese, they fetched the owner who spoke some English.

"My son speaks English well," he said, "I will send him to talk to you...this is your room. Be careful to lock the doors, the station is a bad place, you should not be here!"....*Great.*

'Oh stuff 'em all." I thought and went downstairs to sit outside the bar. The cool air was tinged with the smell of steel sparking onto flints, fuming diesel, wooden benches. I tried to calm down, relax with my cold beer, but within minutes three scallies, larrikins, hoods, had sat around me, examining. I stared straight at them, silently erupting, as they picked at my boots, pulled my gold ring, fingered my shirt.

"Don't do that!" I said calmly, brushing their hands away. I had my boot on a neighbouring chair: he pulled the lace undone. They weren't playing. I went over the edge.

"DON'T TOUCH ME ARSEHOLE!!" I was on my feet, "Or you'll get this ring alright," I said to the first, my fist an inch from his face.

"And you can have my boot," I said to the second, still seated on his stool, the boot hovering next to his ear.

"And YOU!!" I shouted at the one who'd stood up first "cop this!" and I mimed a Glaswegian kiss. Unfortunately, either the drink or the tiredness had ruined my timing. My forehead smashed into his nose, and sparks flew inside my head. *Oh shit!* He shot backwards over the stool and, expecting a full attack, I grabbed my bottle of Linquan from the table and swung to face the other two. They were lizarding away into the darkness. I sat down on my stool, leaning back against the wall and lit a cigarette, and if I'd looked in a mirror I would have seen a cold, grey, manic stare. Three large men moved over to my table...

"OH...FUCK...OFF!!" I shouted staring into space. They shot back on their stools, hands up in mock surrender, smiling. I smiled back, and holding my bottle to the moon, seeing that it was half full, said...

"Same-same...50." I tipped it down my throat 'til empty and they joined in. We were friends.

The moment that the three left, I was joined by Phong (the owner's son) and his teacher. "You keep very bad company," said the teacher.

"Usually, yes," I said, a bit drunk, "it's a gift you're born with, it can't be taught." I offered Phong a cigarette but he'd given up when he was fifteen. He started when he was five. The rest of the evening was full of chatter, and their presence kept away any unwelcome guests.

I woke with the knife still tight in my hand and used it to strip a Pomelo of it's skin, pith and pips, which left little. Shooting out to the bank and then breakfast, I was stopped by the owner who begged me to join them. It was Phong's leaving day. He was going to Hanoi for two years to study English and Electronics and the whole family were there to see him off. The men had been drinking since 7am and the restaurant was rocking. By mid-day I had 'same-samed' my head off, but fortunately the women arrived...and with them came food! and I had place of honour next to the son.

"One day we hope Phong will be just like you." said the mother.

"Poor bastard." I said.

"Yes, one day." she replied, wistfully. Dish after dish arrived; sticky rice, greens, chicken swathed in lemon grass buffeted by spring onion; plates piled high with tongue and more chicken, strange shaped, with ochre rubber skin attached, dangling and to be eaten with gusto. The sister next to me, who'd had a boot in the back - the third since fifteen, handed me a piece with her chopsticks.

"I like this piece," I said "it even looks like a chicken." Holding it by what looked like a comb, I twiddled it clockwise. The dead eye of a chicken looked at my fingers holding it's comb.

I mimed a chicken strutting along the table and jumping over a bowl of soup, then dropped it in with a splash and a squit and it swam like a headless chicken amongst the chilis and onions which must have stung it's eye. Then pork and dog and fried jaberwocky leapt onto the table begging to be eaten, and rivers of beer ran around the table, most of which seemed to flow into my estuary. The drinking game carried on in earnest. The son had retired early after two bottles but the father was shitfaced and practically cuddling me; "You're a really good geezer, I really love you...my son's going away for two years and he won't drink with me. You go to bed now and we will drink together at 4 o'clock. I'll come to your room." *I don't think so.*

But I was there at the table again, eating with the family, while they snatched dread glances at the clock marching on to 8.00 o'clock, when Phong would leave. They urged me to carry on eating and ignore the running around and preparations and crying of the older sisters and aunties. At last it was 8.00 and Phong appeared at the door with his belongings in a tin box, a hush creeping over the room. He was only a boy, but he was kind, handsome, clever and much loved...and it doesn't come much better than that in any old language. He had a great future ahead. He said his goodbyes and turned into the darkness. The father, next to me, gamely reached for a piece of meat and attempted to remain stoic. The tears running down his cheeks gave the game away though and he reached under the table and held my hand. It was then I realised that he looked like my Father, and suddenly I missed him dreadfully and cried like a baby.

I LOOKED out into the station yard with clear eyes and mind, watching the early morning scuttlings of the people. The pregnant sister had put me to bed and stroked my head until I slept. The madness that had been growing in me like a disease over the weeks had been washed out by the tears and the tenderness of a stranger. It was time to carry on.

Packing my bag, there was a great treasure missing. Robert Smith had gone a-wandering and taken the whole of KLF on his back. But I knew where he'd gone. Phuong had borrowed the tape the day before to listen to and in his rush and gloom had probably packed it away in his the tin box with his few posessions by mistake. Or perhaps Robert had so enjoyed tripping down the leafy boulevards of Hanoi he'd slipped himself into the box for a free ride back. I thoughtlesly asked the father if he'd given it to him, or left it in his room. But no. He was humiliated by his son's mistake. I told him it didn't matter as..."Look...I've got another three!" But face had to be saved and my two days of food and drink were wiped from the slate with a very wet cloth and I was packed onto my bike with kid gloves and cotton wool and waved away by the whole family.

And as though she had also been cleansed, Minx took me, trouble-free, through the Demilitarized zone, to visit the tunnels of Vinh Moc, sneak past the Forbidden city at Hue and on to Danang. And it only took two Lotabas and one bamboo hut.

*

92 THRAN PU, HOI AN

THE ANCIENT and gnarly pantiles lay heavily on each other, staggering up the roof. Foliage tumbled down their steepness, in places holding the broken tiles together in a mutual bond. The buildings below huddled up to each other in a ragged row, discoloured, broken, like an old man's teeth. Down their faces and over the edges of wrought iron balconies dripped frangipani and honeysuckle, that lay their scent on the heavy ozone rolling through the streets from the sea.

Pagodas stood amidst narrow lanes of shutter-clad villas shouting *'Attention!..Francais! Chinoise!'* unheeded, as the seeds sewn in the cracks centuries before, had now matured into a hybrid; strange but interesting. Vespas scooted along the waterfront, flapping the edges of tablecloths, that bore fresh baked bread smeared with confiture, quail's eggs with pepper and strong black coffee that drip-drip-dripped into evaporated milk. But passing behind the condiments and hillock of bread, a fishing sampan could be seen, nets flying out and skywards to land *thwaackk!* on the water; and sink silent. Hiding here and there in nooks and crannies were artists bashing out pictures in a Vietnamese style, but painted with a Chinese brush that had run through the tricolour on a rainy day.

*

I rammed Minx nastily up the kerb to a stop and winces decorated the faces of the local crowd I'd parked amongst. I'd left Danang station at nearlight, Minx's feeble headlight failing to reach the three feet to the road, and knocked off the 60km to Hoi An by 6am with a sense of a mission accomplished.

Hoi An had, in the 17th and 18th century, been one of the most important ports in South East Asia, and driving in it seemed to me that it could hardly have changed in appearance since; though a lot quieter. I liked it already.

"No rooms," said the owner of the hostel. "No rooms today." So I sat in the front restaurant and drank coffee and coffee and coffee until. I was running along the ceiling. A couple leaving, hove into view, so I grabbed their key before the receptionist could reach it.

"Now you have a room...and so do I." I said to her, signing my name in the book. By noon I had showered, eaten and was swimming around in the China Sea with a lazy grin and even lazier backstroke from where, even with my myopic eyes, I viewed a sky high and wide. It seemed to me that the Chinese had taken it's sky and pulled it tight and thin to all corners to fit the land, whereas the Vietnamese had let theirs wander up and away in every direction that it fancied. Looking back to the beach through the gap between my half-submerged feet, I watched a herd of cows pass along the beach, driven from behind by an old man, his cane swishing down onto their skinny rumps.

Later, the sun and salt-water still clinging warm to my skin despite the cool of approaching dusk, I cycled back to town amongst a convoy of old, stiff-backed bicycles. As they rode, chatting, the evening reduced the riders to dark shapes, resembling the bats flitting around above, so that they spoke to me in Vietnamese in error. I answered loudly in English which silenced the flock, but having explained that I was from England and my name was Howie, they rode closer. From in front and behind I heard my name and country being bandied back and forth. Unseen hands patted me on the back if they overtook and blank faces uttered 'Hullo' at me if they were dropping back. I suddenly felt at ease and my troubles fell away, leaving me weak and smiling in the dark. I whistled a silly song (I don't remember what) and many riders joined in, tunelessly, so that as we entered the town people ran from houses to look and toddlers ran in to hide from the din.

I lay showered and cool under the mosquito net, which made ghosts of my room-mates, whilst Gregory Issacs massaged my head through the earphones with a Jamaican beat. A thought nosed it's way in and I wondered why I hadn't thought of it before. Why didn't I sell Minx? Yes, I *had* been collecting some unique experiences, but I wasn't seeing much of the countryside and I was taking a hell of a beating. I hadn't met a single traveller between Hanoi and Hoi An; surely that was good...*or not?*. I decided to let the idea float for a while. It was my birthday the next day and I wanted no worries on my mind, so I decided to limber up with a meal at the much recommended Cafe des Amis on the waterfront.

After a cold beer and a chat in the hostel, I found myself heading out with two Americans, a pony-tailed Englishman and a Vietnamese girl called Ha. She wore the finest silk *ao-dai* to match her perfection and was a doll in all respects. They told me that she was acknowledged as 'The most beautiful girl in Vietnam' and I could see why. Her Uncle owned the Cafe des Amis. It was full, but they made a new table for us at the head of the cafe in full view of the passers-by. We had the standard meal. Any superlative above standard would have struggled,

71

apart from perhaps...perfect. The dishes only stopped arriving when you were fit to bust.

So out of the kitchen came shrimps in Rizla thin pancakes that had hopped briefly in chili sauce. Flamingo pink crabs, twice-dressed with garlic, marched sideways round a huge platter. A formation of mussels sneezed in, all lemon and peppery. Then a very smart troupe of giant prawns in sugar-cane jackets heralded a huge grilled fish, with lemons and bay leaves as scales. Calamari balls, filled with mixed seafood and herbs, brought up the rear where they were smartly caught up by a new wave of crabs, rampant with ginger.

Then cries of..."Enough, enough!" brought golden creme brulees to finish the carnival, and the mellow night breeze blew in to clear the table, the mind and the palate, and carry me home to bed, tucking in my mosquito net; already snoozing into my birthday.

I was sitting outside the Post Office before it even opened, fingers and toes crossed in anticipation, eyes crossed and tongue out in play with two children in the middle of the dusty road. There was something for me. A thick and battered envelope, which I hugged greedily. My first mail in six weeks. Back under the mosquito net I read and reread them all. A birthday card and letter from both parents, a letter from my brother, notes from my niece and nephew with drawings; they all tugged at my heart. I was happy in Hoi An and hoped that they could feel it. If they'd known what I'd been through since leaving home, they'd have been shocked. Good job they didn't, ay?!

And there was one more letter, forwarded from Israel...from Keron. She'd returned home to great trouble. Her fiance had heard tales from many Israeli travellers about her 'affair' with an Englishman! She 'felt less of me now' and would I please not contact her anymore. I laughed, genuinely amused and throwing it in the bin, decided at a stroke that the Israelis were a bunch of insecure, self-opinionated, jingoistic, tell-tale-tits; that is, apart from the Kibbutzniks. I also realised suddenly how nice it was, (as the Israelis couldn't get into Vietnam) not to see their flocks and gangs and platoons marching around dressed as hippies. All the travellers I'd met in Vietnam had been alone or in twos, or had at least had open minds, travelled with other nationalities. But then I also felt sorry for them as they seemed unable to leave home behind and be free. I didn't have time for it; it was my birthday and I was going to the beach. On the way I stopped for a leisurely breakfast by the river - eggs, bread and sweet coffee accompanied by the song of flying fishing nets. I paid one of the boatboys for not taking his boat out for a ride and strolled into the market.

Stale odours of melting ice, giving up it's fishy captives from rushes and baskets, rose up; ranks of mirror eyed fish, stone cold dead in the market; a paint box of spices piled in shifting dunes, each one's colour brighter than the last, their fragrances fighting and mingling and clutching at the ankles of passers by. Dogs lay too hot to snarl, their dry tongues lolling onto the baked earth. All manner of roots and vegetables, dwarfs, giants, yellow-skinned, green-haired, gnarled, twisted, reed-thin, bloated, stood in their cliques, still clinging onto the moist morning earth they were brutally pulled from; the earth putting up a damp, musty aroma that hung heavy in the electric dry air. The chattering of questions and answers, chickens squawking, metal beating, sounded dull and muffled under the cane and tarpaulin ceiling, but out in the naked sun the sound rose in pitch and bang-bang-banged.

I scooted the bike around the corner and passing the blazing, flapping flags of the Chinese assembly hall, swung my leg over the saddle and pedalled off to the beach. I'd arranged to meet my roommates on the beach and there they were, waving me over to their encampment, surrounded by children selling 'pineapple!' 'peanut!' 'cold drink!'. They were Jerome and David - two Gauls, and Katherine - an American girl.

The boys were outlandish and 'plein de la joie de vivre'. They imitated the sounds of birds and animals which delighted the children. Jerome mimicked their pidgeon English and chased them around the beach, flapping his arms like wings. David painted watercolours, using sea-water in a shell and an ancient French paintbox. I wrote and swam, and swam and wrote. Katherine was blond and attractive with a tan and her legs wove together like a plait. The combination of our little colony overwhelmed the locals and peddlers alike and being ourselves was it's own entertainment. The day ran long and light with sun and rain and laughter. I was wearing a broad smile way after the sun dipped behind the mountains and we moved off home in the dark on our cycles: once again wobbling and weaving, hooting 'hellos' and 'bonjours' with the Vietnamese, like owls amongst blackbirds.

At the hostel, my companions announced, "We are going to stay in the room tonight Howie, we are all very tired, I hope you don't mind."

"No of course not," I said, and didn't mind at all. As I showered I thought how nice it would be to sit alone by the river, silent, eating good food and contemplating the past and the future. I was content. Tripping half naked through the kitchen (to the delight of the giggling girls working) I entered my room. There, in a row stood Katherine, stunning in evening dress and long-brushed hair, David and Jerome in white T shirts with ties painted on.

"Taraagghh!!" said David...frenchly, "only joking, you silly Englishman. Did you think we would not celebrate your birthday? we just wanted to test your English politeness. Baaahh! we eat and drink and dance. Let's go!" We did.

At midnight Jerome was chasing children out of the circle of friends into the blackness, squawking and flapping his wings like a crow on speed. The charming thing about Jerome was that he was very handsome and could so easily have spent his time trying to be cool on the 'Rive Gauche', Gauloise dripping from the his lips, self important and shallow. But he got his kicks with games and noises and chasing children. Consequently the locals and travellers alike thought he was cool; which is exactly what he was. The night tumbled on and we spoke of England and France and America, until at last we swayed home, arms linked, lovers, and tucked each other up in bed.

As THE sun geared itself up for another busy day, Jerome chased one last posse of peddlars round the waterfront before jumping on the motorbike behind David. He donned his white pith helmet.

"I hope to see you in Bali, you silly Englishman," he threw back over the noise of the engine. And I knew that if on some beach I saw children fleeing, laughing, from a great crow making machine-gun noises, I would be wearing a huge smile to see such fun again.

'Au revoir mes petit pomme de terres!'

Sitting outside Ha's restaurant, tickling a plate of crab dumplings with fresh chilis and garlic, a summer storm crept up over the pantiles. They closed up like clams, jiggling together. If I stretched my hand out to the right it disappeared through a wall of water. I kept my cigarette in my left hand. The leaves were humming 'tra-la-la', turning greener with delight. The storm stormed itself out and the street was bathed with the scent of sighing leaves, their blossoms breathing out sweet honeysuckle perfume. Suddenly, firecrackers banged along Le Loi St., a thousand double-barrels being fired in ragged procession. The retorts jumped through windows onto sleeping babies, crying them, and crowded in unruly gangs round buzzing motorcyles, striking them dumb. Billowing clouds of stinging cordite swept the street of perfume and, turning the corner, barreled along Kna Kach Rd. Then; a chinese magic trick. As the smoke cleared, each explosion had turned into a vivid vermilion petal. The street floor was the colour of a cardinal's underpants, and petals were still turning in the air, light, then dark and floating to the carpet to join the fun. The wedding party tripped along this an inch above the ground with a terrible clanging of bells and a parade of silk in all the colours of a tube of Smarties. As the procession passed by the petals seemed to brown and tire, limping into the gutter to rest. A strange melody followed along behind, the theme tune to a spaghetti western with a disco beat. It came from two orange-box speakers fixed each end of a bicycle, and sitting slouched between them - a Mexican bandido with wide brimmed hat, eyes narrowed to slits, looking each side into doorways and windows for Clint Eastwood to jump out. It was the Ice Cream Man who had joined the party in the hope of extra business, and I thought...'It's no stranger than Mister Whippy cruising the streets of Manchester's Moss-side, playing Greensleeves in an armoured ice-cream van.' But I bet he didn't have a jumbo cornet with a flake, only a chili lolly.

I sit in evening gladness outside the Hoi An cafe with Ha sat to one side, glowing in the dark, illuminating my writing. She blinks her big eyes and occasionally flits a sensual but sad smile across her kissable lips. She listens, trilling, head swaying side to side to heavy Jamaican reggae, and smiling at me alarmingly. Having recognised her job at the restaurant, (to attract custom) and knowing her mission, (to marry a foreigner) I'd been coquettish with the little Crepe Suzette as I had little to offer. Her little brother brings the visitor's book for me to read. Scanning the endless comments I see it's full of worldwide praise for the cuisine, but more for Ha. It seems that her fame travels up and down Vietnam, like Minx, as 'The Most Beautiful Girl in Vietnam' and each page holds many desperate pleas from Scandinavians, Europeans and Antipodeans promising the earth and asking for her hand. Some travel far to Hoi An just to see Ha and leave proclaiming 'It was worth it.' Stealing a long look I admit to myself it's probably true, but to share electric air and sounds and smiles is enough for me. I think my stand-offishness is affecting her. I don't want her, and in the perverse world of men and women, that is exactly why she wants me. I ask her.."Ha, this book is full of men who want to marry you, look after you, take you to Europe...why haven't you gone yet?"

"I wait for the right man." And she throws a look at me that nearly bursts my trousers. But I might as well marry a Martian; she's as stupid as she is beautiful, but it still leaves that nagging question... what about one night in paradise? I know the answer. You have to pay the piper.

My account of the trip down had spread around Hoi An like a bush-fire and having casually mentioned my small desire to be rid of Minx, offers started to pour in from locals I passed in the street, on corners, even in the sea. They must have been circulating my photograph. The amount being bandied was much lower than I could get in Saigon but the thought of losing my burden was oh-so tempting. I could leave, rested, with just my bedraggled backpack.

As I sat basking on the beach I noticed two burly men seated near and behind me, sunglassed. They were watching my every move and were obviously uninvolved with the beach life. After several hours and dips in the sea I was getting worried, but I had to pass them to leave the beach. I had no choice, I was hungry. Fronting it out, I walked nonchalanty past them looking straight ahead. "Where are you going?"

The tone was inquisitive, not menacing, so I stopped and looked at the four of me in their glasses. "Are you going back to town?...you have been in the sea a long time, you like the waves?"

"Yes" I said "but the waves aren't big enough. I like to surf."

"Then I will take you to China beach, they have big waves there. There are also the best girls, I will get you one." And standing now, he mimed screwing which made both of them smile.

I suddenly remembered the film 'Apocalypse Now' and the mad commander flying over China beach with his helicopter attack -

"See there, it peels right and left, must be four foot. Get in there soldier! You either surf or fight." "But sir! what about the enemy?" "Charly don't surf son."

"How much would it cost?" I asked.

"No, I will take you as a friend. Also, can I come back to town with you, I want to buy your bike." He was actually the agent. It was a young lad that wanted Minx but he couldn't speak English and didn't know how to buy her. We wound through the back lanes of Hoi An, seemingly into the middle of a maze. This was where the proloteriat lived in crowded poverty, tumble down shacks made from bits, so it was impossible to see where one ended and the neighbour began. I was once again in the dodgiest part of town, alone, and although the thought crossed my mind that I may never emerge from here, I felt quite safe with the agent. Crammed into a small room were the agent, a commission man, his friend, two friends of his, some men passing by who came in to watch and a man asleep along a bench, his feet alarm-ingly close to an electric fan with blades like a supertanker's propellors. After some negotiation, we arrived at a price slightly lower than the ceiling under which we sat. One and a half million. The lad had been saving for years and each note was of small denomination and carefully folded in four. The agent looked embarassed and smiled weakly at me. The lad tipped them onto the table from a shoebox.

"That's alright" I said, seeing the possibilities of the afternoon disappearing, "I'm sure it's all correct."

"No, said the agent, it must be counted in front of you." With checks and recounts and a lot of elastic bands it took an hour. It would have been quicker, but the sleeping man, rolling over, put his foot into the fan sending a blade flying like a scimitar across the room into the neat piles. They shouted and insulted him for interrupting the counting as he lay groaning in agony. I was happy. I'd sold a wreck with no front brake, suspension; clutch teetering on it's last, leaking oil and petrol, for $150 dollars. I'd lost just as much on the deal but I figured that the expedition had paid for itself. I'd learnt a lot about loneliness, despair, frustration and I didn't think anything could ever stress me again. Also I wouldn't have it on my conscience selling Minx to an unsuspecting backpacker. These boys knew what they were buying and knew it's value as a hire bike. Bikes were hard to get in the middle of Vietnam. But then the bubble burst. The agent, examining the papers that came with the bike, looked at me suspiciously and said, "This is a photocopy of the licence, it is no good."

"Pardon?" was the best I could manage. I hadn't even looked at it before. He explained it to the buyer, whose face crumpled. I felt like a cheat, albeit unintentional. "Shit! what can I do?"

"You will have to take it to the office in the town it comes from. They will give you a proper one."

"Where does it come from?" I asked, praying it wasn't Hanoi. Scanning the page he announced, "Na Trang." Na Trang was best part of the way to Saigon. It seemed that Minx and I were destined to stay together.

"I am very sorry," I said pushing the pile of money back across the table.

"No." he said, and shoved it back at me. After a long debate with the whole room he said, "We will mend the bike so that it won't break down and when you get to Na Ttrang you must get the papers. If you go to the Thong Nhat Hotel a man will take them from you and drive the bike back."

"It's very kind of you to trust me with this money." I said.

"No," he replied, "we will know where you are all the time." I believed him. I knew now that the Vietnamese were very thorough. Apart from when they fixed motorbikes of course.

The next morning while they fixed Minx, we rode up to China Beach on his motorbike. As we dodged potholes and cyclists he gave me a running commentary. Passing by Danang, he pointed out the airbase where the Americans first made a foothold in Vietnam. We were motoring up a piece of tarmac road which he explained was made by the Americans. "My parents helped to make this road. They were Koreans who were brought over to work on the road."

"Do they still live in Vietnam?" I asked.

"No, they were killed while working on the road; by an American bomb." About then, as I was struggling for a reply, his bike stalled and we came to a halt in the middle of a bridge. I thought 'Minx has a twin!' Lorries were crashing past, horns blaring.

"You might like to stand over there" he said pointing to the side of the bridge. "Yes I might just do that" I said, and did, as he seemed very happy to work on the bike in the middle of the road. It was soon fixed and we reached China Beach. The surf was flat.

As with any surfing beach around the world, wave-starved boardies hung around waiting hungrily for a swell to arrive. The agent took me amongst them and we talked surfing.

"Tom Curren No.1"

"Martin Potter No.1"

I told them that I was on my way to Australia and Hawaii which was greeted by a chorus of sighs 'aaaaagghh!!' The agent had been right, the girls were as beautiful as the surf was flat and they were circling me! As evening drew in food arrived from god knows where, cold beers attached. I insisted they took some money and pleasingly they accepted, but handed it to the stunning girl in the middle that my eyes wouldn't leave alone. The sky was darkening, streaked with runnels of pink and orange, when the agent stood up and putting his hands on my shoulder said quietly, "I am sleeping at my friend's house, I will pick you up in the morning." and walked off.

Dumbfounded, I watched him all the way up the beach and when I turned back there was only one person left sitting by me. Smouldering. To cut a long whatsit short, I wrapped the blanket round her in the morning, still warm and naked and smiling in the sand, jumped on the back of the motorbike and as we raced off back to Hoi An, thought... 'It's absolutely wonderful to be alive and kicking.'

*

NHA TRANG

So, as though leaving the hotel room of a six day love affair, clothes awry, I slipped out of Hoi An at dawn. I pointed Minx's front wheel south, whispered 'Nha Trang...home' in her ear, and set off, startling a dog licking his nuts outside the guesthouse. It was a cool start. The sky was like a drystone wall, all blocks of grey, and the miles fell away behind me. There wasn't anywhere in particular I wanted to see along the way and I'd noted the night before that my time in Vietnam was running short, so I fixed my head to the task. The sun knocked the wall of clouds down and grew and grew with the morning.

Minx broke down. I passed the cigarettes around: electrics.

Minx broke down. I chased the kids, David style: water in petrol.

I found a 'Lotoba' in a nowhere town and stayed the night.

It was a cool start, but not for long. By mid-morning I felt I was riding the rim of a huge foundry wheel, white hot so I couldn't stop, ashen dust for smoke, scouring my eyes and tearing at my nostrils: the same shack, paddy, flick-tailed lizard, passing by to the left and right. Above, the sky was one great sun that defied a glance and beat my eyelids into slits. The road was regular as a canal but potholed, scarred, beaten, it's surface loose and wicked, pulling the tyres into the dusty verge or a hard edged dent, which would hammer the bike into my spinal column, forcing a grunt as it winded me. It followed the path of the railway, holding hands on their walk down Vietnam, sometimes skipping to one side or crisscrossing so they could swap sweaty hands. When they reached rivers they held each other tight so that they were one, and rode piggyback over the swirling brown waters on the backs of creaking, rocking, complaining old bridges. Tacked on the side of the bridges were narrow footpaths, incomplete heartstopping collections of strapped-together logs and river jetsom; seemingly an afterthought that carried the walkers, cyclists and motorbikes. At these Minx shied and whinnied through her wasted shock absorbers and threatened to push her wobbling wheel through the flimsy guardrail, so I struggled to keep her straight and miss the missing pieces. And back on the road I kept the throttle open, trying to stay away from the cloud of brown dust that was tied, swirling, to my back wheel.

On a stretch, virtually empty of shacks and sales cabinets, the road bent lazily to the left; Minx didn't; she headed straight for the sole domicile. The handlebar repair was shot. Once again I laid Minx on her side, my leg trapped underneath, and we crashed through the bamboo wall. I came up in cloud of dust trying to escape the burning exhaust pipe and as things settled down into quiet, saw the family backed up against the wall, eyes round.

"I'm very sorry, I'm English, the bike is Russian!...Chao Em" I said to the pretty little girl with one hand in her mouth. She giggled.

They ushered me to sit down and poured me tea. I drank glass after glass as I gave them the background slowly, with the aid of the phrasebook. The mother, seeing me examine the burn on my leg, rushed off and returned with a pot of gunk which she spread gently on the wound. I'd left a hole in the wall, but unlike in cartoons, it wasn't man-shaped, and I mimed to the father that I would help him fix it. He shook his head, took me round the corner, showed me a pile of concrete bricks, sand and cement. He was going to build a wall anyway.

"Yes" I said "I can lay them for you." I mimed bricklaying. His face lit up and he slapped me on the back. "Tomorrow" I said.

I ate with the family. Grandmother had been brought out to the main room now to listen, and I passed round the photos and explained who all these strange faces were. The little girls *ooohed!* and *aaaghed!* over Bumble and held him to their cheeks. They went off to bed later with Gran and I smoked with Dad. They put me to bed eventually in Gran's bed, well, they only had two. It was only a bare board platform but I had a piece of it. The little ones snuggled up front and back, falling straight back to sleep, while I struggled against the furore that was issuing from Gran's mouth. It wasn't just her mouth, her whole face snored.

The family were up at first light. A neighbour had come round and taken Minx away for fixing, so we set to the wall. Dad seemed to think that my bricklaying was brilliant which was amazing as it's actually crap. The neighbours and passers-by also stopped to watch. I was back in my circus again and the family were puffed with pride. Minx came back late afternoon just as we were cleaning the tools, and I was asked to stay. I was delighted. It was a very full house that evening and many a bottle of beer arrived with visitors, who inspected the wall and me.

Gran could have snored through a megaphone that night and I wouldn't have heard it.

I set off early the next morning for the push to Nha Trang as I figured that the man waiting may be getting a bit worried.

Minx broke down. I did the coin tricks: spark plug knackered.

Minx broke down. I tried breakdancing: Water in the petrol.

Minx broke down. My fault: no petrol.

At last, in the early evening gloom, we arrived. Minx, like an eager dog, ran on home, sniffing with pleasure the lights and fumes of Nha -Trang. The man was waiting.

*

THE THONG NAHT TRAIN - SOUTHBOUND

MY TIME was nearly up, so after a brief tour around Nha Trang I bought a ticket for the night train. Hard seat. But they wouldn't let me into the hard seat carriage. I was ushered into the soft seats and placed next to a young girl who, when she stopped crying, explained that she was going away to technical school in Saigon.

Unlike the Chinese, who liked to turn every trip into your worst nightmare, the Vietnamese made theirs more like a picnic. Cool, wet handcloths dangled from luggage racks along with spare clean clothes.

The floor was swept every hour by a smiling lady and her perfumed broom who, just like your Mum, chuckled as she made you lift your legs, man, woman, monk and all. Food wandered in the carriage every couple of hours and inbetween, an orange or a bottle of mineral water would appear like magic when you opened your eyes from a snooze. Now and then a guard rushed through, Mr Jobsworth, barking at the people to put the mesh back down on the windows. There was an explosion to my left. A rock fragment spun through the grille, creasing my forehead. I leapt up, threw a *"Fuck!!"* out the window and putting my hand to my face it came away smeared with blood. The mother opposite was sharing her seat with her two daughters, who she'd been lovingly cuddling, stroking, fanning and towelling with a cool cloth. She put her babbies to one side, where they instinctively clung to each other and went back to sleep. She brought her damp cloth over and, kneeling in the aisle, wiped my forehead; spoke soft and cooing to me. It was such a shock to the system I almost pouted with quivering bottom lip...the *"Not the iodine Mum!"* The whole carriage was indignant that a European had been hit. He may be a foreigner, but he was their foreigner.

Minutes later, another missile hit further along the carriage, showering a table of four and powdering their soup with bullock dung. The Vietnamese lady brushed her hair with her fingers and carried on slurping. The monk that shared the table however, jumped up, and though barely five feet tall his head was visible above the seat - ablaze with anger. A look that could penetrate steel and rip through mountains lasered from his eyes back down the track. The young girl explained sweetly that the culprits were only children and it was a game to hit the white face on the trains. At this point Mr Jobsworth returned and beckoned me to follow. "You go with him," the girl said. "Take your bags."

He led me to the next carriage and into a sleeper. There was a spare berth and the three occupants motioned me to it, said 'Hellos'. Two returned to their books, but I sat by the window with the other sharing a silent conversation, both watching the same things fly past, agreeing on form and colour. We handed each other cigarettes at the exact time we each wanted one and once, chivied our butts through the grille and reached for our water bottles simultaneously. It brought a smile across the divide which was only two feet, but also eight thousand miles. When we could see no more of the dark-cloaked countryside through the inch square steel-ringed holes, we made our beds and lay on them.

I'd only been slumbering a short while when the sliding door flew open with a rush. A hearty and husky *"My Friend!!"* hurtled in, the words dragged out long, containing the whole of Vietnam in one breath. He was well dressed, so much so that I'd noticed him on the platform and nodded to his smile.

"You like beer?...yes!...come with me!" He ushered me with great booming sentences to the compartment next door and handed me a cold one. My soul went *"Aaaaaagghhh."*

There were only twobeds; three men, a woman and child, a dog, and the best part of a department store, but they found room to turn it into a party.

Vodka and beer flew back and forth fuelling Vietnamese, English and drunken gibberish. Under the influence I became a writer, because it was easier to say than graphic designer or photographer. This made me blood-brother to the one that couldn't speak English as he was a writer in Saigon; the result...another session of 'same-same'. Empty bottles scatted end over end through the smog of the compartment, on through the corridor and dodging passers-by, to exit through an open window. The woman and child slept on. During a stop, where the bottles smashed against the station building, 'my friend' slipped eel-like and hunched, through the chaos of legs, and dived through the open window. He was stopped at the waist, which was bigger than the hole, his shouts muffled as he hollered into the darkness, his legs wriggling; like Winnie the Pooh after the honey. With his friends pushing from behind he popped out and was gone for several minutes. He shot back in the carriage with a giant laugh and cut a clearing through the smoke with a whole cooked chicken as a rotor blade.

He ripped it apart at the seams and spread it on a plate of salad that appeared from nowhere. It was as tender as a joke rubber chicken, but it was for my benefit as they indicated that I needed fattening up.

The writer fell off his box and stayed where he lay, comatose.

The woman, waking, tapped her man gently on the shoulder. He spoke to her gently and then to me..."Bed, my friend," and held my hands between his. I returned to my bed, and though the noise next door must have disturbed him, my roomate raised his hand in welcome and smiled, grimly.

*

HOANG TU HOTEL, SAIGON

4.00am. Saigon was half asleep and dreaming it was Hanoi.

The girl looked as tired and beat as I felt and very lonely at the end of the station bench; the same wood bench you'd find in New York, Hong Kong or Godalming, Surrey, designed to make sleep impossible if stranded at some godawful hour, which was now.

I crossed the waiting room hoping she spoke English. She did, Canadian. We'd both had the same idea, to wait until dawn poked it's head through the door and gave a shout, rather than cross Saigon in the dark looking for an open hostel.

5.00am. Having established that I wasn't a sex fiend or her a miser-able bitch, we wearily carted our packs outside and with a tired barter, took a cyclo each. Pedalling side by side across town, our drivers swopped notes on us, politics and the World Cup, while that great sky painted itself, splashing colour carelessly onto buildings and roads. Cach Mang Thang Tam Street, as long as it's name, headed into District 1 and we watched it waking up and going about it's business as we rode. My driver laughed as his friend went round the wrong side of the roundabout, shaking his fist back at the hooting traffic.

The steel shutters were still across the door of Hoang Tui Hotel, wide as the grins on our faces. Pulling it back far enough to squeeze through, I woke the inevitable security guard sleeping on his camp bed in the middle of the mezzanine foyer.

Do you have any rooms?"

"One" he mumbled without lifting his head from the pillow, "Double...8 dollars", producing a key seemingly from his ear. I looked at her, she nodded. There was no discussion or suspicion.

6.00am. We'd both showered, and in my case shaved, and were lying unclothed in a crisp, hospital white bed knowing nothing about each other, yet everything, and if she'd turned and asked for a cuddle I would have given it, without any motive but comfort. We slept.

I crossed the road later for a breakfast of treacly Moca and warm croissant with strawberry jam, leaving a note for her on my pillow. She joined me around ten, sitting down with a smile and looking for the menu. "By the way, my name's Howie".

"Katherine!" she said leaning over, and planted a soft kiss on my cheek. I'd fretted and bothered about this before I left home. How did this hostel business work?, how do you meet people, share a room with a stranger?. It was as easy as 4.00, 5.00, 6.00 and it fitted like a well worn glove.

*

My visa had only two days left and Katherine had to return home, so we wandered Saigon aimlessly, trying to take in by osmosis what had taken two weeks in little Hanoi. Saigon was bigger and wider, brash and bold. Charm was not a word that sat comfortable. Even the postcard sellers lacked the personality and theatrics of Thuy and her friends and along Le Loi St they looked like the friend of the girl you really fancied, of Samoan proportions with scowls that could curdle milk. One boy had a scar, a railway track running from nose to ear that pulled his eye into a menacing squint when he cursed you for not buying- *"Fug yooo!"* But considering these kids were 'Bui Doi - Dust of Life', being orphans, homeless and usually working for a gang, they had a right to scowl, and spit, and snarl, and cry.

Turning any corner, the chances of finding someone pissing up a wall or squatting in the dirt were as likely as Lester Piggot winning a horse race. My opinion quickly grew that whether it was by constructing ugly buildings, using the river to collect rubbish, sewerage and slum dwellers, or erecting acres of western billboards to complement the river view, Saigon was quite happy pissing in it's own backyard.

My dislike was further fuelled by a visit to the Warcrimes Museum. It had seemed to me that in the North the war had been pushed into the background and best forgotten. Here, the intention seemed to be to show what inhumane bastards the Americans had been. They probably were, but I don't recall the Viet-Cong pulling any punches. The Huey helicopter was for me a lasting impression of that television war, buzzing the skies like demented dragonflies, on Panorama & News at Ten.

Here was one sitting on the lawn of the museum as though it had been invited to tea. It was a tin can with dials and gauges from an old car but it had me cold thinking of it's occupants trying to survive, and the people below running from the hell and damnation that it spat from it's cannons.

Inside the museum I found a photo that had been shot through a sock in a sandstorm. It showed two soldiers standing next to a body

86

and entitled "GI cuts off ear of victim...will he take it home for a souvenir?" The alleged ear was not visible. Neither was a knife. I decided after a long study that it could as easily be entitled:

"After tucking up enemy in a nice warm blanket, GI's take off boots and tiptoe away in stockinged feet". I'm sure ears were exchanged in the conflict but pure conjecture don't amount to a hill of beans.

To speed my exit from this debacle, a party of middle-aged Japanese were scrutinising artists impressions of American torture methods and 'tut-tutting' in disgust. Hypocrites of the world unite.

I learned one interesting fact at the museum of the war between America and Vietnam. For every three Americans killed, an Australian or Kiwi also died: and I didn't even know they were there. It was this that prompted me, much later, to at least skim over the history of Vietnam. I was captivated, enthralled and subsequently my views on Saigon and Vietnam as a whole, were radically changed.

Sitting back at the Sinh cafe, the sugar dust blowing off my fresh cinnamon donut, I held the pages of my book down against the wind that was trying to rush onto the last chapter. The slug appeared round the corner on his second circuit of the morning. With no legs, the man lay face down on a trolley, nose three inches from the cruel concrete. The stumps rested on a plastic sheet that dragged behind, rasping. He had two rubber blocks tied to his hands to pull his way along this horizontal mountain. Hand over hand; the summit never in sight.

The wind brought with it rain, that first whispered it's approach, then roared on arrival. He slithered under a cyclo which left abruptly, the dry patch staining dark and wet in an instant. And while diners fretted over wet newspapers, rain in their coffee and having to move indoors, the road had filled and become a river.

Inching upstream, wheels submerged, the slug was forming a bow-wave with his head, turning it sideways every yard to draw breath, his mouth a great 'O' shape, eyes shut. Looking around I saw all eyes fixed on coffee, newspapers, light fittings and distant objects. I wished he could turn into the flow and drift away clean out of Saigon to a merciful drowning, or wash up on a sunny China Sea beach with suddenly, legs, to walk up the beach, toes sifting the warm sand.

After all, he wasn't a slug, he was a man, fighting the great fight.

The rain spent, the sky streaked with blue, and Katherine and I crossed the city through a gentle steam bath from the road below. We were heading for Maxims (*the best restaurant in Saigon and probably all Indochina. Numerous enthralled back-packers have reported...*

absolutely not to be missed..Lonely Planet Guide) intrigued. On the way we passed by Paris, Biarritz and Marseille, Canton, Peking and Brooklyn, in the guise of buildings. The Ham-bu-go Ca-li-pho-nia had no customers. We strolled along boulevards lined with a classic French salad trees but being Saigon the leaves were limp and dusty. And above them were concrete cloud-kissers that the Americans had thrown up.

Literally.

Just next to the river, the doors to Maxims were open to let in the early evening dusk and early diners. We goaded each other to go in first and eventually pushed and pulled each other through the door like two silly schoolkids, skitting across the lush carpet and peeking into the dining room. Outside, drawing a circle on the path with my toe, I asked " Shall we book a table then Katherine?" not really fancying it.

"Do you want to?" she asked, not really fancying it.

"Not really" I said. "Nor me"

"I don't think I can cope with virgin tablecloths, choosing cutlery; it all looks a bit ....posh for me"

"I'd feel tatty in there with these clothes"

"I *am* tatty in these clothes...shit, let's get a Chinese"

"I'm with you...y'tramp!" While we walked, almost skipped to the soup shop, I thought how I was once comfortable in the very best restaurants and what an extravagant waste it now seemed. We slurped our bowls of 'pho', shovelled garlands of noodles, chewed on chicken wings, dropping the bones on the oilcloth amongst the puddles of water that had run down the sides of the beer bottles: no glasses.

Which is why we decided that we'd been to probably the best restaurant in Saigon, because we liked it.

As we chomped and chortled, dark crept over the railway tracks and slunk downtown. Saigon had put it's face and gladrags on and was shimmying into life. Stepping out to the street, the advertising hoardings were costume jewellery, the ornate hotels- floodlit Disney castles, and flying scooters were disco-lights leading the dance around town.

Passing a brightly-lit colonial garden, we were approached by a concierge, *"Please...come in"*. We entered a false daylight where greens were ultramarine and ferns waved like seaweed. A man in crisp white Fred Perry outfit jogged by swinging his racquet, and nodded a loud *"Hello"* as he passed. Slazenger balls thock-thocked back and forth through the arc lights, landing Love, Deuce & Advantage. As if in a different world, we took our cue and ordered Gin and Tonics, sipping them gently over lime, as Miss Thung trounced Miss Prang

6-0, 6-1, and even applauded as they bent to each other over the net to shake hands and display their panties.

Returning to the piss-stinking street, it seemed much hotter, although only a laurel hedge seperated the two; the city lights gaudy like a cheap fairground. Then the sound crept into my head, that I'd heard all day. On every boulevard, streetboys and girls tapped on hollow sugar canes with sticks while dipping along. It was a rocksteady beat that you hear at The Oval, as England try to survive the onslaught of the West Indies pace attack. No melody. Just a *tap tap tap, a tocka tocka tocka tocka tocka, tap tap tap.* And it gave Saigon a heartbeat that I will always remember. The "Dust of life" were playing up.

Leaving Saigon on the plane next day, I was playing the rythym on a Singha beer can with a plastic spoon, watching Pnom Penh disappear below. Was Cambodia rocking to the beat?, or just dancing to the Khmer Rouge quickstep. A lot of people I'd met were there or on their way, and I knew that a trio of English, French and Australians were being held directly below me with death hanging over their heads like a cloud of mosquitos. I thought...'was I being a coward not venturing into Cambodia?' or just Captain Sensible heading for Bangkok; backpacker's convention town - as exotic and dangerous as Worthing.

Perhaps I was.

"But at least", I said to myself, "I did go to Vietnam, on my own...
...pre-McDonalds".

Tap tap tap, a tocka tocka....

*

KHAO SAN ROAD, BANGKOK

So it was down to Bangkok I fear, and the shock was a shock. With my new found travelling skills I sat on my backpack outside the terminal, ignoring the touts and taxis, and watched and waited for something to happen: as it always does. I smoked two snouts.

Two girls walked past me left, then right, then left again. On their next pass they approached me, their backpacks still holding the creases from the shop, but no flag sewn on to show their homeland.

"Was I going to the Khao San Rd ?"

"Yes, but I'm not paying the 300 baht these taxis are asking. I may take the bus."

"Would you share a taxi with us?" said one of the two extremely attracive girls who looked like Spanish sisters.

"I'd be delighted." I said, and I was.

They were Spanish sisters, on a month trip to Thailand. I met their enquiry... "Have you just come from England?" with a nonchalant:

"No, after travelling China I rode the length of Vietnam on a motorbike". This produced a heavy silence and Spanish eyes stared at me as the taxi moved another ten feet, a myth growing in their minds.

Having seen that Bangkok was concrete and cars and motorbikes all thrashed together in a huge traffic jam I closed my eyes, and leaning a heavy head on the door jamb, sank into a resigned doze. I'd known what to expect from Bangkok but the reality was a bastard to bear.

THE KHAO SAN ROAD. Theme park to all travellers. You can arrive an English public schoolchild, or the EEC equivalent, and in two hours buy all the necessary clothing to look like a hippy, and then you only have to act like one ...man!. It's children trying to be adults and adults trying to be kids: a never-never land of blinkered people travelling to islands and resorts packed full of their like, swopping *"where to buy this, where to buy that, and where's the drugs man, the rave, the full moon party ?"* And the real travellers look on in amazement with their boring clothes and anything but boring experiences tucked away in their backpacks and memories, getting high on coffee and lemonade, ambience and conversation. In China and Vietnam the travellers talked: of the moon, river, mountains, home...life. And going to bed was sense and sensibility, not a matter of ridicule or a challenge failed, for the new dawn seen through clear eyes heralded a great day. I'd touched not amphetamine, smoked no dope and drank only a sober amount of alcohol for two months, and was just a bit pleased with myself. At one time in the past I was taking so much speed I could have given Linford Christie a run for his money: backwards. Only elephantine quantities of Special Brew could keep me from walking on water, or running the world, and sleep was a fairy tale I seemed to remember when I was a child. The after-effects of this were akin to Parkinson's disease with dysentery thrown in, and of course only a another bucketful of the hair-raising shit could hit the spot.

I was now enjoying life through undistorted eyes and ears and mind and knew I didn't have to try and kill myself to die happy. I was, at last, being honest with myself.

Olives are one of those things I've been trying all my life. Trying to figure out why everybody likes them. Each time I'm offered one I think, 'I'll try again, perhaps I've grown up now and they'll taste good.' But, as usual, the cats-piss taste hits my tongue and my mouth curls down at the corners just before I spit it out. People stare at me and say, "Don't you like Olives?" with a look of amazement. It's the same with dope, hash, blow, puff, hooter, skunk, grass, ganja. I've often had a toke, a pull, a lag, on a joint, spliff, cone, dak, but I just don't like it. And that ain't cool man. Apparently. It's not so much what it does to me that I dislike, it's the effect it has on company. I've witnessed too many lively, intelligent conversations turn into total bollocks. People having the giggles over someone else laughing at something not in the least funny, is not funny. It's sad. And when somebody who could normally trounce me at backgammon has a spliff and can't remember which colour they are, sixteen times, it takes the shine off the game. Don't get me wrong, each to their own poison I say. Mine's alcohol and it has the same effect, but at least it takes me a few hours before I talk gibberish. So puff on, just don't ask me to "get one together" or bore me talking about it.

*

UP AND DOWN the Khao San Road bars blurted out Bruce Willis and Whoopi Goldberg videos and all heads, blond and dreadlocked, nap-headed, ponytailed or braided stared blank-faced and blank-minded at the flickering screen, having consulted the blackboard earlier to see what was showing at 2.00 and 4.00 and 7.00. I couldn't be doing with it.

The Sisters Espanol found me outside a bar watching the circus parade, and as though this had been an appetiser to whet the palate, they asked me if I would take them to Patpong to see a sex show.

Being an English gentleman, I was obliged to fulfil my duty as a responsible chaperone. Well, I ask you, you would....wouldn't you?.

We shot across the city in a tuk-tuk, it's two-stroke engine screaming, and avoiding the sneak-eyed side-street touts who promised real treats 'upstairs', went for a large club where we hoped the beer wouldn't climb from $3 on entry to $300 on leaving. We watched paint dry for two hours until Elise complained to the waiter:

"We want to see a show, with ping-pong balls and things."

"After 12.30." he replied and true to his word the show commenced when a girl ambled naked onto the stage and lying at eye level, assumed the birthing position. She produced a string of razor blades from her front bottom, amongst polite applause and intakes of breath, and shredded a sheet of paper with them. Handed a balloon, and feeling silly with all the other balloon holders round the bar, I waited my turn as she blew darts from a blowpipe, accurate as Robin Hood... bang, bang, bang!! My balloon burst when it nudged my neighbour's cigarette end, and as she hadn't reloaded, everybody looked to see if she'd cleverly hit mine with a hidden blowpipe up her arse. She looked over at me with a relieved expression (probably an unsuitable choice of words) but this was explained, as with just one balloon left, she missed with three darts in a row. "Come on darlin!" shouted a heckler from the darkness. She replied loudly ,"It's tired... you try it!" and with an extra squeeze of the buttocks lobbed a dart in a lazy arc over the bar into his lap and as a finale, burst the remaining balloon with her left tit. I never worked this one out, but assume it must have been a slight of the teat trick.

By now I was delighted with the performance and the fact it was meant to be sexual had passed completely over my head. I mouthed at the Spanish girls across the bar " It's good isn't it!". Elise mouthed back "Yes, but I want the ping-pong balls!" She didn't get them but we were content with the next performer who did a good impression of a crab circling a giant birthday cake, blowing out the candles with a bushy mustachioed mouth; although the smell of singed hair did indicate a less than perfect performance. We left while the next girl was halfway down a Marlboro Light and I hoped she'd heeded the Goverment Health warning and left a long stub. The man to the left of the exit, invisible in the dark apart from his card held outstretched in the neon, said, "We have very nice girls."

"Yes," I said, "and very talented too!" We tuk-tukked home to the other circus which was the Kho San Rd, and I reflected that I'd only been in Bangkok for eight hours. Bangkok...mad, bad and sad.

RHANEES GUEST HOUSE, BANGKOK

JUST one back from the Khao San road was a narrow Soi where I stumbled on some small guest houses. Peaceful, chalet-like rooms, huddled around tree'd and leafy courtyards with shade and whirling fan, but no television. The quiet was excruciating and I leapt into the first one that had a room. I found later that my little bungalow had bedbugs, but they were quiet, left interesting patterns on my legs and lets face it, they don't give you any diseases, so we shared the room.

Sitting poised over one of Rhanee's towering toasties I was joined by a fairhaired rasta from Copenhagen whose redshot eyes and racking cough were nothing to do with smoking dope and eating shit food, oh no sirree! He explained, short of money, that he hoped his business would continue to grow and pointed to his shoes. Now I'd seen these pass by me on the left as I was bent over reading and was so fixed on them I couldn't look up. I guessed that the owner was a combination of sub-aqua diver and Peter Pan. They were skin-tight, neoprene, with the big toe seperated from it's brothers. They rose above the calf with three clips an inch apart and rolled down, resembled a pirate boot.

"I make these you know....maannn. A lot of people have approached me about them..." he said " on the Khao San road.....lots".

"Yes,"", I said, "that doesn't surprise me." and he took it as a compliment , smiled a sickly smile and coughed till his buckles rattled.

"Can I finish your sandwich?" he asked coughing in it's general direction.

"Help yourself..." I said "I've lost my appetite."

"That's the heat that does that," he said.

I later saw a few pairs, sloshbuckling down the circus, and concluded that they must have some redeemable quality or use, such as holding a joint between the toes, when wrecked on the floor, but style it certainly wasn't. They also didn't fit into the fancy dress party.

Here Israelis came as Arabian Knights, English as Thais, Thais as Americans, Australians as Indonesians, Scandas as Rastas and the French came as the French. Well they would wouldn't they?.

The real travellers came in their usual garb - the scarecrow, with that certain un-coordinated look.

As the evening inked purple, strolling past the Hello Cafe, I was hit round the head by a blast from Exterminator 2 and at the same instant

93

a hearty slap on the back from....Doron!, and the Kibutznik whirled me around and around shouting "Ta gidli!, ta gidli! (Tell all!) or words to that effect. Turning, I saw Sharon, those dulcet eyes brimming with real and felt tears. We were speechless, but not for long. They were leaving three hours later for the South, so we set about catching up with tales, them shaking their heads and moaning:

"Howie, Howie, Howie" at the juicier parts. They'd parted company with a very confused Keren at Beijing, as the 'scandal' had travelled ahead and met them there, to Kerons dismay. I felt like a shit. But it wasn't my fault, it was the Israelis themselves. They were tell-tale tits.

It was, to use a distinctly out of fashion term, a gay day that we spent together. They took me to an Israeli cafe off the circus where I was the only foreigner; the waiter asked me for my order in Hebrew and we ate falafel and humus and chips. Swearing fealty and meetings in Australia we said goodbye again, and seeing them onto a coach heading south, and feeling more than a tad sad, I retired to the bar opposite for a disconsolate beer and reminiscence of Yangshuo.

The circus interrupted my thoughts, forcing me to leave, and standing up and turning, I looked into the face that rose from it's journal.

I sat down opposite, placed my bag on the floor, and grabbing the waiter who was clearing my last table asked, "A large beer please."

"And a large one for me too!" said Harry before continuing...

" What the fark are you doing here Howie?"

" Drinking beer." I said, and in an instant I'd flown from Bangkok to Hanoi. "I just heard about you yesterday from a man in Laos who saw you arrive in Hoi An and Saigon" he said..

So, in my innocent, bumbling way I'd managed to gain infamy the length of China and Vietnam. Quite an achievement for a stupid old Englishman. An absolute beginner.

We fell to comparism and opinion, sucked on beer bottles with a vengeance and when it still wouldn't go down fast enough, tipped the latch on the forehead, flip-topped the head and poured it in from the upturned bottles. Which is how we came to spend the last three hours of the night in a bar with no name. A bar for gay, Thai headbangers, who fed us whiskey and crisps and dances, heads pumping to White-snake, Aerosmith and Nirvarna.

Dawn blinked furiously as we carried our air guitars home, and Harry tied the ends of the night off with...

"It's Tuesday Howie. Mondays are always such hard work."

We parted again later that day with the certainty of future meetings stomping over any gloom. He was going to Penang, and I was off to a to a new, enchanting country called... Chantal.

Having lost my best pals again, I stepped back on the treadmill to find some new ones. I spied, with my little eye...something beginning with....'A'. A girl. Alone. In a bar. Writing. A very attractive alone girl.

With bashful left at home in England with Dopey and Sneezy, I strode in and took the next table. My approach was crude:

"How's the food ?" which came out garbled, as my head was twisted round over my shoulder. "It's okay". What magic words.

Somehow, I don't recall how, I manouvered onto her table. I wasn't looking for a 'result', just companionship. We were staying at the same guest house but hadn't seen each other. She was Flemish; yes of course I knew where that was... where the hell was it?. At first she was cold, formal, aloof but my first impressions of Harry sprang to mind and I resolved not to make the same presumption again. Her name was Chantal...*mmmm.*

With my work experience as clown on the motorbike in Vietnam, and being in the Khao San road circus, I played the fool to the limit.

This was a side of me that had emerged since travelling and I enjoyed the audience reaction. I noticed now that Chantals eyes were limpid pools, and I wanted to dive into them naked and splash around. Tomfoolery added very attractive crinkles to the corners of her eyes and softened her lips to... oh so kissable. I was reaching the third stage of enchantment, and every time she laughed, she reached in and squeezed my heart. Once again a woman had slipped in the backdoor and was right now strapping gelegnite to the safebox marked love.

She had seen Bumble staring out from my wallet and with a slender hand over her mouth was trying to hold in the chuckles. Her eyes gimlet with tears of laughter, she giggled:

"I'm so sorry, but only you would carry around a picture of a dog."

I didn't know if this was good or not, but she asked to see it several times during the evening and at least she was laughing. It's a very weak and tired safebox that I have and I tend to wear my heart on my sleeve...cuff, collar, lapels...anywhere where it can be damaged, so in anticipation of a brush-off, I kept away the next day, ate alone, and joined her late in the same bar for a few drinks and a bowl of beernuts.

Travelling back from the Post Office on the Chao Phraya Express boat, I realised I was seeing nothing. Wats and Palaces were passing me by like Emperors in their new clothes. I had to make a move of some kind, so I hurried back to Rhanee's where Chantal sat cool and shaded. When I suggested eating out together that evening, the affirmative came almost too quickly. I trepidated, but a few shared beers cleared the floor and like a teenager slipping his arm around his girl at the cinema, I picked up her hand from the table.

"Are you reading my palm Howie ?"

"No...I'm just holding your hand." Her eyes dipped momentarily and for the next two hours we loved each other madly, bayed at the moon, hung upside down and scraped our shoes on the stars. But old doubts were creeping along behind in the shadows. Was I strong enough to handle a parting? An unrequited love? The elbow?

So we kissed briefly and sensibly before retiring, and I could tell she was frightened also.

I said farewell to my bedbugs in the pale morning, paused to stare at the flimsy door seperating me from the sleeping Chantal and dropped my pack to the floor. I wrote a note to her and pinned it to the notice board, promising to meet her in ChiangMai, 36 hours later, where we were both heading. I knew that ChiangMai would either be our swan-song or duck shoot. The old qualms, inadequacies, doubts and pal-pitations were nowhere to be seen. What the hell, like the great phi-losopher Forrest Gump said, "Life's like a box'a choclits, y'never know whatcher gonna get".

*

LEK HOUSE,CHIANG MAI

ENJOYING another fine tray of food with wine and brandy, courtesy of Thai Airlines, I touched down in Chiang Mai with an agreeable Australian girl by my side. But Chantal was already inside.

I went straight to the hostel where I knew she was heading, trying to think of a plausible reason why I hadn't gone to the one I'd been heading for. But then I thought, if you're skating on thin ice you might as well tap dance.

Chiang Mai was a small version of Bangkok, an ancient town that had all but hidden it's heritage with western bars and hotels, and the smell of fried chicken and burgers often rode roughshod over the insensce from the hundreds of Wats.

Chiang Mai was where all the Toyota Space Cruisers went to live and holiday, the tinted windows concealing the occupants. Though the second largest city in Thailand, it was a managable size and it's air was sweet, rolling down from the mountains, frequently washed by clean rain and hung out to dry in the ensuing heat. Unlike Bangkok (Venice of the East) whose canals were a polluted broth, the moats around the city had clean water by which people sat and fished; languid and hopeful as anglers anywhere in the world.

Just as languid, but not quite so hopeful, were the Europeans banged up in the prison in the centre of the city for drug offences. Backpackers were invited, nay, *encouraged* to go and visit and cheer them up; perhaps with a book or chocolate. I was reading Midnight Express at the time and they wouldn't have the munchies in there so I didn't think I'd be much help. I also didn't have a lot of sympathy.

The hostel was a peach. I'd arrived by taxi and walked into another courtyard, quiet in the midday heat. Palm trees, hanging foliage and two Thais, all dozed in siesta. The only movement was a puppy dog's tail, sweeping fallen blossom, glad of a moving person. His yip, yip, yip pulled open the left eye of one of the sleepers who leapt into a laugh and hopped from one leg to the other, pumping my hand.

"I want a room...single."

"Yes! Room 103." handing me a key attached to a large, smiling wooden cat. And looking up at his face I saw the same cheshire smile.

"That'll do." I said, to complete the quickest hostel check-in ever.

"No!" he said, "Look first, you may hate it." I looked. I loved it.

I crunched gravel back to where he sat beaming.

"You're right..." I said, "it's awful; horrible." and as the smile on his face disappeared below the horizon I added, " Do you know of a good hostel around here?" His lower lip was only inches from the floor and snapped shut with a loud "but..." and again, "but..."

"Only joking," I said "it's a great room and you're not having this key back." and tried to match his smile. Jiggling from hot-foot to other and spinning around, he let loose a string of squeals and giggles, cuddled me from behind, massaged my shoulders and picking me up, carried me across the threshold, completing the friendliest hostel check-in ever.

There were several others like him. It turned out they were the trekking guides, who also served the food, checked in guests, cleaned the rooms, and everything at a laughing, hopping jog and "No problem!".

It was an all singing, dancing show and the hostel was the stage.

Waking the next morning, I looked across the courtyard through my mosquito net to see Chantal sitting behind a glass of orange juice, head back, laughing with a pony-tailed, olive skinned man. *Another piggin' Israeli?*. To save face and self respect I showered, shat and shaved for a remarkably long time, dressed twice, and eventually stumbled across the gravel, stubbing my toe on a plantpot. In a gesture of defiance, and perhaps posession, I kissed her hello on the lips. She was still laughing, with me or at me?. They'd been on the bus fourteen hours, and I knew how this threw people together. On a Dulux colour chart I would have fitted snugly between emerald and pea-green, and homemakers would have chosen me for my dazzling hue.

I'd fallen for first impressions again. He was Mexican. Oscar...slight of build but straight and true as an Aztec layline. They'd been waiting for a double room to come vacant but I realised she was shining at me and only glowing dully in his direction. We decided when a single room arose that Chantal should have it and Oscar and I share the double.

This, I found, was a great relief and knew it was the right course of action, as I always held that longing was the best part of belonging and invariably led to the best orgasms. As well as that I really liked Oscar. He asked *me!* for advice about travelling, had no pretentions, and was as respectful as any English gentleman. He was also the first Mexican I had slept with. We got on like a bodega on fire. He'd come all the way from Mexico to study Thai massage at the school in Chiang Mai; he'd seen a leaflet in Mexico!. You could qualify in two weeks and then he could go home, and into business. Did we think that was a good idea?

Oscar was out riding with bandidos somewhere that evening which left Chantal and I watching the stars through beer glasses, and shooting the breeze. We wondered at the determination of somebody, to travel halfway round the world for a two week course and why we, who'd done more courses than anybody needed, were wandering around for a whole year with no plans at the end. I discovered then that we'd both left home the same week. That we'd travelled the same circuit in China and crossed paths at Yangshuo for a few days: that, as I was riding down Vietnam on The Minx, she was on the train, and the day I shunted into Hoi-An she was leaving. Harry and I were scoffing noodles downstairs whilst she was upstairs, ill, in the Blue Lotus Hostel, Hanoi. You could say we felt a strange attraction, or as the puffers would have said..."spooky man!" And as beddie-byes time came around, Chantal slipped around the other side of my little verandah on the way to her room, but stopped and leant over the wall. I kissed her still firm lips, her neck, then across her downy shoulder and back to her...*was I imagining it?* slightly parted and softer mouth. We were still working at each other, bobbing and weaving and looking for a clench.

"I am exhausted Howie, I'll see you in the morning."

"Night Flem" I said as calmly as I could, as behind the wall I was hiding a hard-on a cat couldn't scratch. Two feet away, on the other side of a thin bamboo wall, I'm sure I heard Chantal, as I drifted into slumber...purring like a kitten.

THROUGH the leafy canopy, the Siam sun filtered into our coffee, as we broke our fast. Across the gravel came a Thai, juggling two bucket-size mugs, deliberately rattling them whilst walking an invisible tight-rope. He bounced them onto the table, not a drop spilt, singing...

"Tea for two, and two for tea...me for you (looking at Chantal) and you for me (swivelling to me).

"But we already have coffee." said Chantal.

"Have tea too...ha,ha,ha,ha,ha,ha; no problem, Rak's gift."

It was Rak who was later to take us trekking, and I was charmed by him. Birds were falling out of the trees at his feet.

"I get you a biiigggg!! breakfast, I know you Germans eat a lot."

"But we're not...."

"I know...ha,ha,ha,ha,ha."

I'd finished the huge breakfast and my hand, dangling over the side of the cane chair, was nuzzled by a wet puppy's nose. I fell to playing with him and, perhaps with Bumble in mind, allowed him to nip my fingers and bite me playfully. A while later whilst in a reverie, I noticed a thin line of a scratch tracking across my wrist, round my thumb, and turning my hand over, increase in width and colour into an angry cut. I suddenly remembered the French paper I'd read earlier and surprisingly understood. The particular article that interested me, especially after seeing the scabby curs roaming Bangkok, stated that over 60% of the dogs in Thailand carried the rabies virus and should be avoided where possible. The scratch on my hand seemed to turn into a festering wound and I could almost see wriggly things burying along my veins. How stupid could I be?

It was too late to suck the poison like a boyscout bitten by an adder, so I stared at the wound waiting for the convulsions to arrive. Was I imagining it or was I going blind?

No, the cloud that had crossed the sun hurried along and Rak took away the swelling, returning to the kitchen past me at a jog, backwards and giggling. And Chantal, arriving with a soft, moist kiss sealed the wound and put a cold compress on my heart. Hell, if you're going to go, why not rabies?

Numbed by the choice of treks available, and stultified by the presence of each other, we whiled away the morning, doing nothing.

Rak had brought lunch, and later cleared it away asking:

"You not going anywhere today?"

"Yes" I suddenly decided, "I'm going for a haircut." Chantal looked at me in surprise. "I'm having one in every country, for the sake of it, and so I can tell my friend Carl at home how underwhelmed I am by his cutting skills."

"Well," said Chantal, "In that case I'm going for a massage to loosen up for the evening."

Gosh.

The barber in Hanoi, a *tiny* lady who climbed a pair of steps to do the top, gave me an amazing cut using a pair of wallpaper scissors and a hand operated pair of sheep shears over a tortoiseshell World War One comb. So I had no qualms when the Thai pensioner donned a surgical mask, pointed an interrogation lamp at my head and set to, after a loud *"thrump"* through his nose.

I sat smiling at the absurbity of it all which he obviously took as encouragement, not knowing that without my glasses I can't see the wall in the opticians let alone the chart on it. My smile however was fading after an hour, as I couldn't figure out where he'd found the hair to cut for so long. It was already short before he'd started. Eventually, after stepping up to the podium and back like a darts player retrieving his 'arrows' 37 times, snipping at something each time, he removed his mask with a *"thrump"* and handed me my specs. Fuck me, it was perfect. It was Steve McQueen in 'Papillon' with a Tin-Tin quiff at the front. I laughed. He laughed, nervously.

I slapped him on the back, disturbing a cloud of microscopic hairs he'd managed to create. This was a fifty pound haircut, it cost half a dollar. I gave him two dollars with glee as I loved it, and had the delicious thought that any traveller following me into the chair was going to get the same...not very hippy man!. There was more though. Pulling my hand forcibly from the old barber's grip I left his shop. I spied Chantal entering a cafe after her massage, loose I hoped, and followed her. She turned at the sound of the door and looked. And looked.

"Wow" she said running her fingers up the back, "Wow" again.

"Hey, where did' ya get that haircut man?..that's funky" asked the traveller at the next table. I told him where the shop was and described the old cutter. "I'm going to get one", he said and left.

I turned back to Chantal, flicking my locks. Her eyes were blazing above her smile. She loved it, or perhaps she just loved the fact that I'd done it. It had been a good afternoon's work, but I was to fan the flames higher later, again unintentionally, but very effectively.

*

DARET HOUSE RESTAURANT, CHAIYOPHUM RD

THE TWO of us sat, in the Daret House, facing each other over an unmatchable fish hot-pot; squid slinking in the depths while above, crabs chased chilis, squeezing them amongst waving fronds of lemon grass. I'd grabbed a sly headstart earlier by sinking a few Thai beers while Chantal got ready and was, to put it mildly, fluid; but still in control. I thought.

I was being distracted from the heavenly smile in front by the sounds behind me. *Bip-bap-bip-bap-ker-ping-pong-bip-bap.* For some reason I was turning around to watch the locals playing table-tennis every few minutes. One of them gestured me to play. I politely refused, but turning, Chantal smiled me to go. "They will like it if you play with them".

With no ryhme or reason, I left a crab claw in mid air and took a paddle. Now I was quite good at this when younger and even had a small tin-cup for it somewhere. My solitary cup that sat among my brother's massed army of tall, fat, silver trophies. It had a purpose though, as it collected all the dust and left all his sparkling. My mother, bless her, regularly moved it to the front after the surrounding bully boys had nudged it into a dark corner, and even went to the pretence of trying to make it shine with Duraglit. It never shone how ever hard it was rubbed. In fact it was rubbed so much, the crossed bats became a smudge and my title reduced to 'Table Ten...... ham...'

I took on the first player quite easily and getting my rythym, beat the replacements as they came, each one better than the last.... until the last one. Stony-faced and cool, he matched every shot as the audience grew, but they were clapping both of us. I was pleased to see he was as sweaty as me when we shook hands. I was chuffed, as I had beaten him narrowly, then it hit me. I had left an angel in mid-dinner to play ping-pong. I returned drenched, bowed and crestfallen to the table and sat down. There, again, was that same glowing smile. I'd somehow done the right thing. My opponent wandered over and proffered his hand. "Good game mate... aint 'ad a game like that fer ages". He was a native who in previous years had been a native of Basildon. I told him that I used to go to clubs at Canvey Island and Ilford to which he replied excitedly, "That used ter be my stompin' ground!" We chatted for a long time, Chantal straining to understand the Thai-cockney, chin in hands, and a strange dialect it was to be sure. I'd left Chantal out again; was I a complete arsehole?

We left the bar by the back door as it was long closed, and parting at our seperate doors....we didn't. She leant over, and up, and around, and brushing my neck with her cheek whispered:

"I want you with me tonight."

"Yes, I do too," I said panicking....condoms! I returned to my room where Oscar was asleep under his igloo-shaped mosquito net.

Rummaging in the dark for the packet I knew was there, somewhere, Oscar awoke.

"Hey Howie, how goes man?"

"Very good Oscar, I'm sleeping next door tonight so lock the door behind me."

"S'cool man." and he rolled over naked, conchitas waiting for him in his dreams. My fingers rounded on the Durex, next to the syringes and I hoped the two parties hadn't had a rough journey together.

We danced on each others bones, first a fiery tarantella, then a bouncy bossanova and the bed and the bamboo walls swayed to the rythym and bruised to the beat, and finally as daylight was more than newborn and the morning kitchen sounds clinked and clattered, all that was left on the bed was a pool of sweat and sex. We'd floated through the mosquito net, past the ceiling fan and were sleeping spoons on a cottonwool cloud somewhere in the north of Thailand.

We bumped to earth quite sharply when Coitus Interruptus Mexicanus knocked at the door and shouted through the bamboo...

"I go to school now bambinos, sees you later!" and left for his first massage lesson. Between snoozes we massaged each others egos, hearts and insides, and the dust disturbed from the floor raced around in the shaft of light from the glassless window. The cat had got the cream.

*

It's name was Snowy, a stuffed white toy. In the day it was my friend. Together my bruvver and I rode it, bouncing down the stairrods and drab paisley carpet. At night the landing light squeezed into the bedroom and lit Snowy, hiding under Martin's bed. Snowy frightened me at night.

Tommy Slater could make great machine gun noises, "Ack,ack,ack, doosh,doosh,doosh...pwwhiirrrrr" Mine just went du,du,du,du. Nobody played dead when I shot them. I won a chalk poodle at the fair and took it to school where it sat on the windowsill of the leaded-glass arched window. The sun shone through the window onto the black-

board marked "The Weather Today", and when the monitor banged the dusters together I thought he was making clouds. My brother was told off for showing off. He did a handstand and broke my mums glasses. She sent him to his bedroom. I hated her. It was his 8th birthday. But I cried 'cos she couldn't see and the red marks on the sides of her nose looked sore.

The Budds were the same age as me, but bigger. Their Dad ran the scrapyard. He had deformed arms but still lifted engines from cars that smelt of old red leather and mould. I pushed John Budd in the stingers and hid in the coal cupboard at home. I got the cane.

If you put dandelions down someones back, they wet the bed.

If you threw mudpies at the side of your council house they stuck and when he came home from work your Dad went barmy. I loved pulling the ends of the sheets from the end of the mangle when Mum was turning the handle. The water oozed down your arms from the rubber rollers and into the tin bucket. I put my hands in the mangle once to dare myself. Didn't hurt.

"One, two, three, mother caught a flea, put it in the teapot and made a cup of tea, flea jumped out, mother gave a shout, Dad came running with his shirt hanging out."

We had a 40's sofa and 50's chairs which we pretended were the coal lorry. The cushions were hunderd weight sacks and half hunderd bags. Mrs Brown always had a half.

Snow was the best thing in the world till your gloves and balaclava got wet and the cold made you run indoors hand and ears stinging with burn and tears. Until to be brave you went back out again to stick rocks in snowballs and crack your head on iceslides.

When we stole Jif lemons from the village shop with the rusty enamel Tizer sign, to use as water pistols, Mum chased us with a wooden spoon and broke it with one wild swing on the banister. We laughed, Mum laughed too.

Bonfire night was scary and we had to put a cloth over the goldfish bowl so it wouldn't die of fright. Dad said so. Dad was an engineer. They poured milk on the machines to cool them down and he came home smelling of metal shavings until he went in his shed and came out all wood, sometimes with a boat or a fort or a garage with Shell stickers and a ramp that went up and down.

Once he made a rabbit hutch and Thumper arrived, grey and white and fluffy, it's big ears twitching, but I wouldn't pick him up by them. Thumper got very ill and one night someone must have left his door open. He wasn't there in the morning. I spect an owl got him, Dad said.

*Mum's Hoover switched off at elevenses time and we had orange
squash and biscuits and sat by the radio to wait for the lady to say, as
she did every day "If you're sitting comfortably?" and we would
wiggle our bums..."then I'll begin.? And as the Grand Old Duke of
York's men marched up the hill to a trumpeting...or was it a
trombone....or....I was dragged from Clappers Meadow, Alfold,
Surrey, 1964 to.....*

....the trumpeting, not entirely tuneful, split my dream into pieces.
Where the hell was I ? My arse ached and the tugging at my sleeping
bag was definitely not Chantal. Even without my glasses I realised that
the member, wet and snuffling, snorting my bedding was as thick as a
man's thigh and ..... attached to the front of an elephant! I touched the
yardbroom bristles to confirm my suspicions and it disappeared out the
window with a snort, grey against the dark sky, still half past a
moonbeam. I turned to Chantal and even in the gloom saw her face,
innocent and happy as a sleeping child, felt her puppy breath sweet
against my cheek: and as when people are disturbed but not woken,
she buried deep into my neck with a warm nose.

With the hand that wasn't cradling her back, numb from it's nights
work, I pinched myself hard to remind that I was in a village hut in the
Northern hills of Thailand with a Belgian angel and the elephant we'd
ridden together the previous day. The insane grin that recognised this
kept me awake for a long time and I was glad, as it gave me time to
breathe in the perfume of life; freedom, rain-drenched air, elephant
dung, lingering opium clouds, sweet Belgian musk, and I realised that
this was it. And now I knew at last what "It" was. Tomorrow I could
die happy, knowing that although I'd be missing a lot, I'd had so much;
so much more than most. My candle had burned so very bright through
storm and flood while others' had flickered dimly in a sheltered breeze.

*

RAK'S TREK

THE WEATHER was like a child on an activity centre. It would push the heat button, spin the clouds and pull the string for rain; often spinning, pulling and pushing at the same time. We took boots off to cross streams, put them on to climb a hill of mud, took them off, then, just kept them on whatever. When the cloud hid the sun, the fields and hills were khaki, until the sun cracked them apart and the country turned into heaps and mounds of sparkling emeralds.

We trekked through mud and sheets of rain thick as duvets. The slopes were often steep and slippery but Rak sang and danced and jollied us along even when we didn't need it. Chantal and I sat in our creaking wicker basket as Rak rode the elephant's head, flapping it's ears with his bare feet. He rode it backwards like Pan on a buffalo, standing up, mock galloping. The man's store of fun was bottomless. As we climbed on our bristly juggernaut, it's rolling gait flinging us welcomely together, Rak explained the Opium problem of his country.

"These slopes were once beautiful with red and white and blue flowers but of course the by-product of this beauty was Opium. Over 90% of the population were users and most of the addicts were cabbages. Work output fell, as people didn't want to work. Only smoke. So the growing of poppy was banned, the government brought in a slash and burn policy to rid the country of the menace. For me it is very difficult as I love smoking opium, but it has made my country better and now I see the people happier and working. Large areas were de-forested and the people were encouraged to grow cabbages instead of the so pretty flowers".

And there, as we puffed our way up a skid-pan slope, the rain dripping from the penthouse of our backpacks, were the cabbages. Laid out in neat geometrics, for all impressions a graveyard marking it's former victims, spread up and over and around the hills. I stopped, cotton wool breath billowing, and thought twice about drugs.

Now the number of users had been halved, addicts decimated, and it was one of these I lay facing on the rattan floor, arm crooked under my head, drawing great lungfuls of opium whilst he poked in the bead of bubbling resin with a pointy stick. But we knew that this was tourist class, for fun only, and we wouldn't be taking a trip across clouds of flowers and cabbages. Opium has a calming effect that also heightens the senses and it was in this euphoria, with Chantal stroking my forearm, that Rak was persuaded to tell a tale. The light from the oil lamps crept across the floor, up the bamboo wall and slinked out into the smouldering dusk over the window sills. Rak coughed long and hard into a dark corner and started.

My first trek was in 1979, when I was only sixteen and not a real guide. A hotel owner had phoned me one morning to say that two Germans wanted to go trekking in the hills. I thought it a good chance and went over there in a flash. In the bar waiting for me were two huge German men. Not even knowing what to charge I asked:

"You want to go trekking?"

"Jah, in de mountains"

"Would you like to ride elephants ...it is more expensive?"

"Jah, money is no problem". I left and returned two hours later, all preparations made to give them a schedule. They had gone and the very happy barman said, "They very good customers Rak, they spend 300 dollars today!"

"You have robbed them" I said "even for that amount," as I pointed at a table full of empty beer and whiskey bottles. "No," he said, very upset, "look under the table Rak" and he pulled the cloth aside to show many, many more empty bottles. "Oh God!" I said.

"They said they go to the silk factory and will see you at one" said my friend. I went back to the bar at one and they were there, dressed in the finest silk suits and new hand made leather shoes!

"But we must go now!" I told them "You must go and change!"

"It's OK Rak we have more of these," said the biggest, "Do we have time to go to beer shop?" At three they were ready to go but unfortunately then in come the elephant owner. He saw the empty bottles and the size of the Germans and said "No my elephants cannot carry them." I saw my first job disappearing, and whispered to him,

"They will pay extra.". We had to pay double but they were happy withi it and we left four hours late. The next day, still in their fine silk garments, we climbed up a steep hill, one of them in the basket, one on the head, and the legs of the poor elephant were bending. In my stupidness I stopped to speak to a farmer but I keep my eye on the elephant going away from me. I did not know that over the hill slash and burn was going on and the smoke was scaring the beast who almost was running and the Germans bouncing up and down. The owner shouted and the farmer and myself chased after them and as we went over the top of the hill we saw the elephant charging down the hill. One of the Germans grab hold of a branch as they went under a

tree and his trousers rip off. The other hang on to the flapping ears until the beast get to the river and with a big trumpet...stop dead. The german fly into the muddy river. We pulled him out and all ran back up the hill to get his friend who still hang from the branch with no trousers.

"Let go!" we all shout.

"Nein" he say "the elephant will get me."

Now with a big crack the branch break from his weight. He hit the floor and started sliding down the hill on the mud and passed the elephant who was coming back up. The beast stood up on his back feet as the German went past, trumpeting, and then chased him down the hill. He wouldn't come out of the river until the elephant was gone.

When we got back to Chiang Mai we went to their hotel which was very expensive and when we walked in they saw a group of people at a table and with torn and muddy clothes and bruises and a nose bleed they went up to them. I couldn't find anywhere to hide and I saw my new job disappearing.

The smaller of the two giants, with no trousers said "If you is thinking of the trekking go wiz zis man Rak. It is great but leave out ze elephant riding it is a little uncomfortable".

True or not, Rak tucked the two of us up under our blanket, both chuckling and giggling long into the night, but before I drifted off I heard 'opium man'- our porter, behind the curtain, blowing up a storm on his pipe. A soliloquy to the cabbage.

*

"Tea my little ones" was the morning greeting from Rak, and we scrambled to wake. "No worries!!" have a cuddle, wake up slow, it's raining." And damn me if we didn't spend the morning - wet.

We crossed swollen streams; barefoot, showered under pounding waterfalls; in underwear, stumbled off the narrow strips of green that held in the water of the paddies; filling our boots. Then, through the rain which was sweeping across like a theatre curtain, appeared a hill village, all stilted bamboo and squealing pigs and smoke curling damply into the mist. As I heaped my backpack with the others in one of the huts I watched a small boy, crouched on the packed earth outside, firing a catapult at a piglet.

This was a 'Karen' tribe, the most numerous of the hillpeople and not particularly 'rare'. But we were'nt collecting stamps or Brownie points, just having a look; getting a taste. Initially, children were the only sign of life. Dressed in handmade calico clothes and smoking pipes, they had already learned by heart...'5 baht!' which was the rate for anything; a photograph, a friendship bracelet, a brooch. Eventually however, men strolled into or through the village and invariably sported Adidas stripes or a Nike logo on their jogging bottoms.

Warmed by a rice dinner and tea from Rak, Chantal walked off to the edge of the village and a small hilltop. I left her alone with her thoughts for a time and then followed up the winding, slippery path, nervous. Approaching her, I looked past her to where she was gazing.

Puffy clouds streamed out of Burma, their shadows plunging down the slopes of cabbage, slowing as they moved up the hills. As she turned to me she swept her now dry hair back with her hand and holding it against the wind, took mine with the other. As she looked into my eyes her own were alight, full dark electric pupils like a cat's.

"Burma" she said, knowing that I knew: "I have to leave Bangkok to go there in three days." and as she said it her eyes dimmed.

"Chantal...I have a very hard question to ask that's been going around in my head since yesterday?. I chewed the inside of my lip and winced... "Can I come down to Bangkok with you? When you leave, Thailand will be finished for me." She breathed loudly and pulled me to her, nuzzling into my neck and murmured,

"I dreamt you asked me that in my sleep last night, or perhaps I just hoped you would. Oh yes please!"

And the sadness of parting was trampled over by another three days with each other. So we returned to Lek House, entertained, invigorated; and very much together.

The storm clouds gathered over our picnic.

*

SOMPRASONG GUEST HOUSE,SUKOTHAI

WITH ONLY a brief time left together we opted for a single stop-off on the return; at Sukothai, the first but short lived capital of Thailand.

It had an impressive lineup of Wats but after Bangkok and Chiang Mai I was practically stuffed with Wats. No; with the state we were in we could have stopped off at another planet and not noticed. The area around Sukothai had been flooded before our arrival and we found the river in the town up to the top of the wall, so thick with mud it looked walkable. We spent the afternoon as only lovers can and, strolling out for an early evening walk, the sky gave us a show.

The rumbustious weather patterns were battling it out above, refereed by a waning sun. The spectacle resembled Van Gogh's pallette after a mad canvas. The clouds were every shape from round to square and the only green cloud I'd ever seen was threatening a purple patch that already looked bruised from the conflict. The river was pink, and I was whirling around in the road, eyes aloft, until Chantal pulled me to the safety of the pavement. The mood stayed with me 'til much later when we sat, dark on our balcony, and fortified by my old friend beer I poured thoughts onto the sounds of the night: raindrops, cicadas, cats fighting *screech!*; our hands holding very tightly in desperation at the time running away down the chocolate pink river.

For hours I gabbled on, dredging up old memories, thoughts, sights; talking China, Vietnam, Belgium, England. I was drunk with words and they all wanted to come out. My mouth went spastic. For the first time since I left home I could pour it all out: I laughed, I cried, my voice went deep and hoarse with the effort and at last I stopped. There was a silence like after the crash of broken glass. The rain had stopped.

"Oh god" I said "I'm so sorry Chantal...I've been talking crap for hours, you...." She put a finger to my lips and led me to bed.

IT WAS nine in the morning and the sun was at it. 'Seasoned travellers' that we were, we spurned the taxi driver's special offer of 200 baht for a return trip and headed for the local bus to the ruins. 5 baht.

We had the choice between an open sided affair that could have come from Trumpton, or a charabanc that would have been at home on a day trip to Bangor. We chose the latter, as it looked as though it may be quicker. We rumbled out of the station at 5mph and roared into second gear, several minutes later, just when the engine seemed to be near exploding, the driver jammed it into third and reaching top speed of 10mph, stopped to pick up an old lady going shopping. Chantal and I looked sideways at each other. We calculated, as we had plenty of time, that if we hi-jacked the bus it would take us four days to get to Bangkok. This however wouldn't have been so uncomfortable, as the driver had converted his section into a lounge. A 1970's music centre was on a shelf supported by wrought iron brackets, the speakers above and behind him. A tassled lamp-cover hung round the light throwing a shadow onto the picnic chair beside him, supposedly for guests.

Between it and him, resplendent on the engine cover, was a vase of plastic flowers. Real flowers would have been shaken to bare stalks in yards with the vigorous gear changing, and we saw that we too were being vibrated forward. Only by shifting back continually could we avoid ending up in the guest chair.

Arriving at our stop at the Old Town; bumsore but amused, despite the thirty two stops; two bicycles were pushed at us with -

"15 baht for day." We took them and set off around the ruins. The Wats and Buddahs had been groomed into a virtual theme park, each different area incurring another entrance fee, and the only thing missing was a procession of people dressed in oversize Buddah suits and shaking our hands. I almost expected to see daisies growing on the manicured greens. Virtually empty of visitors, the only thing in abundance were Wats, which were as thick on the ground as fleas on the scabby Bangkok dogs. We took advantage of the situation by using the paths for a game of chase, on bikes.

I caught glimpses of Chantal between Wats, hid behind golden Buddahs, and when a hand tapped me on the shoulder, whirled around to find two Japanese girls asking, "Please, can take picture?"

"Yes, of course" I answered, and ensured that when they got the photo home to 'show the family' they would each have a temple spire seemingly growing out of their heads. We cycled to the ancient dam through pampas-like grass, where lesser Wats stood derelict as scarecrows and cows drifted in and out of the shade from solitary trees. We skimmed stones and hearts across the water, making no promises beyond the night to come. We opted for the 'Trumpton' for the trip back to town in the hope it would be quicker. The name proved apt as at only our third stop, after an exhilirating ride of 11mph, we picked up a bunch of schoolboys, to us indistinguishable from each other in their uniforms. They could almost have been...'Pew, Pew, Barney McGrew, Cuthbert, Dibble and Grub'. Schoolboy humour and bashfulness caused them to giggle and fight and being in a childish mood ourselves we contributed to their state by making faces and winking.

Chantal however, exploded into laughter, which had them straight backed and blank faced with confusion. I shrugged my shoulders at the uneasy line of faces to try and comfort them but Chantal whispered in my ear, "The little one on the end has his money in his ear."

At that point the conductor arrived and glad of a diversion they all turned to her. The little one prised the coin from his lughole with some difficulty and gave it to her and I hoped he wouldn't get any change as the next coin down was much, much bigger. We rocked and roared all the way to our stop where the frowning boys and smiling conductor waved us off and the driver rang his big brass bell. We giggled into the Wagonwheel restaurant for a fiery Tom Yum soup which turned our tears of laughter into tears of pain and joy.

At bedtime however Chantals eyes brimmed with anguish, cutting me to the bone and wishing that I'd never started this thing.

"I want you to come to Burma with me Howie."

"Yes, I want to come with you."

"We have to go our own ways though, don't we?"

"Yes."

If only I could go back and change that word.

We took a last walk along the Willy-Wonka river, reflecting on a magical day in Sukothai, and before I knew it I was standing in the middle of the Kho San road, with a lump in my throat, watching Chantal's bus disappear around the corner to Burma, India and Nepal.

My visa to Chantal had expired.

*

I staggered back to Rhanees and moved my belongings from the double room, where we had spent our last night, into the single boxroom and my old mates the bedbugs, laying out the sarong that Chantal had given me on the mattress. It was no good, I had to go and get pissed.

I walked up and down the Khao San road, friendless, clueless, past the empty green chairs where we'd met; until a thought grew.

Harry was here somewhere.

I scanned the bars with no result until, for no apparent reason, I returned to the restaurant down a side alley where Chantal and I had our last meal. Approaching the chair where she had sat, I saw Harry, waiting. "Hello old friend" I said, "I knew that you would be here."

"Yes" he said "I knew you would find me here."

"I go home to Sweden tomorrow". We didn't look for an explanation or a meaning but merely said our goodbyes over many hours and bottles: went our own ways.

Bangkok had a pall of melancholy hanging over it that spread to the boundaries of Thailand, so to escape, I pulled my flight to Bali back a week, grimacing until departure. Despite my inward urgings, when the aeroplane parted the curtains of the Bangkok smog and sliced into clean blue air, the pilot didn't change course to Burma, but flew unwavering in the direction of Bali, while I wavered in my seat.

*

KUTA BEACH, BALI

THE first sign of things to come glided round the baggage carousel at Denpasar airport. Suitcases, shiny and clean for their holidays. Backpacks were thin on the ground and pushed together like second class passengers. I shared a ride into Kuta with a Kiwi who flew over as regular as a trip to the local Sainsburys to buy cut price goods for his shop. He sold Australian surfwear, from Bali, to New Zealanders at home.

From Denpasar airport it's possible to collect your bags and, in a taxi, change into your Speedos, apply suntan lotion, wrap around the sunglasses, by which time you've arrived at Kuta beach where you can spill directly onto the sand.

Then, catching your first rays, you can look through the basting bodies, dugs hanging, bums burning right up to where the sun don't shine, and you may catch a glimpse of the next planeload skimming in to land, the tops of the suntan lotions swivelling to the ready.

There were more tits to be seen in one sweeping glance than a year of page threes, but surprisingly, hawkers were not allowed onto the sand.

Kuta - half Australian, half European, half hawkers. The latter had been irritating in China but easily ignored. In Vietnam, their extra guile made them harder to avoid but their charm or looks normally compensated. But in Kuta they were dedicated to their craft, though fairly inept, relying on Americans and tourists to fall for their lines and prices. They were downright insulted if you didn't buy one of their copywatches and yo-yos that light up in the dark, or take the boy-girls, on the inland side of Jalan Legian for a good time.

Curious one day I asked the price of a pack of cigarettes knowing that they were 900 rupia in the shop I could see over his shoulder.

"How much?" I asked, pulling out a pack.

"2000 rupia" he snapped, hand outstretched for the money.

"1500" I countered.

"No" he parried.

"OK, I don't want them," sliding them back into their slot. His friend, with an identical tray, joined in, "2000 rupia!"

I took the packet out again and showed them the government price tag showing 1000 rupia.

"I offered your friend 1500, and he didn't want it, so I'm going to buy them in that shop there." As I entered the shop I was hit between the shoulder-blades by a double-barrel..."You fucker bastard" and turning, met four eyes filled with malice; but they lacked the conviction of the Chinese gangsters or Vietnamese veterans, so I laughed.

*

KENNY AND DUGGIE were due in a few days and I was looking forward to spending a week or so with some mates from home. I was hoping I might be able to persuade them to do some 'real' travelling for a short while to show them what it was all about. But I knew that I couldn't stay with them as I was a lone traveller now, and the rewards of going it alone were too great to lose.

Meanwhile, I thought...see how you can fit in with 'real life' so as to speak, and try to come to terms with the loss of a great love.

Chantal was summer on my mind.

I spent the afternoon on Kuta beach, basting with the rest, and surfed a rented board on a messy shore break. Coming off the beach, I made a beeline for the famous 'Surfbar' on Poppies 2.

Past the concrete wave at the entrance where dorks can have their photo taken pretending they're surfing, I settled down to a beer that froze to the side of the glass.

If it hadn't been happy hour I couldn't have afforded it; the other cus tomers seemed to think it was cheap. But, on the cinema-sized screen Tom Curren, the Rudolf Nureyev of surfing was ripping and slashing some of the best waves in the world. I melted into the screen as Ullawatu, Pipeline, Bells, Kirra and all the other famed waves rolled by. I was going to be visiting them all. It made me hungry.

Amongst the jumble of side streets that ran back from the beach, I sat alone in a restaurant writing with this hand, shovelling Nasi Goreng into my mouth with the other, I tried to block out the conversation to my left which was a cheese-grater on my nerves. Gus and Tobes had moved over to the table when it held just two girls. They were English public schoolboys and spoke with an accent so posh, they could have had their silver spoons still stuck in their mouths. I wondered why they were here and not Montecarlo or Cannes.

"Hi girls, mind if us chaps sit down?" They'd sat down anyway and bored the girls pantless for an hour.

115

"Oh yes, parachuting is just the business. Did my basic training at Aldershot..from a balloon. Then gave it the big one at Sandhurst. 15,000 feet free frall." Gus was a bit worse for wear by now and his prey were shrinking back to try and gain some airspace.

"That's right ay Tobes?"

"Yah, but heliskiing is pretty damn close to it for the old adrenalin. I was just telling this luvvy creature how many harses your family have."

"Oh Christ! must be dozens of them."

"Not harses you prat...houses!"

At this point Gus kicked his chair backward to the floor and sprinted for the toilet. "Must have gone to throw up," said Tobes, his head swaying alarmingly.

"Sorry about that girls...had to go an' throw up," said Gus returning on jelly legs, replacing the chair and sitting down. "Just the four now, and the lodge in Scotland of course."

The girls had taken enough and took their leave, grinning at me and nodding at the boy's backs. Gus and Tobes grated on.

"Y'know Tobes, being honest now; never, ever in our time together never, ever thought D'arcy's jokes were funny, never, ever farking laughed once...ever, though one pretends to of course."

"S'right!"

"Never, ever."

"Hey! sis bil correct old chap?" slurred Tobes. "Surely can't be this much! only had a couple of drinks."

"No problem Tobes...got m'calculator with me, can add it up." Gus couldn't.

"Look at this farking loser Tobes at the next table, writing his postcards or something...think he's a dago?"

"Probly" stammered Tobes.

"Should be out looking for chicks...get his dick pulled, must be something wrong with him eh?"

"Hyaaa, hyaaa, hyaaa!" Gus let go a snort that would have won him first prize at a pig show. I didn't want to look up, I'd avoided it so far but I couldn't help myself.

And there they were, Tobes...hefty with bloaty jowels and bumfluff on his upper lip. Gus...weedy, thin nose, no chin, both sporting foppish haircuts, polo shirts, khaki shorts and boating shoes. I laughed as they stared at me with unsteady, watery and I guessed, 17 year old eyes.

"What's your problem dago?" said Gus with all the menace of Sooty.

I very carefully and correctly pronunciated in the proper Queen's English..."Fuck off...and go to bed, before I call Matron."

As they staggered out the door, in through the adjacent one entered a girl. I thought...that's just like one of those little weather houses; out went 'wet and windy', in came 'sunny'. She was an Asian girl. A girl of immeasurable gorgeousness. As though time had stopped still, forks, spoons and food hung somewhere between plates and mouths. Kicks were being delivered under tables by wives and girlfriends.

She sat alone at a table directly across from me and sideways on which meant I could feast my eyes whilst eating. The males in the place were stealing looks while pretending to scratch their ear, or read the menu. She noticed. So did the girlfriends.

I decided to enjoy myself, after all I had nothing to lose. I was past embarassment. I called the waiter and asked him to deliver a note I'd quickly scribbled, to her table. This was seen by all the hungry males who watched his progress across the room, all thinking...'it'll never work.'

She unfolded the note, the waiter waiting, and laughed, beautiful hand to lovely lips, leaving only the impossible eyes visible.

She asked the waiter who. He pointed at me. The whole room pointed at me. I raised my glass and smiled my best smile and, lo and behold, she beckoned me over. The faces watching me thread my way through the tables had "Bastard!" written all over them, but the girl-friends were all smiles.

As I bent down to sit, she grabbed (beautifully) my pendant, pulled my head down to hers and planted a soft kiss. My lips exploded with delight. I thought I was in a 'Bond' movie. A dozen men furiously set about their cooled dinners. Having met at the wrong end of the evening it was a short coupling but a meal was set for the next night. She was from Singapore. She took my hand and led me from the restaurant. I winked and shrugged at every green face I passed.

We had a skeerious meal the next night, I don't remember what, and we must have looked fresh from bed as this time all the males in the restaurant were smiling, lewd, lascivious smiles.

I felt like going around them one by one and saying, "No we didn't; you don't have to you know; but we had good fun, we took two even-ings out of each others life...and shared them."

She was leaving for Singapore at I don't know how much o'clock, so we parted in Jalan Legian after an affectionate hug and kiss.

She asked "Why didn't you try to go to bed with me?"

"Because I didn't want to," I replied, and thought 'that sounds like an insult.'

"Thank you" she said, "If you had tried I would hate you. But now I love you and will remember you always."

Jesus wept!

Oh yes...the note?

That would be telling.

*

I'd rung my brother when I first arrived to ask him to confirm Duggie and Kenny's arrival date. I'd been here four days now, and they should have arrived. I was spending a fortune ringing home and I knew my brother was also spending time and money at home, trying to find out what was going on.

I'd rested, gained some bodyweight and a tan, felt more human, but no less alone. I wanted to get to Ubud, the artists colony in the centre of the island and from there to Mount Batur, the volcano in the north. I'd heard that there were eruption warnings, so I had to be there soon. And behind these, Lombok, Sumbawa and Flores beckoned, tempting me away from Chantal province, who for all I knew had already stashed me away on a dusty page in the back of her passport. It was time to move myself.

"What the hell's going on Martin?"

"I don't know!!" We were starting to get annoyed at each other, an irrational brother thing, "All I can find out is that Duggie's in trouble with the police and probably won't be coming."

"What about Kenny?"

"I'm speaking to his Mum tonight, ring me tomorrow at work, and hey, forget about the others...enjoy yourself. What's Ullawatu like?" And it dawned on me, he was working away at home as usual, looking after the kids and trying to help me out. I was on a dream trip.

"Sorry Martin; I'm going down there tomorrow, I'll give you a report."

I booked a ticket to Ubud for two days hence, hired a motorbike, and bought a toilet roll; act positive. The Balinese were so laid back they laid their roadsigns right back, in the grass; so it was a long trip. I went via Nusa Dua, the opposite end of the peninsula.

118

It was a purpose built luxury resort of no interest to me apart from a telephone. Bowling into a lobby, I phoned home, counting the rupiah disappearing on the screen.

"Can't speak long Martin, what's the go?"

"Duggie's had his passport confiscated, and Kenny won't go by himself. You're on your own Bro'. Do it, and take care."

Bastards! At least they could have contacted me. I stomped out of the hotel under a black cloud, a stream of filth fuming out of my mouth.

I knew I'd made a big mistake. I should have followed my heart to Burma. Instead I'd wasted a week sitting in Kuta. I would have to shorten my trip along Indonesia and shoot on to Oz. From there, with money waiting for me, I could perhaps go back and meet Chantal somewhere. In the meantime, apart from hanging a 'Kick me' sign on my back, I didn't know what else to do. I rode on, a steel band of depression and anger tightening round my forehead; at least I could see some surf.

I passed by the 'Ullawatu Cliff surf beach', through sheer speed, then the 'Official Ullawatu Beach' sign and confused, turned right at the next 'Ullawatu Beach' sign which turned out to be 'Padang Padang-Ullawatu Surf-Beach'. Well...what's an Ullawatu between friends. Negotiating a dirt track equal to any of Vietnam's, I arrived at the car park.

"Need a guide," the first of the swarm said. It wasn't a question.

"You have to have guide to go to beach," another threatened.

"No, not unless it's an eighteen year old Girl Guide," I said and walking off in the general direction of the sea, saw a sign 'Don't get lost, get a guide.' I took a path between some shacks, insults being hurled at me from behind, until it spewed out in all directions, and as though someone had laid a string from source to mouth, followed the flip-flop marks, crushed cigarette cartons and supermarket bags until turning left at a patch of dusty, thorny, scabbage I spied below me a magical sight.

Rolling in, bedecked with twinkling sunbursts, were queues of waves, their tops blown back; white quiffs in the offshore breeze. Sitting amongst this corrugated heaven, silhouetted against the burning reflections, were what looked like a school of porpoises, bobbing over green skylark hills. Even from where I was standing I could see that they measured twice head high. As I watched, one of the shapes broke away from the pack and carved it's signature along the virgin face, signing off at the end with a *'whooop!'* that steamrollered up the hill to my feet. As a surfer of mean ability, the scene below filled me with an electric gush and I had to sit on a rock to take it in. My surfing was woeful, though much enjoyed. I could handle a right hander on a beach-break, but this was a left, over a coral reef.

I watch the next set arrive from the horizon, the energy that has travelled so far, compressing as the seabed shallows. Then finding a solid reef barring the way, it jumps up, indignant, to show it's form and sucks the water in front back up it's glassy face leaving the reef almost dry and gurgling. Along the unbroken face the surfer dances his tune and as the lip of the wave curls over to punish the reef he stays one jump ahead to avoid being used as a missile. Like a matador he teases the shoulder of the wave, flicking the board away and back, a red cape to the roaring bull, foaming behind him. And the ultimate; he stalls the board to let the lip catch up and envelop him in it's mouth, then shoots out forward in flying spray and over the top of the wave, which thunders down.

Having never been 'behind the green door', I can only wonder at the feeling it must impart; but I know that even when riding a 'normal' wave, perhaps stealing up and down it's face, the energy that it harbours runs through the board, your feet and into your body. The buzz that results is unequalled by any artificial substance and is only bettered by lying with a woman you love, making your own waves.

The injuries passing by me testified to the difficulty of the wave and I knew the surfers I was watching were 'hotties.' Wandering into their camp, intimidated and awed, I excused myself with...

"No, I'm not surfing today, just photographing," which massaged their egos and muscles. Offered a board, I came clean. "Thanks, but I'm only a beginner, I'd either get in the way or die." "Good call mate," said an Aussie with a gashed head. But I desperately wanted to be out in the line-up, stroke into an emerald hill, rip and slash my own signature. I knew it was beyond me; too old; too shortsighted; too scared. I envied their youth and skill and a great helplessness washed over me. I roamed the shoreline taking photos, dipping into rockpools, and hating myself for not being out there. I climbed back up the hill often looking back at the joy below. I wish I could say "I surfed Ulluwatu boys!" but I can't. Rounding the last corner, and looking back, the front half of a board was floating in across the reef, alone.

On returning to the carpark I found that they had washed and polished the bike. "5000 rupiahs!"

"That's bloody lovely," I said, "I'm sure the owner will be pleased... it's a rental bike dumbfuck!" Their smiles dropped lower than a monkey's arse as I thrashed the bike round the carpark spitting gravel and dusting their good works, and hitting the road, acknowledged their grasping deeds with a two finger salute. As in Vietnam I was in a dodgy state, from anger, frustration and loneliness. I screamed the bike back to Kuta determined to leave it empty and knackered like me. I cut up everybody, rode through every red light, slid round gravel corners, traded insults with bus drivers and other bikes and on reaching Kuta, rode the wrong way up the pavement, scattering hawkers, tourists and women with starving babies.

I lay in my room at the losmen, flat on the bed, trying to calm down. A brief thought of joining 'the stupid club' passed by. There were times when it didn't seem so stupid, but I knew they'd never get me to join; there were things I wanted to see...

Chantal. My family. A bank holiday. Tommy Cooper. A volcano erupting. Cambodia. Roast Sunday lunch. Bumble. Crisp golden Autumn leaves. Rebecca. Monitor Lizards. A crisp frosty morning. A black run on a ski slope. The Great Barrier reef. Fog. A Brian Moore novel. A cold Lowenbrau. Harry the Swede. My Aunty Gladys. Thuy. North Devon. Tom Yam soup. Another motorbike. Kites flying above Bali. Porridge. Manly Beach. Crisp new snow. Schoolkids- full of the expectations of life. The Merry Harriers. Hanoi in a stormburst. A Madness concert. My Volkswagon camper. Ryan Giggs jinking through on the left wing. Doron and Keren's Kibbutz. A Sun newspaper headline. The colour of Spring in England. My backpack- full and waiting. The Vietnamese sky.....another Birthday.

*

MERTHA HOUSE, THE FOOTBALL FIELD, UBUD

THE WHITE marble table was chill to my hand, which rested face down, fingers splayed, trying to copy the gorgonzola veins of the stone. At the same time my right elbow warmed on the terracotta balustrade, which had sucked in hours of sunshine through it's emery paper surface. Without looking up from my reverie, I saw a hand that wasn't mine, slide a plate into the centre of my gaze. And there, puffed up with pride, was the tuna sandwich I had ordered. I looked up at the waitress with surprise. Puzzled, she asked..."Is okay?"

"Is it mine?" I asked, worried that it may be taken away and re-placed by tinned tuna in Mighty White.

"Yes sir."

From a pregnant pitta bread tumbled a small feast, that hung over the sides of a barely visible cream plate. The bread, fresh and light as a sponge, was steaming, as inside was a sumptuous slice of fresh tuna, scorched crisp on one side to lie on the salad. Alfalfa sprouts, salmon pink shallots and feta cheese mingled together round the sunniest dried tomatoes I'd ever tasted. Freshening the crowd with a shower of lemon juice, I fancied I heard the fishing boats lapping in the harbour, as a Greek sun went down; but looking up, it was palm trees and bamboo I saw, and Monkey Forest road disappearing into the paddy fields.

Thick clusters of white lotus flowers stirred in the sparkling jade-green water, carpetting, running up to the temple.

I lifted a doll's cup of thick black espresso, bitter-sweet nectar, but looking over the rim, the scene stayed the same.

I arrived the in Ubud the day before, almost before I could look up the details in the 'Lonely Planet'. I wasn't used to bus trips of less than a month now, there was too much getting on and off, and not enough time to listen to your tape collection. Ubud was an artist's colony in the centre of the island. Quite apt, I thought, as most artists wanted to be the centre of everything, even though it might be a strange world of their own making.

Here amongst the traditional Balinese wood and stone carvers, German and French expats of repute had set up school and mixed onto their pallettes- Balinese style with Gaugin, Renoir and a touch of Andy Warhol. And to their credit they had remained in the ambience that they'd created. I visited 'Blanco's House'. He was an old French fop, a

Quentin Crisp-Picasso, who had painted some pictures of note, notably for me, a portrait of Cole Porter that I'd seen many times. I spoke to him, between American and Japanese tourists, and he opened with a simpering "Oooooooohh.. you're English!" But followed it up creditably with, "How do you feel about the IRA ceasefire?"

"The what?" I replied.

"The ceasefire...it started yesterday," and showed me the article in The Times. I decided he wasn't such a bad lad, even though he was now churning out prints for the tourists. The house was as bizarre as his work, with artefacts old and new, Eastern and European, scuffling with photos and presents from movie and pop stars, politicians, despots and deadbeats. The shockingly blue swimming pool also looked like a painting, a very wet one, but although I'd been told I may be invited in, I wasn't. But I reminded myself that it was Sunday morning and I wasn't lying in bed with a hangover waiting for the pub to open, nor braving the 'Fuckwit Shuffle' at Sainsburys. I was in Ubud, about to ride up to Tampaksring. 'Up' being the operative word. 25 kilometres of up, on a pushbike.

My thighs burnt and the sweat stung my eyes and stuck the once pale- blue denim shirt to my back, navy wet. The reward at the end was the most impressive ruin I'd seen since Barbara Cartland, and to me, the best in Asia. Not the size, intricacy of detail or dazzling colours, but the setting and it's balance with nature. Hidden in a deep and steep-sided valley, the remains of a burial temple straddled a rushing water - not quite a river, but certainly not a stream. Pocket-sized paddies climbed up the valley walls, shaded and tended by palm trees and flowered shrubs. Whilst these all reached up to the warmth of the sun, dancing downwards to the cool were waterfalls, sluices, and sometimes just rivulets issuing out of tiny crevices, or oozing through sponges of moss. 'Verdant' is a word that would have fallen limp in this valley. I climbed high as it was possible and reaching the top, looked down into Nirvana. Then, I looked further, clear round the world and back, asking "Where are you my love?" and finding no answer but the babbling of monkeys, great sadness flew out from in every direction leaving me empty and alone.

I looked back to the temple which wasn't forced onto the landscape, to exhibit it's glory, it was part of it and now, worn by time, it fitted snug with the surroundings. It was one of the things I liked about Bali. Every house is a temple and every temple a house. They built the shrine first and the house around it. Each losmen was a gaggle of shrines, rooms and the owner's home spread in no particular order.

Breakfast was likely to come from round any corner and it was dificult to place where conversations, laughter or windchimes were coming from. Their religion is in the air, water, flowers, the house, the kites that play above. The stones of temples or statues grew ferns and flowers in their cracks to keep themselves alive and new. This day was a celebration of metal, so my rental bike had a posy of grass and petals and a burning incense stick on it's handlebars. The incense had finished burning just as my legs started to.

But now I had the long cruise home, downhill the whole way, shirt tail flapping. I saw a small boy coming towards me up the hill and steered straight for him. He changed course to the other side of the road. I mirrored his movement and he tacked back to the middle. His face had grown a mask of confusion and then, as time grew thin on the ground, I hunched down over the handlebars, poured a wide smile at him and screamed *"Yaaagggh!"* With a child's instinct, he saw the game, and jumping left and right, matched my laugh. As I flew past he shot me with his invisible gun. Looking back I saw him alone, punctuating the middle of the road, a big full stop on a line of dashes, hand waving in the air above his head.

I arrived back in Ubud late afternoon, and grabbing a cold beer from a bar full of Hitler Youth, crossed the pitholed tarmac to sit, legs dangling in a dry stormditch, awash with supermarket bags and weeds, swaying togther in the breeze. It was time for the daily match. At night this plot was stray-dog town, the darkness broken endlessly by howls of fighting and fucking. In the day it was the football pitch. One heavily pregnant bitch had held her ground in the daylight and was curled up in a depression with lip curled back. A snarling corner flag. And there stood in front with his back to me, was Stanley Matthews; red and white-hooped socks leading up to billowing shorts that finished half-way up his back, his collared shirt buttoned up tight under his chin. But turning, I saw that he was about fifteen and proud as punch of his outfit. He was standing on the 'T' junction of centre line and a touchline marked by a row of discarded shirts, which more than once brought down players with sneaky ankle attacks. At it's zenith, 43 players raced up and down the dusty pasture, the ball bouncing like a ping-pong ball on the granite grass. Under each progressively lower bounce a Thai boxing match took place in midair, the ball still at liberty, until the flailing limbs sent it willy-nilly. It was a giant size pin ball game.

The game continued, the ball's progress marked by a rolling dustcloud, misty figures inside, the other players disappearing into the squall at intervals. Some were engaged in small groups, discussing their boots or shorts, and some in pairs wandering the vacant half of the pitch hand-in-hand, stirring the dust with their toes until the approaching dust-cloud interrupted their intercourse and dragged them into it's vortex. After long periods the ball would escape it's tortured trajectory. I saw it fly like a bullet across Monkey Forest road, knock the sign for the 'Dew Drop Inn' off it's hinges and cannon into the hands of a portly spectator on a bench. He stood up, laughing at the coincidence, and hoofed the ball back to the centre pullover. Still eyeing his one contribution to the game and stepping back, he tumbled over the bench. His chubby brown legs stuck up in a perfect 'V' sign, shaking in rythm to the hooting that was coming from the unseen half of his body. The 43 players became screeching monkeys, slapping their thighs, backs, and the dusty ground, causing the occupants over in Monkey Forest to quiet in suspicion. When the ball eventually flipped past a goalkeeper, half blind with tears from the dust, the scene resembled a 1934 'Charlton Athletic versus Preston North End' game. Polite applause came from all the players with cries of ...

"Well done old chap, cracking good shot from that angle!"

Just one player, the closest, would shake the scorer's hand as adequate appreciation, whilst the other 41 resumed their positions, quietly and efficiently.

An Englishman joined the game, his carrot-top head blazing above his Chelsea shirt. As the ball arrived at the feet of a local, 'Ginger' cut his legs from under him with a tackle that would have shamed Eric Cantona. As the boy lay contemplating a life in a wheelchair 'Ginger' took off down the pitch, dribbling manically, jinking left and right, past this player, round that one, the FA Cup in his eyes. He ignored his teamates and carried on his own path to glory. The opposition were letting him pass, I presumed so that they could keep their legs intact, until 'whaaackk!!' he fired the ball past the goalie, cringing on the floor. 'Yeeessss!!' he shouted turning and running back to the centre. It was then he noticed that all the other players were pointing at the other goal, the one he should have been scoring in. His face matched his hair.

There was no time limit to this game and only bad light, a bus-load of backpackers or starvation usually ended the game. This day, with light waning rapidly, the dust cloud raced diagonally across the pitch then hesitated, as the ball bounced alone to roll and bump into the indignant corner flag. After discussion, the smallest boy was sent to retrieve it and in only shorts, he had the least protection. The boy, anxious to impress his elders took a running baseball slide at the dog and flicked the ball away with his toe. Now, with only escape in mind, he scrabbled to all fours, frantically searching for a toehold in the dust.

As he came off the ground, his shorts dropped to his ankles, anchored in the bitch's teeth. He shot out of them across the pitch, buttocks jiggling, hands cupped in front of his groin, and ran a zigzag gauntlet through the sea of players trying to catch him through helpless laughter. The man on the bench was once again a 'V' sign, legs shaking. This brought the game to an end as efficiently as two sharp blasts of a whistle, followed by one drawn out one.

Leaving the post match analysis, I sauntered past the temple on Jalan Raya, the Balinese music cacaphonal on the deepening dark air. I slipped in a sidegate guiltily, and for an hour stood transfixed as the Legong Dance Troupe put rhyme and rythym to the noise, translating the syncopation to movement. With eyes and fingers they sang of love and loss, sadness and fury, sweet gladness. They were fluttering bees, strutting princesses, their tiny steps tied to the beatmaster's drum. I fell in love with them all and joined by the boy from my losman, he asked,
"You like the girls, they are beautiful...yes?" I nodded.
"Would you like to meet them after?" I would, but thinking they might be a little young for me, perhaps sixteen or seventeen I asked,
"How old are they? How old is the princess?"
"She is twelve...the others are ten." He laughed at me wincing.

I pulled myself away to a restaurant where the music followed me in and once again rattled around my table, a discordant noise.
Duck in hot, sour sauce. Aloo Gobi - sweet potatoes with delicate curry spices, spinach hiding Anis and chilis in it's greenery. The sounds were mellowing and with some persuasion from a bottle of Kerem over ice and a twist of lemon, it became a lullaby. Drifting, a short time later, I clung on long enough to run back over a day in Ubud. How could a day like that be matched, compared to? It is a treasured day, a halcyon day. A Sunday. I fell asleep smiling.

In an effort to equal Ubud, I jumped on the first bus north to Mt Batur, a spectacular dormant volcano with a crater the size of Guildford holding a lake. At dawn the sun crept up, peered over the rim and poured sunshine into the bowl and liquid fire onto the lake. This was what normally brought travellers to the spot but I had an extra reason for hurrying north. The word was out that the volcano had shaken off it's slumber and was awake with a raging hangover. I wanted to be there when it really lost it's temper or threw up.
Arriving at Kedisan in the afternoon, I strolled the lake. Swallows or swifts plundered the upper air, the lower air claiming the surface of

the lake, whipping it up into thei smallest of waves. The concussion from the volcano flattened the ripples that necklaced the bathing children and shrouded their shrill cries. I stripped off, apart from my now frayed Marks and Spencer pants (well I didn't want them to laugh too much, they might drown) and joined them in the warm water.

Back on the sand, they performed a 'Monkey dance' for me, all *'kejak, kejak, kejak!'* and giggles, while my toes wriggled in the sand with delight. Further along the shore by an outcrop, their mothers and sisters were washing clothes in the lake, bobbing up and down like drinking hens, shrieking, spraying metallic bursts of speech like bullets round the rocks.

Sulphur fumes wafting by, acrid and homeless, overpowered the inscence that drifted down on gossamer breeze from the cremation celebration in the village; an incantation away up the slope from us. I saw a cotton wool cloud appear above the volcano and three seconds behind it came the *'bbooooooomm!'* Mount Batur was hardly Krakatoa but it was bubbling away like a pan of boiling potatos. On the sonic scale of explosions it was a single handclap in the Saturday Anfield Kop, which of course was now extinct. But it made me wonder what it sounded like standing near Krakatoa, or when Mt Helen decided to relocate across country very quickly, taking a few insignificant objects with it; a lake, a forest the size of Surrey.

We left at 3.00am in a race to the top before the sun could pull back the covers and jump up, excited with the new day. Torches struggled to distinguish the black rock from the coal- black night, especially as we only had one between four of us and the batteries had come from my Walkman. At the steeper inclines we were on all fours, scrambling up loose scree, barking shins and elbows and loosening lava onto the people below. Some had stopped, exhausted, some terrified, rooted to the spot. The guides' powerful torches were flashing way above and below our position They were trying to sell Coke and Sprite to other climbers who couldn't reach their wallets on all fours, their fingers straining for a safe hold.

The explosions to the left were growing as we reached the summit, sweating, despite the chill morning wind. Facing the awesome sunrise I was distracted constantly by the 'crack' and 'booom' behind me and turned to watch the false dawn of molten lava flying skywards. We had breakfast of eggs, cooked in smoking fissures in the side of the rock, then carried on over the mountain until we were above the core. The helmet would expand and glow red veins, then explode red jism into the sky. Following this would be a 'woooosh' until the sky exploded with an 'Oh God!" and the concussion waves knocked me sideways.

The guides looked worried. An almighty blast sent lumps the size of a Mk 1 Cortina skyward, brake pads, and coils and tyres whizzing in all directions. With an insane grin, I turned to see the guides scurrying up the hill as red hot lumps rained down. They eventually persuaded me away from my perch, hunkered down laughing like a fool.

We descended into a now fully lit Tolkienesque landscape, all folds of ugly black rock, crushed up upon itself and everything petrified. And if I'd seen what we'd been climbing in the dark, without aid, I'd have been petrified too.

Having swum in the lake, climbed the mountain, felt the power, seen the sunrise and many scams and rip-offs, I decided to move on to make this the shortest stay of the trip. I was in and out of Kedisan in under twenty four hours, and arrived at Padangbai to the east in time for a swim and a walk around the rocks in the sunset.

*

I WAS getting around, slipping in and out of rooms, quicker than a whore now. Some of this was to do with the 'The Bible'. No, not the one where 'stories' are true and bad things happen to good people, in a black cover. No; this one always has a yellow cover:

'The Lonely Planet - South East Asia', mine and every other back-packer's bible. Spawned by Tony and Maureen Wheeler, twenty years previous, The Lonely Planet has taken over the mantle that Baedeker relinquished. Without this, many travellers, me included, would spend weeks in Canton station, months on the wrong trains or buses and years at home wondering how the hell to do it. It's information comes from travellers, for travellers, and as a result is honest, truthful and essential. Though I wondered what the Japanese, the Swedes and the like made of it. They had their own versions but always preferred the Yellow bible, in English. So at times they must have been confused by the anomalies scattered around the book.

"Hanoi - a drab, sometimes pleasant, charming city." Can these three live in the same sentence? If the information on a town or service was inaccurate it was joked amongst the travellers that perhaps Maureen had PMT that day or Tony, a hangover.

So they wouldn't win an award for literature! they deserve the Travel Writer's Guild Award for truth and the MBE and a hearty Tory slap-on-the-back for encouraging tens of thousands of recession blink-ered and disillusioned British to roam the world. A percentage of these would return home, enriched and wordly, to serve the country better: in their absence disencumbering the social security system and reducing the unemployment figures. It's a wonder there isn't an MP for Gatwick, Heathrow and Dover, there just to shake the hands of departing travellers.

The lonely planet is a currency of it's own, sold and bought along the way, swapped and borrowed: it's value based on the date of the edition, an old one likely to direct you to a quaint fishing vilage which has since sprouted a nuclear reactor and it's locals, extra legs and heads. At the Micky Mao cafe, after the gangsters and police had left, I held the 'LP' in my left hand and threatened to write a letter with my right. The owner was more scared of getting a bad review than he was the Triads and spilled the beans, bottom lip quivering. For entertainment and elucidation it just can't be equalled. Eat your heart out Rough Guide, the disciples carry the word and the word is the truth - 'The Lonely Planet'.

*

LITTLE BEACH, PADANGBAI

THE LONELY PLANET was right. Padangbai was a small, quiet, fishing village where ferries popped in and out from Lombok and Nusa-Lebomgan, avoiding the reef, and passing the beach that the outriggers clung to; each painted in children's colours; lazing in the sun 'til their night-time's work.

The bamboo hut I was wearing, was a weak stone's throw from the water and good value at 9000 rupia a night. The banana pancake, as it did in Kuta and Ubud, arrived dutifully each morning with the monotony of a metronome in an empty room.

My alarm clock was a Mynah bird that had no snooze, or ON/OFF button. What it did have was a catchy little tune that defied recognition or sleep.

Waking up abruptly I sat up, Chantal's sarong twisted around me, my comforter and tormentor; and looked through the lattice window that had no glass to keep out the scent and taste of the sea.

Lying alarmingly pale on the crest of the beach lay a girl, a new arrival. Legs bent up,supporting herself behind on her elbows, she was an 'M' and protruding from the first downslope was a deadheat in a Zeppelin race. Tits, though I'd seen a million of them now, still put a smile on my face. I suppose it's because my favourite part of a woman is the small of the back or the nape of the neck. Tits are comical in comparism. So, amused, I set off for Little Beach and looking directly to my left - it was still a dead heat. And I sang to myself as my toes hit the hot sand..."*Sunshine girl I'm looking down your bra,* (hopping onto the road)...*I see two round things, I wonder what they are?* (skirting a sleeping dog)...*I ask you brightly, if you'll invite me,* (stumbling over a boatrope)...*to squeeze them tightly,* (kicking a runaway football back to it's game)... ..*my sunshine girl!*

I walked by a shimmering pile of Barracuda, still menacing, and rounded the ferry quay that thronged with comings and goings, threats and promises. Climbing up the headland, all solidified bubbles of lava, I looked back down to the bay. Snaking away from the quay was a chalk-white line marking the trail of the now invisible 12 o'clock ferry to Lombok, which lay sunbathing over the horizon.

Crackling and rustling, to the sides and behind me, made me imagine I was being followed...even surrounded, but when I stopped, the sounds didn't: not like in mystery films. The trees, eucalyptus-like, had pods which were exploding like firecrackers and shooting out seeds, leaving the dry husks to rattle down through the branches in a chain reaction. The falling seeds scattered lizards, who scuffled leaves, so that the whole wood was alive.

Viewing the beach before me, it seemed the same, yet somehow different. The Germans, as usual, were stormtrooping the waves which, as though in defiance were tumbling people gin-gan-gooly, filling their swimsuits with sand and throwing them up the beach, breathless.

Sitting, knees drawn up on my towel, there seemed to be tension on Little Beach. The clouds were playing up, interrupting the sun, and drawing scowls from the worshippers. The hollow plunking from the wind chimes, tied to one of the shacks, sounded discordant and in league with the breeze that was flicking sand in people's faces. The hairs on my neck stood out, and I watched goosebumps gobble up my arms. I'd bought a coffee and the glass tankard sat squat in the sand next to me with a domed red lid that echoed the sunburnt mammaries all around. Lying prone, supported by crooked elbow, opium smoking position, I could line the lid up with the rocks at the end of the beach where a blowhole sent spumes of water skyward with a bellow. And though I waited; and waited; the acrid coffee grounds refused to sink to the bottom and stay calm.

The only happy thing on the beach, a kite dancing and spinning above, perhaps oblivious of the troubled air below. As if caught un-aware, it spiralled down into a sunburnt leg with an oucchh!

Angry voices rose above the gloom on the beach. A fearsome row had broken out between the hawkers and machetes were being bandied about. I'd watched one of the women scalping a coconut earlier with one and, as she chased another woman with it aloft, my stomach turned. I prayed the blade wouldn't swing.

I'd befriended a small boy the day before, a drink seller, who was quick and funny and just a little boy called Rahm with an engaging smile. He was dodging amongst the swirling arms and legs, eyes wide ans scared, until they took his drink box away. He fought them; flaying at them, spindly but indignant, knocked to the sand over and over. As the tide of trouble swept over him he was left on the sand, crying his heart out. And for a long time, a guilty long time for me, he lay alone, shoulders heaving, sobbing into the sand.

131

Between sobs, he looked up and seeing me, he raced over. Arms clinging round my neck, his head jerked under my chin and I brushed the sand from his back as though it would help.

I noticed that, hanging on a threadbare string around his neck, was a handsome, silver ring. I told him, "This is a very nice ring Rahm; I would like to buy it if you give me a good price."

"He won't sell it to you," said his elder sister, squatting in the sand a few feet away. "It's his best one. He found it under the waves and has worn it for a year now. He has two others but that is his best one. When he has two more he will sell them all and buy a bicycle. Many people have wanted that ring."

I wanted that ring.

I lifted the little head by the chin until the helpless eyes fixed on me through the tears.

"Rahm, I want to buy your ring."

His head bobbed down onto my chest mingling suncream with tears as it shook in a silent "No."

"You can buy a same ring in town for 15,000 rupia" whispered his sister. Rahm looked daggers at her and warily at me. I slipped it, still on the string, onto my little finger, the only one it would fit.

"Rahm, I will give you a good price for this ring."

He straightened, snuffling.

"Hold out your hands and close your eyes tight." He did this and the tears squeezed from the side of his eyes and rolled down his cheeks. I rolled 50,000 rupia into a tight roll and slipped it through the ring where it expanded and filled the hole. Opening his eyes, he searched his empty hands and my face. I nodded at his chest and he looked down, the sun casting a shadow from his chin that pointed to the ring.

He unrolled the money, added up the notes, squealed, then grabbing the girl's pineapple knife, slashed the string and put the ring on my finger. I felt like I'd been crowned.

His face grew a sunbeam and he cartwheeled round the beach, waved the money in the faces of the harridans, shouting "na na na nergh nergh!!" like children do the world over. He was a richman. He was a boy. He was eight years old. My nephew Russel, floated before my eyes. He had computer games, a mountain bike, clothes, a future, but he wasn't spoilt; far from it; he was just fortunate to be born in Guildford and not Padangbai.

It was probably the best 25 dollars I ever spent. I gained a silver ring that had lived beneath the waves, sliding amongst the shells, to be fished up by a wee boy who wore it for a year like a treasure; his crown jewels; his fortune.

The next day he screamed when I hit the beach and ran over, tumbling to the sand once in his hurry, to show me his new drinkbox. His mum, who cooked food in one of the shacks, had made him buy a new one so that he could stay in business. The rest of the money she was saving for his bicycle. His sparrow chest was puffed with pride. He had a Coca-Cola box...blood red, and bandage white, not an old wooden one.

His eyes still darted to the ring on my finger and I told him,

"You don't need a ring, you need a bicycle and a childhood."

He made me a kite. It was red. We flew it all afternoon over the exploding trees and the roaring blowhole. I had to say goodbye. His mum let him walk to town with me, his hand so small and hot in mine, but when the time came to leave he cried so much I had to take him back to the beach and his mum.

I caught the next ferry, two hours later, and rounding the headland, Little Beach came into view, a white crescent with a red kite flying above. My red kite. I waved, though I knew he couldn't see me, and said quietly to myself, "Bye-bye Rahm, take your time young man, don't you rush to get old." And finding myself desolate and a long way from home, I gripped the rail 'til my knuckles whitened, in an effort to stop the tears from flying out like poison arrows and frightening the locals.

*

AMPENAM POST OFFICE, LOMBOK

AMPENAM was the westerly of four towns that had joined up along a single road over the years. 'The Bible' said, *"Ampenam fades out before the old dusty port and grubby beach."* It didn't. It was faded from the start of Sweta, the most easterly town, carried on in the same tatty fashion through Cakra and despite a brief flowering of fancy Government buildings and offices with sprinkler fed lawns in Mataram, faded all the way to the grubby beach. *"These days, many visitors don't bother with the town at all, preferring to stay on the beach at Sengiggi or head straight toi the Gili Islands,"* said 'The Bible'. Which was exactly why I bothered, and as always, the surprises kept on coming. I'd get to the Gilis in my own time.

As I tumbled out of the minibus, the man reclining against the tumbledown wall asked, "Where you from?"

"England," I replied, hoisting up my pack, adding the tired old travellers joke, "and are you from...here?"

"No," he said "I'm an Aborigine."

"Ah, a native of Lombok!"

"No, an Abbo from Australia." Looking at the lumpy eyebrows, splayed nose and eyes set deeper than an opal mine, I saw that it was fair dinkum. My first Abbo. In Lombok! Which, I reflected later that evening, wasn't so unusual as a hop across Sumbawa, a skip onto Flores, and a jump from Timor would land you in the sandpit of Northern Australia.

A stroll on the beach confirmed that it was spectacularly grubby. The sea was characterless and brown, the sand grey and brown to match the rusting- brown oil tanks that dominated the top of the beach. Dead fish lay dull in the scummy froth at the water's edge and as I walked, hosts of flies rose humming from innards scattered along the sand.

A young boy, naked, squatted in apparent meditation ahead of me and I realised as he wiped his arse with his hand that this was also the toilet for the ramshackle fishermen's huts. A complete family stood, as if being photographed, outside their hut, smiling, until I veered towards them and shouted "Hullo!" Their smiles turned to stone. One daughter ran off into the hut, the other, quite lovely, hid behind her father.

I rejoined my footmarks in the sand and walked on. Finding three more children, splashing naked in a lagoon, I decided to stay quiet. They spotted me however and took to their heels, the smallest one howling as though chased by a banshee. It struck me that it must be very unusual for travellers to stop here these days.

On arrival I was the only passenger on the minibus to get off. The Germans, who'd been stormtrooping the waves at Padangbai, were heading for Sengiggi and a hotel, presumably so they'd have somewhere to park their towels. The French couple didn't seem to know where they were going. Le Monsieur, however, looked quite envious at me alighting, as the hardcore techno dance beat had been pounding from the doorspeakers the whole way, extracting a regular *"Merde...arretez le musique!!"* But they couldn't hear him or chose not to. His wife looked sick. The Germas looked at me blankly, wondering why I wanted to stay in a grubby hole like this. Well, I had a reason. A big one. Two miles down the road, marked 'Poste Restante, Mataram, Lombok', could, or should be an air mail letter from Burma.

As I returned back along the beach to the town, I thought, 'at least the sky is blue', and saw a stream of starlings fly, seemingly out of the sand, and head inland like a column of ants looking for a picnic. A second stream crossed the first, diagonally, and kept their formation. Two flocks of pigeons circled each side of this with a roaring of wings, forming a game of noughts & crosses on unlined blue paper. 'Perhaps it's a sign or an omen' I thought and turned in the direction of the Post Office.

Ponies with twinkling brasses and jingling bells trotted by, proud heads bobbing, pulling small traps behind. These were the taxis, and every other one slowed to my pace and asked if I wanted a lift, but I wanted to walk; to think about the letter. It was three weeks since Chantal and I had parted. What had happened in that time? I knew so well now how time was accelerated whilst travelling. Routine, events, sights, sounds, meetings and partings; that would fill months at home, could be and were compressed into a single week on the road. It was the most tiring thing about backpacking; fitting all the experiences into a vessel use to much less.

If the letter were there, what did it contain? If it wasn't, what would I do? I was nervous. It was like waiting for Christmas to arrive and hoping you got that football game that you wanted, But anything would do really. Wouldn't it?

I'd only walked the first two hundred yards before I was joined by the omnipresent young lad touting, "Where are you from?" "Where are you going?" He asked if he could accompany me to the Post Office to practice his English. I knew that, as in China, Vietnam, and Thailand, English words learnt were a currency to be stored away and used to obtain some kind of a future. However hard they tried, Esperanto would never be taken up, English is to be the future language of the world and it's the world saying that; not me.

It would also take my mind off the letter so I slapped him on the back and said "it'd be a hooter!" "Excuse me?" he said.

"What's your name?" I asked; "Hallan;" "Ah! Alan is an English name" I teased, and his grin touched his earlobes. All along the route, people on bicycles, hanging out of windows, walking, trotting or just standing asked him the same question, to which he replied,

"England...Post Office."

We talked about his ambition to become a normal human being. He was seventeen, had no house; so lived with his uncle, had no job; there were none here, and no money. Without these, he could not get a wife. But despite these obstacles he was hopeful ofi getting a job at a hotel or hostel in one of the resorts as his English was getting better (It was good), and he could cook! He could do fruit salad, omelette and banana pancake!

"Then you and I are same-same" I told him.

"What a faintly preposterous hypothetical comparism of human prosperity" he countered in his own words, which sounded very much like a laugh. I explained to him that at home, I had no home. No job. No money and certainly no wife.

"Then we *are* same-same" he said smiling..."Broken Wing."

"Excuse me?" I said.

"People like you and me are called Broken Wing in Lombok."

And I thought to myself 'that sums me up perfectly,' brought down from heady heights by divorce, bankruptcy and unemployment to flap helplessly in the dust of Asia. Would I find a way to get aloft? or be pancaked into the road by a ten-ton truck leaving two tail feathers sticking up: a last 'V' sign to the world. I carried on flapping and, we reached the Post Office.

It was high and wide inside like Grand Central Station; tidy, efficient-looking, with clean air wandering around the marble floor that led me, optimistically, to the Poste Restante desk. There was nothing under 'C' in the box for me, nor in the cross-referenced, carefully written journal with one clean line between each entry. I was heading towards panic and asked to look at 'H',. She refused, as it wasn't in her journal...see! I tried to explain, and under her stiff scrutiny, found it sandwiched between 'Ferguson Helen' and 'Jalatasin Horas'. There, in black and white, in her best handwriting, crisp as her blouse collars, was my name. It had never looked so good. In my relief at finding the red and blue edged letter in the box, I helped her sort the other boxes, all blushes and apologies, horrified at her system breakdown.

With that precious missive folded in my pocket, I gabbled on, all the way back to town and I don't think Hallan understood a word. *I* don't remember a word I said. Back at the bar where Hallan lived, his Uncle nodding his consent, I bought him a Coke and sipped my cold beer while I read the letter, and with incredible politeness he looked away until I had finished. He was too well mannered to ask me outright, though his eyes were pleading, so I told him who it was from, and where, and read some pieces for him. Later it occurred, that to him I must seem to be very lucky and I wasn't really 'Broken Wing'. I wasn't trapped like him. I was lucky. I had a letter from Burma.

I remember every word it said. I still do now. Chantal had sent it shortly after arrival in Burma. Harassed by locals in the Post Office, she wrote it in the corridor. She felt the same as me; desperate. She missed me; terribly. This made it all so much easier didn't it? We were on different continents, moving in different directions; what could we do?" No answers fell from the sky or popped up from the sunbaked soil. Happy to be still wanted, but tragic to be parted from her, I sentenced myself with local transport to the Gili Isles in the hope it would occupy my mind.

The first Bemo; small, covered truck with bench seats along each side, dropped me at a crossroads of no significant purpose. The old lady sitting beside the Northern tributary, skin like a crocodile, working over a Singer sewing machine, looked up briefly and nodded in the direction she was sewing. She muttered "Gili" and pointed at the dirty, scrubby bush opposite. She followed up with, "Bus" and putting two and two together I crossed and stood on the patch of sunhammered grass that most resembled a bus stop. From a hundred feet above the crossroads it would have resembled a scene from a David Lynch movie.

Two strangers; one, right foot pedalling her old machine, tick... tick..ticking along the cloth, sunlight glinting off the spinning wheel; myself standing motionless, opposite. The bus stopped on the southern side of the crossroads and glared at me, the radiator and lights a grim smiling face. I had an eerie feeling that if I walked towards it, the bus would reverse away; stop if I stopped , return if I returned; baiting me. But it disgorged a passenger and drove the thirty feet across to me, jerkily. There was room for me inside, but not my pack; so squeezing through the bodies, human and animal, alive and dead, I gave it up to the conductor who put it on and clung to the outside of the bus for the whole trip. A bunch of chickens that had been on my seat, legs tied but very much alive, now sat on my lap. I was growing quite attached to them until one of the four took his profession literally and started a cockfight. Unfortunately the nearest contender was in my shorts. I leapt from the seat and threw the bunch like a bride's posie down the bus where they flapped amongst a huddle of schoolchildren, who tossed them between each other as though they were hot potatoes.

Fortunately, Colonel Sanders seated next to me seemed as amused as all the others and offered a small pig as a replacement, which I politely refused on the grounds that it may hunt through my pants for truffles.

Our passage through the villages attracted great interest as it appeared that a backpacker had run for the bus too late, with the doors shut, and had hung on for grim death, banging on the doors to be let in. But it was only the conductor signalling the driver to stop for a passenger or carry on, my full pack threatening to peel him from the side and drop him onto the monkeys that lined the roadside of Pusak Pass, grinning, scratching milestones.

The trip ended at Pemanang where the pony and traps (or Dokar) waited to shuttle travellers the last two miles to the harbour. I decided to walk, eventually shaking off the persistent Dokar driver, shadowing me, at the half mile mark. He looked puzzled as to why anybody wanted to walk at mid-day in headbanging heat.

When the booking office at Bangsai had enough passengers to fill an outrigger we crossed the choppy strait to the Gili Islands.

'Gili' meant 'Islands'; three beauty spots on the cheek of Lombok, and I'd chosen the largest and furthest away.

*

GILI TREWANGAN

*If you held a picture postcard at reading distance; azure perfect
sea lapping over coral onto white sand, a single cotton wool cloud on
a flawless sky; then dropped it, the scene would still be there with just
the words 'Gili Trawangan - A tropical paradise' missing. But we all
know that paradise doesn't exist, don't we children?... The palm tree
cropping the left corner of the postcard has a nice line of spray paint
at it's base and under, enjoying it's shade, is a tired hut sporting a
wall bearing the niceties of the world. 'Don't fuck with the locals',
'Hell sucks', 'No money - no honey', 'Gili boys take it up the arse',
'Shit' (a hidden message in that one I think or perhaps a succinct
comment on life as a Lombokian)*

*Just escaping the lens to the right, a goat is chewing away at a
black and white striped grocery bag, the tip of a mound of rubbish
that will take him years to get through. Behind are ramshackle huts,
some so tired they've lain down in the dust, which, kicked up by wheels
and feet, hangs heavy on the limp foliage. Lying eyes closed, alone, in
the centre of the postcard, I hear sleighbells approaching and stretch
out my fingers soporifically to check I'm on white sand and not snow.*

*The pony canters past, high kicking, bells and harness
jingle-jangling and the little banana yellow cab bouncing on it's
rubber tyres. The swirling dustcloud momentarily obscures the
number '28' painted childlike on it's side.*

*As the dust settles, so does the noise. A dog barks, so far in the
distance it seems a memory*

This was the only transport on Trewangan and it was a feast to the
ears after the bellowing horns of China, the buzz of motorbikes in
Vietnam or the tone deaf traffic jams of Bangkok. The only noise rising
above the gentle lapping of the waves and a Mosque calling the faithful
to prayer was the put-put-put of the next outrigger arriving at the
harbour. The harbour was a fallen tree that the boys tied the boats to,
after running up the sand with the rope. This was the signal for the
sunbathers to sit up and watch the only entertainment available.
Backpackers would have to leap from the boat into the shallows and
frequently they would lose balance and topple forward or back into the
waves, where like a turtle on it's back it was very difficult to regain the

vertical. This was great fun for the people that had negotiated the landing previously and a comfort for the ones that hadn't, their belongings spread out at their hut, drying in the sun. It was like watching someone slipping on a banana skin, once an hour.

Having seen two duckings in an hour and tired of sunbathing, I moved on home. I regard sunbathing as interesting as collecting car registration numbers and if the time wasted on it was spent solving the world's food problem, we would be a planet of fat people. I strolled along the beaches looking at the peaches, with two stops for a chat: one English - Carol, fair hair, soft pointed strawberry cones; one Austrian - Isabella, dark hair, wicked eyes, firm, round with maltesers for nipples. I wondered if they'd melt in my mouth and not in my hand. I decided I needed a cold shower, and heading home passed under an exploding Kapok tree, the banana-shaped pods bursting out a snowshower of white fluff.

The toilet and showers were combined and called Mandies. So I took my clothes off and slipped into Mandy. I'd always wanted to. The water was warm and salty and was one of the features of the Gilis - no fresh water and no electricity (apart from a small section in the middle of the beach). As I was ladling the water over my head I heard a shouting outside. It was Ronnie and Man, the two that ran this cottage. Loosely tying my sarong around for modesty I slipped out of Mandy and into a duststorm, and bumping into Ronnie, he grabbed my arm.

"Run Howie! whirlywind! whirlywind!" We rushed into the calmer dust of the yard collecting Man on the way, who was hooting. Looking back, we saw the spout come through between the two cottages with the speed of a Granny on a zimmer frame but with the force of Mike Tyson. It lifted the corner of my roof like an adult looking into a doll's house. We were all three following it along, smiling skyward. Ronny squealed "My towel!!" and there it was, a hundred feet up, spinning; Bob Marley smiling down at us.

"Come back Bob!" shouted Man through cupped hands. The assorted yard rubbish had been sucked up with it and wouldn't come down for nearly ten minutes. I had a favourite goat in the yard, jet-black with a startlingly white patch. It had a strange bleat that was too human and looked like one I had on my toy farmyard when I was young. Tied by a washing line to a stake, he wasn't going anywhere. We all three realised at the same moment that goat was on target. We grinned at each other wickedly; it was too late to reach it anyway. Honest. It pulled his front feet off the ground first, then rocked him back onto them and picked up his back ones. He was like a bucking picnic table and at one stage was aloft on his rope spinning round and round; a balloon with legs. Then he spun down like water going down a plughole. We were helpless with laughter now and Ronnie, seeing that my sarong had slipped unnoticed to the floor, fell on his back kicking his legs, dreadlocks brushing the dust and shrieked,

"White bum! white bum!" I joined him on the floor trying to breathe through the spasms. If the goat had broken his moorings I think I would have wet myself so it was a good job I was naked. Ronnie's towel didn't come down, but a toilet roll, complete and unrolled, fell down on the goat like manna from heaven and he set about eating it in the now unruffled air. There were no red shoes poking out from under the cottage so I figured it hadn't been a dream.

Later sitting reading on my balcony, by a hurricane lamp that would have struggled with a gentle breeze, I had an impulse to sit blank, and stare at a video-screen, with no conversation, making no new friends. So I did.

The bar was full but could have been empty, every head glued to the same spot, the glare from the screen spread across the faces of the watchers, the soundtrack on megabass. I joined in. I pointed and signed to the waiter to order my food. I tutted when somebody went to the toilet, momentarily blocking the screen. I apologised to the person behind when my food arrived and had to sit forward to eat it, blocking his view. When the laserdisc had to turn itself over, there was a thirty second gap, and the screen was blank. The heads all swivelled, indignant, and initiated conversations, but the renewed soundtrack cut them short and pulled them back to the screen. I realised I was amongst zombies and I was one also. The film? It was a masterpiece about a rebellious maiden in the times of Richard the Lionheart, who, teaming up with a circus troupe, leads an army of children against the wicked Baron. Phew!...But it put up some memorable lines. Seeing the Baron bowling a maiden over, the short-arse heroine punched him with a chain-mailed glove, to the floor.

"Wow!" said Dexter Fletcher, "We sure could do with a girl like that in our gang." These gems of screenwriting brought gusts of laughter from the British in the audience and perplexed the Scandinavians and Indonesians. Why were we laughing? It wasn't a comedy, was it?

As the credits rolled people had to look at each other and talk again, but I noticed that on exit they were all going next door. I followed the herd, which was now coralled in 'Rudy's bar', and the blackboard at the entrance announced - 'Party night, dance and get drunk. Free popcorn.' How could I turn down such an event?

I sat alone at a table on the fringes, slightly uncomfortable, being the only lone reveller, and I couldn't see a group that I could break into. My mind however was soon distracted by a figure hitting the empty dance floor. He was a Gili boy; baseball cap back to front, three vests and bright orange trousers cut off at the knee. On arriving nonchalantly at the exact centrespot, he looked down at his feet as though to check they were still there and command them to dance. And there they were in a huge pair of wellies, the toes curled up with age. They shuffled and jiggled, they did the gumboot boogie. They were good, and he seemed to just sway along above them, a sort of helmsman steering his boats around a parquee sea.

The floor filled and I was joined by my neighbour, Laurie. She was half-Arabian, half-American, but had lived in Switzerland most of her life. To her misfortune she carried the unquestionable whining drone of the Californian valley girl, which took away the charm of her Arabian features. But she was great company and we played the nationality game, matching clothes, dancing style and behaviour to the country.

The British danced either with a stiff upper limb or the wild abandonment of Rave-goers. Austrians and Germans danced waltzes and Polkas, twirling each other round, a century behind the times.

Americans; bad shirts tucked into white shorts, white socks and sandals, danced conservatively like presidential candidates afraid to make a mistake. The Indonesian whiskey had flown down at $3 a bottle, the game taking on hilarious dimensions, and either of us would race up to anybody round the room shouting at their sweaty faces "You're English!"..."Etes-vous Francais?" "Deutschlander?" and signal across the room at the other a victory, with a raised fist and a 'Yeesss!' or in defeat, a 'V' sign from me or a raised middle finger from Laurie. The loser got a whiskey, so there were no losers in this game; an opinion I didn't agree with when I woke up at 6am on the sand; tongue of sandpaper. Apparently I'd loaded Laurie into a pony and trap, as she couldn't walk, and forgetting that I lived at the same place, set out for a hostel that didn't exist. I never got there.

The party moved next door the following night, to the Paradise bar. The same warm-up boy waggled his wellies. We watched the same people doing the same dance, to the same tape. We realised that we knew the order of the records. Bob Marley, UB40, The Shamen, Bob Marley, Cypress Hill, Bob Marley, Bob Marley, Bob fucking Marley! I used to like him. We grew weary of the video and the tape by the third night and returned to real life, sitting with our hurricane lamps hissing at the darkness. After a quiet meal under a spangled sky, we told each other our secrets and sadnesses, happily uninvolved and uncomplicated by each other. Early next morning, through the bamboo wall, I heard Laurie leaving.

"Have a good one Laurie" I shouted with nightcroak.

"Have a better one Howie, go back to sleep." she twanged back.

I slipped away again but before I lost consciousness I was conscious I'd lost another friend. As is common in the early morning, my dreams were vivid, disjointed and disturbing. All of my lost friends flew around and about in strange places, and they couldn't remember me, though I shouted at them, *"Harry!...it's me, Howie, where are you going?" "Remember Hanoi, Hoi-An?"* And Chantal said, *"I've never been to Thailand,"* in Belgian, but I could understand it.

I woke up sweating and ready to move on but, counting up my Rupiahs and underestimating my beer bill, found that I'd left it a bit late. I had to leave immediately and I was on the beach half an hour later waiting for another fourteen paying customers to gather. Two hours later I had swum and dried twice in the sun and I was still alone. Knowing that I couldn't afford another night in a cottage I resolved to sleep on the sand. I was joined by three Javans who offered to charter the whole boat and split it four ways. It was all the money I had but I could hitch back to Mataram to a bank.

As we were dipping along in the outrigger, I trailed a hand in the water, elbow crooked over the bleached wood side. One of the Javans pointed at my arm and said "You are very brown."

I was about to say " not as brown as you..." when I realised I was. Considerably.

A flight of flying fish skimmed past on the same course as us, like silver direction arrows, and I had a vision of a cormorant swimming along underwater with the fish flying above in the air, and then swapping places endlessly in confusion at each other's station in life.

I chatted to the three about my travels and one just sat staring into the distance repeating over and over, "China, Vietnam, Thailand, Indonesia, Australia, New Zealand, America, England," until I started to think to myself 'Yes, it is a bit dreamlike isn't it.' When we reached Lombok they asked me how I was getting to Mataram.

"Public bus," I lied "it's more fun." I walked the first stretch to the main road, solitary, but noticed a vehicle following along behind at the same speed, tailing me. It was a black space-cruiser with mirror windows. Eventually it pulled alongside and kept pace with me, until I thought... 'Here we go,' and stopped, glaring at it. I heard laughter from inside. The window slid down and a beautiful woman, looking straight into my eyes said, "The public bus has arrived." The other doors flew open and out popped my three Javans laughing at the look on my face.

"I knew you had no money," one said "I saw your wallet was empty when you showed us your dog." Which was how I came to ride back to Mataram in air-con luxury in just under thirty minutes, passing the same monkey milestones through the pass, one with his lipstick out, pissing a small arc into the middle of the road.

They dropped me outside the Losmen Kambodja after I declined their offer of dinner; their shout. "I have things to do."

They smiled at each other, a car load of very wealthy Javans. I had my pride. When they'd turned the corner I put my back to the hostel, went to the bank to get the very small amount of money I had left, and slipped along to the post office.

I drew a blank. "No letters for you Mr Cobb," said the crisp-bloused girl as I walked in. Her system was obviously working now.

I still wasn't used to the dull ache of disappointment that came from these unfulfilled trips. I invariably left the post office muttering under my breath and hissing "Shit, shit, shit!" in time to my heavy footsteps. The doubts flew around like leaves in a breeze. Does she not care? Has she found someone else to hold? Where are you my little Flem?

The next morning, the sky could have been anything, I was in a hurry. I skipped down to Lembar, caught the ferry, and took a lingering look at Little Beach as we sailed into Padangbai.

I raced across Bali, stopping in Ubud to return a book and get my deposit money, and then deposited myself in Kuta.

Bagus bar was rocking to the Aussie rules football final, beer cans bouncing off the screen to shouts of "You're running the wrong way Lambert y'fuckin poof!"

"Hey mate..." said one, to the waiter scurrying past, ducking the beer cans, "is the chicken curry spicy?"

Either honest or confused he answered "No."

"I'll have that then mate."

There was a letter from Chantal, from India, and describing Burma.

"I spent hours on the balcony watching the life on the river, the sunset; drawing. It was wonderful. Hard sometimes to describe the feelings these places cause inside of you. In the evening the Burmese came out of their houses, playing guitar and singing, words which came straight from the heart. I went out and sat with them listening to the songs of which I could not understand the words, but just through

144

the emotions they put in their voices it was like I understood...was beautiful. My favourite place was Bagan with it's 2000 temples. I biked around these for 5 days by myself again. Spending sometimes hours on the roof of a temple listening to the silence, watching the sun going after the mountains, colouring with it's last light, the temples and the sky with heavy orange colours...it was just so beautiful and perfect and sitting there a feeling of almost total happiness could fall over me that tears well up in my eyes. I discovered things inside of me, did a lot of thinking. Hope you have a wonderful time in Australia, again take care. I think about you all the time. Miss you."

*

CAPTAIN COOK'S. CAIRNS, QUEENSLAND

LEAVING 'the footie' and The Bagus heaving with insults and beer-cans, I went to the Garuda office to bring my flight back a few days. The flight went in four hours, or a week's time. I was packed, checked out, taxied and checked on the plane in one hour.

It lifted it's belly from Bali and we powered out over the sea in the dark, Kuta's tinseltown lights mirrored and wobbling in the surf to our right. We flew into the sunrise which rose doubletime because of our approach. The dull purple sky glowed red, then burst into lemon yellow when the sun nudged above the camber of the horizon; first a thin slice, then a segment, and almost too quick to notice, it pulled itself away from the rim of the earth with a quiet plip! And there it was...day; blue and gold and new, but with the remnants of it's day in England still clinging or falling to the earth in weak morning rays.

We set foot on Australian soil in the transit lounge of Darwin airport. The security guards, custom men and pilots, wore tight shorts, white knee-high socks and bush hats, on top of their 6-7 feet frames.

The smokers milled together, lighters and matches at the ready, eyeing the no smoking signs. "Where can we smoke please?"

"Y'can't smoke nowhere mate, not in this terminal. But I'd slip into the dunny if I was you an' have a crafty one on the crapper. Mind the smoke detectors though mate, else you'll have a soggy smoke!"

And then we were in Cairns.I joined up with Stacey, an American girl, and we chose the first hostel courtesy bus available that had rooms left: a double. We rolled to a stop twenty minutes later beneath the spread legs of a fifty feet high Captain Cook, his lumpy hand pointing to the centre of the town. Checking in at 7.30, we took our prison-issue sheets and went to our 'unit', my first one.

The door opened into the kitchen, with all it's equipment in the sink, empty instant noodle pots clustered together. The kitchen became the lounge as the lino gave way to a trashed carpet, and sported a bum-sweating vinyl sofa. It also held four bunk beds occupied by bodies, backpacks, ash trays and more kitchenware. The wall had a dolphin mural leaping through Magic Roundabout flowers; very hippy, except that a fat penis had been added in biro, and a speech bubble exhorting the watcher to 'Piss off!' The flowers carried on round the corner, at one stage growing on the carpet, stopping briefly at an open door where four more bodies could be seen, 'vogueing' in their sleep.

Then, next to the bathroom, an empty room with a small double bed, or large single, lay empty. We shrugged our shoulders, dumped our packs, locked the door, checked the door was locked, re-locked it, and took a walk into town.

8.30. A weekday. The roads should have been busy; people hurrying to work, ferrying kids to school. They were empty and wide. Then I remembered where I was: Australia had an abundance of space in which to fit the people. Standing on the central reservation, to each side would be two lanes the size of the M25, a hard shoulder, grass run-off, storm ditch, more grass strip, a pavement, a wide grass strip that ran up to the picket-fences, and then, set back in the distance of a garden almost naked to the invisible eye - a house.

Looking down one of these roads, it ran clear and true to the distance-faded mountains, without a vehicle in sight. Turning back to face the way Captain Cook was pointing, the traffic lights were flashing *Go! Go! Go!* at an empty road. People weren't in gardens, at windows, walking the pavement, cycling, skateboarding, following sleepy behind wide-awake dogs, starting cars *nnngh-nnngh-nnngh,* hanging out washing, shouting *'g'day'* across the street.

The truth was, there was too much space for me. After Asia, where every inch was occupied by people and bicycles, and rice grew right up to every building in every crack, and sometimes crept indoors without knocking, it was alien. It was spooky, and I felt lost.

We sat at a waterfront cafe, sipping dusty coffee that came with two steaming cinnamon donuts, free; my first 'Australian special deal', and watched the street really liven up. A few people moved around; some backpackers crawled out, bleary eyed and slackjawed. But it still resembled an English High street on Boxing day.

It was right then that a depression rolled in from the horizon and formed a cloud around my head. It felt as though my trip had ended; or at least faded. I wasn't in a foreign country anymore. Asia had never really appealed to me: until I got there. I never expected to love it the way I did. Chantal was still tripping on, falling over new sights and sounds, bumping into experience. So I had to tell myself: there are things to see here as well, things to write about, people to meet: make the most of it. We returned to Captain Cook's along the esplanade, the tide out, leaving the mudflats bubbling and browning to the horizon, small mango bushes punctuating the sludge.

The 'unit' was awake. The room had been tidied. There was 'Kick'-
a sheila, 'Matt' - a bloke, 'Jill' an Essex girl, Bournemouth 'Andy', and
'Rory' a slow Kiwi. Three of the bodies had left but they were replaced
that night by three Essex boys who were as interesting as Dagenham,
and as articulate as Sooty; but they soon moved hostels. Stories and
characters unfolded over the following days and I'd walked into a soap
opera, a theatre. The unit had a harmony and it was our little home.
The odd arrivals were treated like houseguests until they either gelled
or left.

'Kick' was a reformed heroine addict, aged beyond her years; she
still hung out with the dealers, abbos and shady characters. She'd been
on the fishing boats before, grafting hard and fast in the Torres Strait.
Kick lived in the odd world of Australian optimism. Plans whirled and
grew in her mind, changed by the day.

*"Yeh!, Matt if I get on this prawny boat in the Gulf for a month,
with a 5% cut, I should clean up 15,000 dollars...yeh!. I met Buddah,
y'know, the dealer down at the Big 'O'; he accused me of buying
smokoe behind his back, cheating his fucken cut, yeh he did!, anyway
this guy with Buddah there say's I could get into the
boatyard...mmmh, mending the fucken nets, starting tomorrow
morning at seven. Could you give us a shake in the morning Howie, I
reckon I can get up...yeh! When y'going up to the cape Matt, I might
go up with you if this netting falls through... mmmh, that'd be the
go,...yeh!. But I'd have to come back on Monday to see the cops, so I'd
have to hitch back, do me community service, and try for a boat...yeh!
that'll be a spin."*

There was always a short gap before *'yeh!'* or *'mmmh'* as she
thought briefly about the next thing or what she'd just said. She was a
rough diamond, but she was a diamond, sharing anything she had with
anybody.

I settled into the game - 'What can you get for 10 dollars?' To start
with at Captain Cook's you got a bed in a unit, then the choice of two
swimming pools, one freshwater, the other seawater; a gym, launderette, television room, the free bus service to town, a travel office, a
bar with disc jockey. Then there was the food; a free evening meal,
meat or fish, two kinds of pasta, potatoes, beans, cabbage, rice, salad,
fruit plus music and flashing lights. The arrivals from Europe, perhaps
with a stopoff in Hong Kong or Singapore, thought it disgusting. The
post-Asian travellers and Ozzies thought it great. I'd been eating Nasi-

Goreng for three weeks, so I was aghast at the variety; and no banana pancake either.

Then to wash the meal down, the next game was to buy a pot (a small glass) of beer in the bar, after 9.30. This entitled you to an inkstamp on the arm. Other hostels had small stamps, ours was the size of the saucer. With the ink smudging on the arm, the free bus would shuttle you down, at 11.00, to one of the clubs in town, End of The World, or Samuel's; free entry. Then, when all of 'Cook's' were assembled, three deep along the bar, banging their empty beakers in rythym, a keg was opened and was free until empty. Trying to hold your place at the bar, you sculled the beaker as fast as possible and held it out with your armstamp showing, for a refill.

Matt and I found we could manage about seven or eight in the fifteen minutes it normally took before the shout..."Barrel's done!" and we'd face each other grinning manically at the childishness of it all, belching short, small burps to relieve the swollen stomach and avoid puking up. Then all too soon we'd be creeping home at dawn, along the esplanade, the chirruping wagtails telling us off like a Jimminy Cricket on the shoulder.

On any night in town, free beer could be found between 9.00 and 9.30 here, and 10.00 there; free cocktails for ladies at this one, 3 dollar jugs at another. On alternative nights free beer could be won in our own bar, by picking the right cane toad in the racing, naming the record being played, wearing glasses. It was the Captain Cook hobby; the serious side was trying to find work, which didn't bother me at this stage.

But I had a big reason for going to Cairns; I'd always wanted to learn to scuba-dive, and it was always going to be on 'The Great Barrier Reef'.

Which was how I came to be standing in wetsuit and mask, air-tanks on my back, hangover dissolving in a Hockney-blue swimming pool. Through the prescription mask to the left of my nose, I spotted a sign, *'All children (Yes yours as well!) must wear bathers for obvious reasons'* I chuckled in a snorkel full of water and toppled, Blobbylike, backwards into the deeper water, spurting and snorting to get air.

Wriggling along the bottom, pretending we were in the sea, the swimmers above were joined by four very hairy legs, thrashing along the lanes, up and down. A muted *baaarrk!* thumped through the water. I signalled to my buddy and we both laughed eyes at each other, again choking, and surfaced. It was a Brindle-hound, head raised high but beard still in the water. I guessed that warnings had already been given,

149

as the tannoy was still crackling, and then a hard reedy shout from an old harridan... *"For the last time, get that fucken dog out of the water before I drown it...scuse my French, but I will!"* He carried on his lengths as we returned below, the bubbles that roared from my mouth-piece racing to the surface to burst with a ha! ha! ha!

We slipped away from Yorkey's Knob on a barely wrinkled sea, the sky growing in confidence, the sun. bathing in it's own glory. The white deck threw the light back up in handfuls and I had to screw my eyes Chinese to watch the land shrink into the sea. Turning to face New-Zealand, I saw a glistening hump break the surface here and there, in front, then behind. It was a blue dolphin, enjoying the company of a giant friend, it's propellors churning the water, while he slipped in and out as smooth as a call girl and her stockings.

We anchored on a millpond with no banks. Below us was the largest living organism on planet earth. Almost before I knew it the weight of the diving gear, that had had me sweating and straining, nervous, on the back deck, was taken away by a single stride into the ocean. We were bobbing corks, drawing loud breaths raggedly in anticipation. Our man motioned us down and we followed, sheeplike, bleating into a brand new pasture and clinging to our buddies; if not physically at least emotionally. We sunk to the seabed, trying to concentrate on the technique, whilst spots, stripes and splotches floated past on the sides of fish. Down from the surface, great spears of sun pinned the sea to the floor. A parrot flew past my windows, it's beak opening and shut-ting in silent song, fins flapping in place of wings. Then I saw a chess-board, a girl's summer dress, a neon sign, an acid trip, a giant striped humbug, all sticking to their cliques or running with their own gang.

We settled on the bottom, a nervous semicircle schoolroom, and following the dryteaching, pumped air in or out of the buoyancy jacket, until the point I'd been waiting for arrived...I was buoyant, suspended, weightless in a new world. Now, with a single breath, not only did I carry on living, I also rose up, and exhaling...swooped down. I was flying. Like most people I'd often laid back on a clover-strewn lawn, or summer-stubbled field watching skylarks wheel above, a skein of honking geese returning from a bombing raid; envious. And now I was flying! My breath raced in and out with excitement, sending me bobbing up and down like an errant balloon. We followed our leader for a first trip around this underwater garden. It's shrubs were all packed tight, the borders overflowing, rockery bursting and all tended by mobs of multi-coloured gardeners, some lying amongst the blooms, others pruning coral branches. I breathed myself over the top of a huge science fiction brain. Taller than me, it looked indestructible, but was fragile as butterfly's wings. A wrasse overtook me to the right, slow enough for me to run my hand along his blue-green flank, a doll's hand against his bulk. It stared hard at me, mouthing sweet nothings. A small manta ray flew across the false sky above, silhouetted in the descending sunlight, like a Batman sign above Gotham City. Feeling a tug on my elbow, I turned to Melina, my attractive Swiss buddy, who signalled up! I checked my air gauge, which was in the red - beginner's exuberance. We broke the surface and taking off our masks, hung there looking at each other for what seemed like minutes.

"Howie, that was amazing!" she said, as though we'd just come together. "Yes" was the only reply I could muster. We were wide eyed, drunk with delight. Melina was nervous when snorkelling so she asked if I would hold her hand to swim back to the boat. Once again, I thought to myself, and to the stay-at-homes, 'I'm snorkelling across the Great Barrier Reef, sun blazing in a lapis-lazuli sky, hand-in-hand with a lovely Swiss girl, a new world just below.' The Australian visa application had the query 'If you are over 25, explain why you haven't applied before.' Speaking of travelling generally, I would have to answer..."God knows; I must have been mad!" If you're still 'thinking' of going travelling, don't. Just get down to Trailfinders, book a ticket, hoist up your backpack and put one foot in front of the other.

We grew in confidence, dived for two days, then took a written exam. To my surprise I passed, just, and armed with a piece of paper and a congratulation handshake from the instructor, said "Yes, I'd like to do the night dive."

We were to follow him by torchlight down the anchor rope into the unknown, and gather on the seabed like glow-worms in the dark. Last to go, I checked with Melina and we dipped down from dry dark into wet dark. Almost immediately I saw that Melina had left the rope and was drifting away in the current, checking her torch or gauges, I don't know what. She was also going down fast. The rule is 'stick with your buddy whatever' so I dumped the air from my buoyancy jacket, and emptied my lungs. Shooting down to catch her up, I was going to grab her tank, breathe in, and inflate my jacket; which would stop us both. As I reached her, the pressure build-up in my ears was critical. I pulled my hand back to pinch my nose and equalise, but it was too late. My left eardrum burst. The escaping air made a farting noise as it rushed out...*pppssssschrrthrruuump*. The white anchor line went up, sideways, around; my head was spinning like the newspaper in a gangster movie that stops to scream in two inch capital letters - 'Valentine's Day

Massacre.' I saw that below me Melina was still going away, I had to go up. I had visions of blood pouring from my ear, attracting sharks. It didn't.

The seawater took the whole night to drain out. Every ten minutes, during which the pain built up from uncomfortable to agonising, a single drop would escape into the pillow to sleep. The cycle then started over again. By seven in the morning, the pillow resembled the target of a baccy-spitting contest. I surfaced then, to meet the first dive coming back in, elated. It had been perfect diving conditions, the sea as clear as alpine air, the fish on full parade. My buddy tried to console me, but I could see the gleam in her eyes from the dive, still burning bright. I was pleased for her, even though it had been her mistake that was now to keep me out of the water for six weeks. No swimming, and no surfing. 'Might as well work then' I thought, the money I had wouldn't last all the way down the coast.

Looking through the paper with Matt for a job, I came across an advert that read 'Gay bloke - seeks Aussie bloke who likes a real good time.' "What do you reckon that's all about Matt?" I asked.

"Well this bloke, the first bloke, would greet the other bloke at his front door with - 'Hi mate, I've got some cold stubbies in the fridge.' Then they'd watch the telly, probably Ozzie rules footie, swill beer with the odd trip to the toilet or to the door to pick up the pizza delivery; a pizza the size of a duvet. When they get to the point of collapse or puking, they'd retire to seperate rooms with a last minute 'Yer a good bloke y'know.' 'Yeh!, I had a really good time.'

Matt was twenty five and been out in the world since fourteen. His father was a multi-millionaire, his mother, a money grabber. Matt had been put through public school but had dropped out, and dropped into a dodgy Sydney scene. His CV ranged through drug dealer, marine biologist and diver, to protest organiser for Greenpeace. He'd lived with Hell's Angels, Ferals, Hippies, academics, Abbos, scientists and backpackers. When I met him he was sleeping with Shaharazad, a Lebanese freedom fighter, 35 years old, beautiful and fiery. He asked her jokingly if she carried an Uzzi around at home when she did the shopping.

"No," she said coldly, "Uzzi is Israeli weapon, we carry Kalashnikovs, smaller output but more accurate."

Matt could never say her name, so we had to constantly coach him. After my experiences with the Israelis I was glad to have the chance to talk to their enemy. I could tell from her explanations that the hatred was as ingrained as theirs; *no*, born in. I believe it's human nature, and have no answers. When she left for home I asked Matt if he missed her. "No" he replied, and meant it. He'd enjoyed his time with her and it had come to an end. I wondered...'why can't I be like that?'...instead of agonising, pining, wishing my time away. But the only answer I got was that Matt was Matt, and I was me.

Despite conceding twelve years to me, he had seen and done as much if not more than me, so we balanced well and bounced off each other. Bill and Ben. Walking back to Captain Cook's one arid evening, we passed through Abbo park. This was where the Abbos held a perm-anent picnic, with bottles of pop; radios for music, dancing. But if you looked closer, it was alcohol and the dancing was stumbling, swaying drunk. They pretended to leave at night, but the fact was they lived here, waiting for their social cheque each week, or the genuine ones, waiting for a relative to get better in the hospital so they could go home. Lost in conversation, we hadn't noticed the large, knobbly Koorie (the respectful name for an Abbo, a name now considered an insult) emerge from the shadows.

"This is our fucken land!" he shouted, "black's land, fuck off y'white freaks, we'll kill you all!" He was one of many in a dark huddle under the slumbering tree and the situation looked ugly.

"Hey Vincent!" Matt shouted back "Have y'got a light?"

"Aaaaghh Matt, how's it going mate? got any grog? smokoe? no? it's okay, any black fella trouble you, tell 'em you're a pal of Vincent Bobbolino, best fighter in Cairns" and he shadow boxed in the shadows, his bare feet scuffing up the dust. Matt told me that Vincent had seen a John Travolta film when he was a boy, and had taken the character's name. He'd even met John Travolta and a very skinny, decidedly black, John Wayne. We reached the giant Captain Cook and looking up at it, his arm looked weary from pointing down the road.

"He's a bit excessive, isn't he?" I said to Matt.

"Yeh...but we have to have something, he's better than many I've seen."

"What do you mean" I asked.

"A big thing," he said, "Yas has a sheep - forty feet high, Kew - a big axe. I've eaten fresh oyster in the second floor restaurant of the giant oyster, there's a big banana, a mammoth prawn at Ballina; crab, pineapple; you'll see them on the way down. But as far as I know...there's not a big dick anywhere."

"Yes there is," I said, "He's right above us. He made the bad mistake of finding Australia."

"Fuck off Pom!" he laughed, and we walked along to room 106, arms around each other's shoulders like two schoolkids in the playground; which was exactly what we were. When he ran out of money, I paid for his beers at CC's so he could come out for the free keg. I paid him in a nightclub. He smoked my cigarettes, He never asked, just took them, and drank as many cups of coffee or tea I would make him, eat any food I cooked. When his money came through, he bought me a huge pack of cigarettes, a six pack of beer; he bought the Sambucas at the club, 'Shooters' in the bar; all out of my price range. When the money ran low, he'd had enough. Cairns was too city for him. He went bush. He left for Cape Tribulation, to set camp, plant a little crop away from prying eyes. He walked the opposite way to Captain Cook's pointing finger, barefooting down the highway, a bag of rice and beans in left hand, his right - empty, in anticipation to seize the day.

I sat sipping the chocolate froth on the cappucino, watching her; a commanche squaw, sloping forehead, proud nose flattening to flared nostrils, full wide lips, burning eyes. A blue tattoo braceletted her bare upper arm. I left the coffee. She pushed a leaflet into my hand, smiling.

Two days later I was climbing a steep cliff behind her at Cape Tribulation. Rebecca was half American, half Israeli, wearing black lycra minishorts, black bra and boots, and a film of sweat. She was frighteningly sexual and we were to leapfrog all down the east coast, she breaking men's hearts at every step and smile, me holding onto mine tight. We'd travelled up for a three day stay at PK's Jungle village; set deep in the forest, but holding hands with a white sand bay that swept up to a headland, huddling under it's tropical leaf canopy. It was really just a transplant of a backpacker's hostel to a different site. We were hoping to see Cassowaries - a ridiculous bird made from spare parts of other exotic birds and fancy dress costumes. We wanted to see Koalas - a soporific blend of Teddy bear and Valium; Kangaroo - a mix of giant rat, grasshopper and a handbag; and Crocodiles - handbags with teeth.

Cassowaries had a habit of stopping people, stupid enough to be jogging, by headbutting them with the hard crown on the top of their heads; Koalas of doing nothing; Kangaroos stopped motor vehicles with themselves and Crocodiles stopped at nothing. We saw nothing but trees, and bushrats- a rat that looked like it had eaten too many bushes. Even on a nightwalk, with a local guide, the only things moving were the trees growing...slowly. For entertainment, I dropped to the back of the line and every now and then threw sticks and stones into the darkness, to watch the rest of the group swing their torches onto an unsuspecting branch and hear from 'Ol' Dave - "That was probably a bushpig or a rhinosceros!". The only torch that didn't fall for it was Rebecca's, who in complete boredom, was making faces with her's under her chin, shining it through her hand and signalling SOS to me from the front. The interminable walk finally ended and we were the first two off the bus and into the bar. Before the condensation had chance to run down the side of the beerjug, we were joined by some real wildlife - 'pointyheads' or 'inbreeds', the sort last seen playing banjos and hunting Burt Reynolds down in 'Deliverance'.

Matt had explained that in the bush the choice of mating partner was pretty limited, so any relative, however close, was fair game for a 'root' which led to new everyday sayings like 'Bob's yer Aunty!' and mutations in appearance such as pointy heads, eyes wandering round to join the ears, brains leaking down the spinal cord to drop, never to be seen again, from the arse.

So, sitting himself the thickness of a cigarette paper from Rebecca, ogling her tattoo, was one who'd acquired all three of these and whose mother must have mated with a Kookaburra.

"I'm Clem mate, woshers names?" I heard banjos in the back of my mind. Without waiting for an answer, he carried on, "I've just got out the slammer today!" and let out a cackle that would have frightened Hannibal Lechter. Alarm bells had joined in with the banjos. Looking at Rebecca with one eye, me with the other, like a human fish, he said

"These me mates,.....Jed!" Jed was made of eight dozen, flesh coloured, hot water bottles, blown up to bursting point and tattooed by a maniac. The only hair that had the affrontery to appear between the decorations, sat above his lips in a great hairy bush. He said 'hello' by knitting chainmail with his eyebrows and narrowed his eyes 'til they screamed for light. "and...Johnno!" Johnno was tall. He could have been the granite outcrop that holds up Edinburgh Castle. He stared at me until my sphincter got cramp. "...we're out on the piss!!".

It was the news I'd been waiting for all my life. Rebecca was pleading with me with her eyes to find a way out. Clem explained that they swapped pigskulls for tattoos and showed me a twenty 'skuller' on Jed's arm. It was a bushpig with a knife in it's eye. Clem showed me his 'killing tool', a foldaway knife from the Vietnamese war. With real concern he hissed, "Careful mate it's razor sharp!" Unfolding it, a part transformed into a pair of pliers. "That's f'pulling teeth out mate!" Clem cackled, and even Johnno's shoulders shook with an approximation of an earth tremor. My Saigon 'T' shirt had fascinated Jed, and he asked me - "Are those fucken gooks still hiding under the ground?" then extolled the virtues of napalm as a skin conditioner. My forced smile was wilting like a chocolate bunny in a heatwave, as they ranted that all tourists, especially Japs and English, bringing their stinking diseases

155

into Oz, should be mugged...killed. Rebecca was visibly shaking, so I turned to the full table behind, "Make room for two on that table!" They looked hard at me for a while; "Now!" I almost shouted, and they wriggled up. I motioned Rebecca up, fixed a smile, and said to the boys, "Well, nice meeting you, but we ought to join our friends now." and moved. Clem laughed like a stuck pig.

"What's the problem?" our 'new friends' asked.

"Those three nutters behind" I said, not looking back.

"But there's nobody there." Rebecca looked at me with bottom lip trembling, eyes black with fright. "They've disappeared!" The darkness was held at bay by the fluorescent light of the bar. They'd slipped into it; they were out there somewhere. We went back to our huts mob-handed and I dreamt that night of pigs burning in napalm.

We returned to Cairns, my big friend Captain Cook pointing the way to Samuel's, The Pumphouse, End of the World, and raged for days on the free-drinks tickets that Rebecca was paid, for giving out free drinks tickets.

We had new guests in our room.

Jack came from a small village hidden under Nottingham's skirt folds. He was a Lobby Ludd; gangling, shambling and stooped; with a mop of a hairstyle. He hadn't left the village before, or his parents and sister. His sister had given him a photo of her fish to take away with him. Written in childish hand on the back was 'Lydia'.

"Your sister's name Jack?" I asked, seriously.

"No silly, the fish!" he guffawed.

"That's sweet Jack...how old is your sister?" I asked, imagining a pigtailed schoolgirl with horn-rimmed glasses, hair like Jack's hiding her shy face.

"She's twenty." he stated proudly. Jack came to Australia with no shorts, but six pairs of heavy trousers, neatly folded. Jack had no idea how to converse with people or integrate, which made things difficult for him in a cramped dorm for ten. But he had party tricks. He could wobble his eyes like Nookie Bear on acid. He could regurgitate whole slices of bread. Jack got mugged by Koories, walking a girl from Sydney back to her hostel. The girl was raped. Jack had been away from home for seven days.

Anders, a Swede, came into the evening meal at CC's as usual, but this time the side of his face resembled 'elephant man', the colour of beetroot. He'd walked home through the park. He didn't see it coming, or his ten dollars going, but just before the foot crashed into his eye, he saw it belonged to a Koorie. Vincent Bobbolino...allegedly.

THE UNIT was stuffy, someone had stolen my shoes off the line, and I had a hangover. I needed to clear my head. Stepping down from the hostel bus, I set off for the esplanade and the fresh air that blew onto it from across the mud flats.

Strolling north from the pier, carefully avoiding the cracks in the pavement, I pushed through the smoke from the bushfires burning across the bay, and mentally photographed the scenes that passed by.

*

The tree hung full of screeching and scrawing. The birds resembled Dover-grey doves that had flown headlong into a set of children's paints.

*

The rainbow was complete across the silent Sound, a multi-coloured Sydney Harbour Bridge. There was another, fainter, adjoining it and basking in it's glory.

*

The two labradors had led a dog's life and were sleeping it off. The owner sat between them sporting the longest face in Australia. It stretched from Cape York to the bottom of his chin. His Panama suit crumpled, hiding some of the stains, but showing off the rest. It was the same colour as his skin and the dogs. The notes squeaked from his old flute, the tune as thin and stretched as his frame and the blood red tie that seemingly held up his Adams apple.

*

Hammerhead clouds stood guard like smoke detectors over the bush fire.

*

As Lake St went it's way to the left, four pelicans sailed by on my right in Quadrille, dipping their outlandish beaks to an unheard beat, in perfect time. Prima Ballerina Pelicanus.

*

The day trip boats were coming in, gleaming white. Catamarans, diving boats, dinghys, full-rigged yachts, glass-bottomed boats; all straggled into the harbour like sheep into a pen, the approaching night a vast black Border collie driving them home.

*

The Jap, playing the saxophone, was facing the sea, throwing manic scales across the mud. His buddy sat cross-legged beside him, counting the notes and waiting to catch any bum ones that fell to the floor.

*

157

The juggling balls tumbled over and over in an arc, flashing red-yellow-blue. One ball was banana shaped. It was a banana; without any bruises.

*

The stick was long, brown and smooth and looked like a dog turd, a barkers-egg, that had been lain on the move. It was a seed pod that rattlesnaked when shook; after you'd prodded it with your shoe of course.

*

Pausing, while handing the fish and chips to the backpacker, the girl nodded to the salt and vineger and sauce, and asked...

"D'ya want heaps of shit on y'dinner?"

*

Across the road from the Grand Hotel and the reception, the Groom and Best-man sported red bow ties and bottles of beer, and passing close behind I heard, "Yer married now mate!" and he pounded his extra wide and shiny lapels.

"Congratulations" I offered.

"Aah yeah, thenks mate!...thenks heaps." He was sweating in his penguin suit. I walked on with a smile for his day and his pleasure, but before I'd covered the length of a cricket crease, I realised that I'd cleared my head but my eyes were full, for my own failures.

*

I STOPPED dancing, suddenly, in the middle of the club. I'd just heard 'I like to move it, move it' and '100% pure love' and knew that the next one would be 'Thank god I'm a country boy'. Despite our best efforts, Rebecca and I couldn't keep up with the drinks vouchers: they were building up. It was 4.16 am: I had to leave Cairns for my health. We'd been living high on ten dollars a day. Costly days were ahead. I was on the bus in the morning, waved off by room 106.

*

THE EAST COAST TRAIL

WITH a Greyhound pass to Sydney, I decided to leapfrog down the coast on the backpacker's trail to see what the attraction was. The first lily-pad I landed on was Airlie beach, gateway to the Whitsunday Islands. It didn't have a proper beach, it didn't really have anything, just a half mile strip of cafes, shops and hostels. But it had a post office and I was expecting a letter from Chantal, so I was stuck in Airlie until Monday when it opened.

I stayed at the Whitsunday beach village hostel which, if cleared of backpackers and the amount of beds per room reduced, could rate as a four star holiday village. There were three of these on 'the strip' and Chungking Mansions seemed an awful long way off. But although cheap by English or tourist standards, it made Cairns look like a soup kitchen, at fifteen dollars a night; no free food or beer. I realised that my meagre amount of dollars was actually paltry; chicken feed. In one month I'd spent the same as had kept me in Asia for four and I had a cash-flow problem that only some work, somewhere, sometime would solve. I'd heard all the horror stories on the way down about the fruit picking. Stone Island, Rockhampton, Bundaberg, were all being raided by police, and backpackers without permits were being ejected from the country. On top of this there were poisonous spiders in the bananas, picking with pointyheads - high on dope, snakes, bad pay. I made a half hearted effort to get a photographic job in the resort. Meeting two girls who'd caught up with me from room 106, we carried on where we left off. But they didn't allow dancing on the tables, unlike Cairns where it was encouraged. I tried to enjoy it but I was hearing those same records again.

I sat on my porch, a spit away from the kidney shaped pool, and greeted my new neighbours, three Swedes. At first glance, Swedish-looking as a smorgasbord and as outgoing as rollmop herrings, one of the synchronised spending team introduced himself, and I saw that his eye had vastly improved since I last saw him at Captain Cook's. We talked travelling and lives and loves, and he grilled me about travelling alone. He was tired of being one of a group.

I got my letter from Chantal on the Monday morning and took it to the beach that wasn't quite a beach, to read.

There was a stiff, chill breeze blowing up my shorts as I stared at the stamp of Ghandi. The letter was, as usual, edged with red and blue, but this time also tinged with frost. It was a brief note informing me of change to her travel plans, and a promise to write soon. There was no tenderness squeezed between the lines, or affection scenting the paper. The panic buttons didn't start to ring as they might have once, but the white flag was starting to run up the mast. It was only six weeks ago, but it was starting to magnify.

There was a Greyhound leaving the traps; I jumped on it, and ignoring my own rule for once, bypassed Magnetic Island. So many people had said it was crap, I figured it must be.

Instead I landed with a plop at Hervey Bay, with the intention of a hop to Fraser Island on a four wheel drive trip. Within hours of arrival I'd drawn a blank with work at all the hostels and was signed up for a three day trip to the island. There were eight in the group, old friends of at least ten minutes; seven English and one Belgian; a Flemish girl actually.

The highway on Fraser was a hundred mile beach, the 'inland' roads - sand and stone tracks. There was total fire ban, with a twenty thousand dollar fine attached. We had two tents, eight slabs of Victoria Bitter (Vitamin B!), some food and ourselves.

We sat on Indian Heads and way below, in a sea as clear as air, saw turtles swimming with the grace that land takes away, manta-rays swooping and gliding and reef sharks darting here and there, John Major grey and seemingly as aimless. Rejoining the highway we scooted north, the ozone so thick it slapped you in the face. The only obstacles were the soft sand at the top of the beach, the wet sand at the waterline and the streams that trickled down into the sea. We waded waistdeep upstream in the immaculate water of Ely Creek, until the overhanging foliage threatened to strangle, and then floated down on it's current over pebbled shallows, past limpid pools, under rickety bridges; like a game of Pooh sticks. It was still only mid-morning but in celebration of an already colossal day, the first slab was pulled from the jeep.

"God I needed that!" said Hilde the Flemish girl, as she sculled her first and cracked open another. She threw me another with,

"Are you joining me?" she asked. 'That's my kind of girl' I thought.

"Shit yeh..." I said, "I'll drive tomorrow."

"You're beer monsters!" Matt exclaimed, and joined in.

We managed to avoid the other jeepfuls of backpackers that were scattered around the island as we swam in champagne rock-pools, scaled ten-storey sand dunes - to slide down; walked, talked and bodysurfed. I was persuaded out of the waves by a reef shark, (or a lump of seaweed), and came out with a jellyfish sting from ear to ear, like a clown's smile. The trip drifted along on the breeze, picked up and moved from lake to river, forest to sand-dune, by an untiring sun. Below it we moved from strangers to companions, and some of us went the whole way to friendship in that unknown way that you do.

We sat around the carefully shielded fire, cooked up, kicked back and cruised, the moon smiling at us cheekily. Hilde and I cruised way after the kiddiwinks had retired to their tents, billowing the canvas with their snores and dreams.

We lay in our sleeping bags watching the stars make eyes at each other, emptying cans of Vitamin B. The dingos starting coming in, wearing the darkness as cover. A rustling from the barbeque snapped Hilde to the vertical, "What's that?!"

"It's a dingo..." I slurred back, "turn on the torch." The feeble beam crept over the twigs, pebbles and empty cans, and raised it's weary head to rest on a startled dingo with a mouthful of silver-clad potato. Like extras in a film, several more milled around in the background and slunk away into the dark. Hilde turned the torch off and as the darkness returned, so did they, padding around us to snatch blackened sausages from the still hot griddle. Matt came out of his tent in the murky glimmer of dawn, spying Hilde and I and a pack of dingos amongst a mountain of empty cans.

"Shit!" he hissed, as I raised a blearly head, "Are you mad?, have you seen what you've been sleeping with?"

"Yes" I said, "Hilde...also known as 'Dances with Dingos'" and went back to sleep as her hand, warm from sleep, found mine and held it. We returned to Hervey Bay, tired as a group of children after a day at the zoo, and handing back the jeep we were suddenly no longer a unit, team, outfit, we were back slotted into our allotted dorms. We clustered together for the evening, reliving in-jokes and moments of gladness, and as the plot of the day thinned and tired, the kiddiwinks retired to bed. Hilde and I were the soul survivors again.

"I don't want to sleep in my dorm, I don't like the girls." she said softly.

"Don't then, sleep with me." I suggested.

"Yes I will." she said, and we walked to mine.

There were two lads still undressing as we entered, one leg in and one out of their jeans, hopping to pull them off. I could see them doing sums in their head - one bed, two people, one of them a girl.

"It's that one up there" I nodded, as Hilde slipped out of her clothes and into the top bunk. Looking round the room, the lads were still half dressed, books were left mid sentence, jaws dropped. I dropped my trousers, shrugged my shoulders at them and leapt upstairs. We were Siamese twins, soul mates, and we fell straight to sleep gorged on comfort and the warmth of two people who didn't know what they were to each other yet, and didn't care. Hilde cried out once in her sleep, but it was only a night bear. I tumbled back into sleep.

Roast potatoes were better than boiled, but not as good as mashed, with butter. "You've got potatoes growing in your ears" Dad always said. The Beatles were better than the Stones, Mods than Rockers, Fruit salads than Blackjacks, Tizer than Dandelion and Burdock, Saturday than Sunday, Littlehampton than Worthing (It had a funfair, even though we weren't allowed in it).

Life was black and white; blacks were Sambos, Piccaninnies or Pigmies and unknown to us in our rural outpost they were flooding into Liverpool and Bristol and London to make a new life that I would eventually become part of and enjoy; find no more unusual than rain, cricket or the Golly on the jamjar. It was just a logo, I was more worried about the strange horn on the back of Sunny Jim's head.

Sunday morning we had to stay in bed until 8.00 reading books and comics. (Only 'the Victor' as it had stories, not just pictures) Bruv or me would go down and make a cup of tea, take it in to wake mum and dad, then squirrel back into the still warm bed, reading and farting for another half hour, until the smell of eggs and bacon and the local butcher's chipolatas crept up the very steep stairs.

'Family favourites' surrounded the breakfast table - Puff the Magic Dragon, Three Wheels on my Wagon, My Boomerang won't come back and a host of other such crap, squeaked from the trannie. But sandwiched inbetween were the Kinks, Troggs, Amen Corner and the Hollies. "You're not taking the bikes out 'til they're clean, 'til the morning's wood is chopped, the firegrate cleaned out, the fire laid, the lawn mowed!" said Dad, wiping his last bit of egg with a chipolata.

I went through a martyr stage where I would go out and chop sticks, fingers blue with cold, all the time thinking, they'll love me more than Martin 'cos he said no and he's in our room in the bad books...but also in the warm. But I was chopping sticks like a madman, I was the best woodchopper in the history of the world, and if my fingers fell off with frostbite...it would serve them all right.

If the bikes were clean we could go out...anywhere!. We had no boundaries. Our village and surrounding countryside once blended into the next, and thousands like it, to form England. Now they're all cut off from each other by abduction, rape, murder. The boundaries are fear, and start at the end of your garden, if you're lucky enough to have one.

Kevin Jelly had drunk too many Brown Ales. He was older than us and fat, and got served in the pub. We walked home with him to see if he would fall over or puke. He said he could smash a window with a punch and not cut himself. He stood in front of the fag machine that had three wired windows - Picadilly, Number Six and Guards, and punched the middle one which was strange as he smoked Picadilly. He showed us his knuckles, fist closed - "See!" At first we couldn't, then a red spider's web appeared, getting fatter, and the blood dripped from his hand. "Yeah! good one Jello" we shouted at a distance, as we knew the fat prat would wipe it on us. "Do the shop window with your head" I hollered, running away. Some stitches put the tendons back together, but you could never get No'6 from the machine again, which was Kevin Jelly's contribution to the downfall of that atrocious cigarette.

'God,' I thought as I crawled into consciousness, I was dreaming about 1970, most of these travellers weren't even born.

I peeled myself away from Hilde's back and went to the toilet. I looked in the mirror and looking back was an old man. I don't know who he was, but by gum it wasn't me.

We trundled south (the core of the group) to Noosa, where Matt and I checked out the surf that wasn't there. I attempted to bodysurf in the wishy-washy waves and leaving the water to join Hilde and Matt, who was out of the water due to mashing his hand in the ceiling fan, found that my chest was feeling very tight. I tried to walk straight but left a 'Teach yourself the Foxtrot' pattern in the sand, reaching them on a wide arc. I had another jellyfish sting, that had wrapped itself round my front and back like a bandolier. Hilde was worried; I was touched. After a couple of fruitless days waiting for some surf, Hilde decided to move on. I felt attached and asked if I could go with her.

"I'm going to North Stradbroke Island." she said. "What's there?"

"I don't know, but it sounds nice, are you sure you want to come?"

"Are you sure you want me to come?" Did she want me to?

Did I want to? Why was I asking questions?

*

STRADDIE. In Ozzie tradition, North Stradbroke Island, almost a whole sentence, has to be shortened to two syllables. By the same rule, Tasmania - shortens to Tazzy; Bundaberg with one too many - Bundy; Rockhampton - Rocky; Alice loses her Springs and Sydney, with the correct number remains Sydney, apart from in Melbourne where it has totally silent syllables. To keep the balance, any names foolish enough to have only one syllable are instantly allocated an 'O'; Johnno, Davo.

STRADDIE is sensibly anchored off the coast of 'Brizzie' and 'Surfer's', which to us, passing through, resembled sattelite-cities of Tokyo, in appearance and population. Booking onto the Straddie ferry, we back-packed aboard and having deposited the packs in a corner, joined the other passengers loading boxes of groceries from the jetty. The bus to Point Lookout, Outlook Point, or Pointout Look, a name I never got to grips with, carried a mixed bag of schoolkids going home, office workers, shoppers and two backpackers.

"You two's going to the hostel?...my name's George." said the driver. We trundled off and we listened to the chit-chat of a close community. "Hev you f'gotten me today George?" piped up an old lady with Dame Edna glasses.

"Agghh, sorry Ivy" said George, chunking the bus into reverse and driving back two houses till the door of the bus was in line with the white picket gate. George sprinted ahead of Ivy with her second bag of groceries and opened the fly screen door while she entered.

"Bang the door when you go George!" she flung back, her voice fading as it disappeared inside, and George finished the unheard half of the sentence..."Cos it clears the screen of flyshit!"

After Ivy's we stopped in front of wire gates, shopdoors, the steps of caravans, and Point Lookout hostel. We checked in, in what looked to be a family lounge, the TV blaring, a five and a three year old blaring at each other. Welcoming us the mother shouted, "Stop it Tim, Edward will get hurt!" as Edward's head hit the wall with the sound of a hammer hitting a cantaloupe. Holding a squawking Edward on one hip and our sheets on the other, she said, "This one is 'Seek' and the one looking all innocent is 'Destroy'...here's your room."

It was a dormitory that Snow White and the short things would have been proud to sleep in, and without doubt the nicest I'd seen in all my travels. There was a girl from Brisbane in the next unit, but apart from her we were the only backpackers on the island.

We took the seperate room that was curtained off for privacy, ("Yes we are a couple" I'd had to tell the owner on the phone, "We don't like any funny business" he'd said.)

Sharing the bottom bunk, we awoke in the morning to the sounds of a vacuum in the kitchen. These grew louder as the hoover attachment came through the curtain, closely followed by Edward, who intent on

164

his job, reached the end of the bed. Spying us in the bed, he just stared, while the hoover cleaned one part of the floor, immaculately.

"Hi Edward" we said as he stared a gazely stare.

"Edward!" came a shouted whisper from the kitchen, "Get out of there!" Edward stared on, the hoover straining to find more dust. As we stifled our giggles, Edward smiled a very naughty and knowing smile.

"Edward get out here...now!" His smile drooped but he remained staring.

"Edward...you wanker!!" his father roared, out of sight, and pulled him out, the corrugated pipe tight under his arm, and the coloured plastic blinds swung back together like a grass skirt when the sailor removes his hand.

We wandered the cliffs and beaches, slunk into gullies, lazed around Blue Lake and Brown Lake, revelling in being the only 'visitors'. We sat outside our dorm and ate pasta with lashings of garlic, whilst the night grew loud and dark. A trio of kookaburras cuddled up on a telegraph wire above, telling each other jokes before bedtime. They would giggle until the punchline and then burst into laughter 'til their sides split. As they eventually ran out of steam, got to a chuckle and "Oh dear, no more," one would tell another joke and set them off again. We laughed along with them.

"Wotcha eating?" said a small voice from the blond head, eye level to the table.

"Pasta...Edward, do you want some?" "Naarrgh, bums." he said.

"What do you like to eat?" I asked. "A cake." he drooled.

"What...Chocolate, Birthday, Christmas?" "Naarrgh, bugger cake."

I hoped it had nothing to do with the chocolate starfish.

"And what do you make those with Edward?" Hilde enquired.

"Bloody beetles 'n bloody cockies and red and black icing 'n bloody eat it. And if y'can't eat it y'squash it with y'foot, and spit on it."

It made the pasta seem quite dull, so seeing a mean looking spider scuttling up the wall I pointed to it and asked Hilde, "D'ya want that in y'bloody pasta or shall I just spit in it?"

Heading back for the ferry, we thought we were on the wrong bus, but *there* was George. Apart from us the only passengers were toddlers, here a group of three, there - two sitting silent looking at each other, and single ones spread around, unworried, unabashed, unwashed. We stopped outside a gate with a huge daisy on it - 'Kindy'.

The kids trooped off the bus, some in a hurry to get to school, others still at home cosy in bed, dreaming of rabbits and bugger cake.

The teacher tripped down the path like Julie Andrews and leapt aboard the bus.

"Anymore down there?" Feeling as though we were late for school or skiving, I answered "No miss."

"Could you look under the seats, they sometimes go to sleep." So we became seat monitors and reported "No there's none left"

"OK George, full body count, y'can go." she said, and I swear George said "Yes Miss." We trundled off to the ferry and then left the place where five year olds can cross the island unaccompanied, without fear, and still imagine cakes made of creepy crawlies; where the only two people sharing the beach with beached jellyfish, straight out of Doctor Who, were the two of us.

WE CROSSED to Brisbane, shot through the transit centre, where I had a cup of coffee with Rebecca; who was also in transit, and raced down on a Greyhound to Byron Bay and another hostel.

"Two beds please." "Yes we can fit you in - are you a couple?"

We looked at each other and shrugged "Yes" in unison.

"Right then, you'll be in the double room."

"Oh no, we can't afford that, a dorm room will do."

No, it's the same price as a dorm but you share with another couple, two double beds y'see." We didn't at first, but entering the room, we did. The other couple, John from South Africa and Anna from Norway were in bed, with the sheet nearly up to their nipples. Anna left the bed naked and dressed, while we chatted sociably, and then left. She came back while we were still talking and removed her clothes. While Hilde visited the toilet John asked -

"Are you two going to be hanging around a while?"

"Just a few days." I answered "No, I meant this afternoon."

"Oh, ah..oh, no..we were going to go for a walk along the beach" I replied, thinking that we were in the way.

"I just thought, if you two wanted to spend the afternoon in bed, we'd go for a walk along the beach, wouldn't we Anna?"

"Yaah."

"That's alright, we've already got clothes on" I said as Hilde returned, "we'll be about an hour, will that be long enough?"

"Plenty" said John, Anna looking daggers at him.

BYRON was cool man! a half surfing, half hippie town. We checked out the surf that wasn't there and then the hostel with the art gallery, log cabins and teepees. Rebecca was there, but she had a man in tow like a lost puppy, and we agreed to meet in Sydney, soon.

We sat on Cape Byron, the easternmost point of Australia and watched the whales migrating past, breaching, slapping their mammoth fins on the sea like giant backhanders.

We cruised the surf shops, me dribbling at the thought of the waves to come, and leaving a bottle shop, fully laden, spied a very Swedish looking man sitting on the kerb, scoffing a burger.

Anders had taken the plunge, and left his friends in Airlie. He was having a great time going solo, his eye healed. We agreed to meet in Sydney, soon.

All too soon it was Hilde's time to move on; she had to visit friends in the Sydney suburbs before heading home to Belgium. I wouldn't see her before I got home, but we said 'it's only six months', and I asked myself: 'what are you doing? what about Chantal? and the answer came the next day.

I saw Hilde off onto the bus and traipsed the town for work to take my mind off her. I asked in every bar, pub, hotel, cafe, restaurant and surfshop, drawing a complete blank. I felt dismal, very much alone. I was almost broke. On cue the weather came to town and unloaded it's suitcase, the wind blowing the rain off the sea into the town centre; not a rabbity, choppy wind, but a full blown head of steam with a thousand mile push behind it. As moody and restless as the sky above, I slunk into the Post Office for shelter and finding myself right next to the Poste Restante, asked if there was anything for me. I wasn't expecting anything, but there was Ghandi staring back at me again, but this time he looked a little guilty. Stuck halfway between town and the hostel, I found myself a bus-shelter and read the letter in a dying light.

It was India, painted in technicolour words, vivid and alive; temples, people, the River Ganges all hurried across the pages in a tumble. And then the colour drained away and all I saw was grey, and perhaps a little red -

"...I'm just a memory, I'm not even the same Chantal you met. I don't mean to hurt you, I know I have by writing this, but please forget me. I still wear your sarong, it's very precious to me...and we do still think about you. Anyway...everything what begins has to come to an end, the bad things and the nice, and relationships too, whether it's death or other things what seperate two people. Take care." Chantal
x

I stepped out from the shelter into the rain, which swept across like a theatre curtain, and stood there for the longest time.

"Shhhiiitttt!!" I cried out in a great bellow: stood there, lit up by orange gas and the whining headlamps of the odd passing car, then walked home like a question mark.

The likelihood of decent surf arriving stood hand-in-hand with the chance of getting a job. I rang Hilde in Sydney.

"Hilde, I've given up on the idea of working here, would you mind if I came down to..."

"Yes! yes please Howie, how soon can you..."

I was on the Greyhound.

*

Except that this time it wasn't a Greyhound, but McCafferty's. The only difference between the two was the letters on the side of the bus. In all other aspects, the experience was the same.

This was my fifth. They usually started with a dreadful video; Whoopi Goldberg in Sister Act 2, on another you may be lucky to see Sister Act 1, the sound almost always inaudible, or drowned by the driver and his relief talking. Sleep was not a viable alternative as, even with a vacant seat beside, your legs would be stepped over all night in the aisle, vertically up the window or squashed into your chest by the seat in front, cramp gnawing at your bones. Or, it was what the Chinese call fishing, your head drooping down to the chest until the neckpain wakes you and your head bobs up to start drooping again.

And then there was the neighbour. They could be drunk, boring or smell; usually all three. I seemed to attract old ladies. On my trips I'd had fat old lady, dribbling old lady (Who used my shoulder for a pillow), non-stop talking lady, and scared old lady. She had her gear packed up and clutched tightly in her hand, fifty miles before her stop, rising up and down out of her seat to see if it had arrived and eyeing me suspiciously through the sides of her X-ray specs. I didn't move an inch for fear of her crying rape or murder. She peered out the window away from me until passing through a tunnel, the window mirrored my face and she started, with a gasp. I offered her a sweet, but she just stared at it as though I'd pulled it from my pants.

I couldn't make any movements next to fat lady as my right side was pinned immobile, as though stroke-ridden, and soaked with thermo-nuclear sweat. She was quite comfortable during the night on her waterbed arse and half of my seat, and I slumbered between the aftershocks of her snoring. She never spoke.

Mrs Talky never stopped. From Byron Bay she talked me through to Grafton. Her son - Kevin, hadn't taken after his Father who was a pilot, but gone to Melbourne to study medicine; he always worked hard at school. ,Was I going there? perhaps I'll meet him!' By the time we reached Coffs Harbour, Kevin had got engaged, married Sally and had two kids - Stephen and Eleindia - E..L..E..I..N..D..I..A, such an unusual name, don't you think? The film started and despite my staring hard at the screen and leaning forward, straining to hear the dialogue over the details of Stephen's education, she rolled on with the bus and worked her way through Eleindia's dance career- 'Good toes, naughty toes!'.

"Oh I'm sorry Dear, you're trying to watch the film, I'll shut up!" She didn't. Kevin Costner had super hair, the wolf was just as loyal as a Corgi she once had, the Indians were so cruel at times, but then it did look very cold where they were. And when Kevin (the actor) rode off round the hill, straight through the 'D' of 'The End' which was perched on the hill in Western script, I was relieved to get back to the real life Kevin who was now galloping into middle age as we rode into Port McQuarie. Her husband survived until Newcastle, though he'd been ill for years and just outside of Sydney I almost asked if I could marry Eleindia as she sounded perfect in every way imaginable.

"Are we there already" she said "Gosh, the journey goes so fast when you have someone nice to talk to, doesn't it?" I felt I'd been on the bus for two years.

The coaches had comfort stops. This was where you emptied your bladder, filled your guts, had a fag and a break from the neighbour. The choice was to eat in the restaurant or buy fast food from the service station. The former was normally themed so you could eat, say in Vienna, visions of the Danube behind your head, shnitzels, sausages and strudels waltzing away behind the glass counter, the waitresses in lace dresses and mopcaps.

Next door in the service station they had 'buttons'.

Press button to release Mexican meat pie, remove packaging, press red button for squirt of sauce, add creamer (as you've pressed the cappucino button by mistake) put in micrwave, press button marked Mexican Meat Pie, press Cappucino button for luck, and juggling the nuclear-hot pie on it's pathetic paper plate, pay the man. After a bite, press the 'press' sign on the bin by the door, deposit the pie, go outside for a cigarette.

Arriving at one comfort stop, I felt I'd wandered onto the set of a science fiction movie. Spread around the carpark, orange under the sodium glare, were a dozen figures, each facing a different direction, shuffling from foot to foot like zombies, looking down to the ground or heavenwards. Each had six shadows like umbrella spines surrounding them. To the left, a vast mutant sheep was giving birth to a small restaurant. *They* were the smokers, drawing desperate lungfuls before reboarding their Greyhound; *It* was a big thing, a big merino shielding a theme restaurant - Hungarian. I ran into the next one at Newcastle, but this big thing was small - a miniature Ayers rock. And as we all know, Ayers rock doesn't have windows, so nor did the fast food and souvenir shops inside, bathed in a fluorescent glare day and night.

Outside, the zombies shuffled and smoked until it was time to join the sensible passengers who'd stayed on board, avoiding Austria, Bulgaria, Mexico and the Twilight Zone. They'd also slept undisturbed for forty minutes.

On the lemonside, the Greyhounds had a toilet, drinking water, two drivers, no hard seats, 41 people on a 41 seat bus, curtains; they didn't break down or slide into paddy fields, the drivers always had friendly names like 'Bob' 'Bill' 'Tom' - even a 'Nobby' so when I felt cramped or tired, I thought of China and laughed.

*

GLEBE VILLAGE HOSTEL, SYDNEY

I ENTERED Sydney by the backdoor and checked into Glebe backpackers. Glebe reminded me of Brighton, one of my favourite places. It straggled over the slopes above Darling Harbour, terraces of villas, their wrought-iron verandahs smothered in geraniums and honeysuckle. Thelonious Monk and Charlie Bird, fluttered out of record shops into the coffee bars, milk bars, and bars, where beatniks, punks, trendies and travellers caressed their copies of Kerouac, The Face or Lonely Planet.

Glebe was busy doing nothing and just allowed itself to be preened and restored by it's new owners and kept quiet so that Kings Cross and the like couldn't see what a good time it was having. Hilde was staying across town with friends and the hostel was a silence of cliques, so I set out downtown to introduce myself to Sydney.

The old lady's nose, supporting a pair of Grouch Marx glasses, was squashed against the glass of the pawnbrokers, and she hurred up the window with her Steradent breath. She grabbed my arm and pulled me over.

"You look like you've got good eyesight young man, how much is that ring there?" "80 dollars" I replied.

"How many carats?" "Six" I said.

"And that one?" "110 dollars...12 carats"

"Do you think that blue one's nicer?" I priced and assayed nearly every ring in the window, and had it narrowed down to four when I started to lose patience. "Look I have to go now."

"Oh thanks lovey." Something intrigued me, so I turned back.

"Aren't your glasses any good?"

"Oh no dear, I bought them in here a couple of weeks ago an' I can't see a bloody thing."

The wino staggered backwards across central park, "It's Wullie's buthday...and he'd love a cigarette!" he said, correcting his passage, and shot past me at a trot. Willie's top half rocked back and for, but his legs, below the knee, stayed put as though stuck in clay. His eyes were stuck too, askew.

"Wull y'have a drrrink with us ter shellerbrate hus buthday?" he slurred as he passed me on the right in an arc, desperately trying to get to the spot in front of me. Willy spun the lid off the new bottle of Lochinvar malt, and it hid in the grass.

"Fug it Wullie, we'sll huv t'drink ut orl noo."

I handed him two fags, as he passed my left shoulder crablike, and pushed away the bottle Willie had pushed in my face.

"No thanks Willie, I'm going to meet my girlfriend, she'll give me shit if I smell of booze, but Happy Birthday mate!"

"Aawwh! s'awright Wullie...if it's his hens buthday th'man shoo get along...giv hur a buthday kiss f'me orkee?"

I'd been in Sydney for two hours and I'd only spoken to a mad-woman and two Scottish drunks. As I walked through the city, shoppers shopped, tourists toured and the businessmen scurried up and down wearing self-important frowns. I felt small amongst the glass and marble monoliths, and then I walked out of the shadows into the light.

The coathanger straddled, and the nuns stood up to their necks in the wind choppy harbour, posing for the Yashicas, Minoltas, Nikons and the occasional discerning Hasselblad on sturdy tripod legs.

Directly in front, a litter of harbour ferries suckled the quay, water-taxis skimmed the surface and helicopters dragonflied across the bot-anical gardens that crept out into the bay. I shuffled through the past as 'The Rocks' led me down to the bridge and showed me up steps where I watched the harbour craft skywriting on the water.

A noise rose above the honking of the streets and the hooting har-bour and spun me round by the shoulders. I looked down on a play-ground; the wall painted so that the gay balloon and the sky, and the mountains it glided across, appeared to be made from bricks.

The kids were six, seven, eight, nine, I don't know which, and were playing a sort of volleyball for people not big enough to hit the ball back. The teacher counted down from ten, and the ones holding the ball at zero were the losers. There was one player who caught my eye, dashing around his friends with great excitement, shrieking and laugh-ing. He had short sleeves but they were empty and flapped as he ran. And once, as the ball dropped from high, he followed it down with rounded eyes and headed it back over just as the teacher shouted 'one!'. His friends slapped 'high fives' to his sleeves and 'Yip yaahhed!'

He was normal you see.

I. crossed to the other side of the bridge and looked down on my own past. *There,* were the customs sheds where the liners came in,

172

nudging up to Oz, disgorging thousand-upon-thousands of Pommies - overdressed and overawed, into their new home.

We had one trunk each, in which we carried the whole of our England and some souvenirs of Egypt and Ceylon.
We arrived on Christmas Eve. It was 102 degrees. My Mum cried. My brother and I had a tin car each. Just one. I think we were happy with that. I think we were scared. We lived in two rooms. The Polish landlord was the only snowplough dealer in Australia.
I went to the big-boy's fence in the playground and cried for my brother. We ran around Sydney playing truant and looking in other school's windows. I was seven. One day Sydney disappeared under a flashflood. Martin and I paddled around in the flood instead of going to school. Alan and Terry shared the room next to us and caught us. They dried us off and looked after us until Mum and Dad came home.
"Sorry boys, had to tell them" said Terry. We didn't mind. Alan and Terry were from Chelsea, they were groovy. We lived with my Mum's Auntie for a while; somewhere. My Mum packed her bags and we ran after her crying. "Don't go! don't go!" She didn't. She wouldn't have; ever. She just wanted to. She had to work in a chip van at the Oval. She looked very hot in the van frying chips. It was 95 degrees outside the van. The teacher asked for a word starting with 'F'. I said 'Fag'. She told me off and all the Ozzie kids laughed at me. We moved to Manly. A new school. My friends were Yugoslavian, Chinese, Canadian and Ozzies. We started surfing. We rode the ferries across the harbour; it was better when it was rough. Luna park had a wobbly walkway and it blew air up girls skirts and showed their knickers, and a revolving barrel and an upside down house. You walked through a clown's mouth to get in.

There it was opposite me, with a smashing new set of ivories; and further out, like a children's arms hiding it's exam answers, were the Sydney Heads. We'd drive up there some weeks to wave at friends, on the Oriana and Canberra, sailing home, the streamers still hanging from the ship's rails like a gipsy girl's curls. Although I loved Australia I wanted to be on that boat, waving at us.

Our turn came, so we sailed home to a bleak midwinter. I wished I was back on the Heads again, waving someone else off.

*

173

I headed across Sydney to meet Hilde at her friend's house in Miranda, and realised as the train closed the distance that I was heading into hell - suburbia.

"I couldn't possibly change the seating arrangement Peter, I've planned it!" Susan seemed to have something smelly under her nose.

"Would you like to have a shower Howie...freshen up before we have dinner?" I didn't, but I had one just to muss up the visitor's towel for her. "Do you want to see our wedding video?"

We had three desserts and strawberries dipped in chocolate. They tasted of straw. It never occurred to them that I could stay in one of their numerous rooms, so I was shown to the station at a civilized hour. It took me two hours to cross Sydney on the post-pub midnight train, through the areas it was recommended to avoid. The last time I felt that comfortable was sharing the buffet car to Guildford with the Man United Southern army who'd just been beaten 4-1 by Arsenal. The buffeting was energetic and then the claret flowed, thick and fast.

Hilde, embarassed, escaped the next day, her sanity barely intact. Meeting her at Circular Quay I rang for the job I'd seen advertised on the hostel board.

"Yes I was a painter and decorator" I lied.

"If I had dollar for every Pom or Mick who told me that, I wouldn't have to work. Have you got trade papers?"

'I haven't even got cigarette papers' I thought. "Yes" I lied.

"When did you get those?" "About twelve years ago" I lied.

I was grimacing at Hilde who was smiling, hopefully.

"Alright I'll give you a start...I'll pick you up 6am Monday." Hilde was happy for me, and we had the day left together.

We went back to Glebe where everything shone and laughed, it was 90 degrees and 'Festival!' The heads filled the road, stretching up and over the three hills of Glebe Point road, in and around and about the stalls; where people of imagination laid their ideas on trestle tables. The smell of cooking rose hissing, bubbling into the air; Chinese, Nepalese, Lebanese, Thai, Indian, Indonesian, Turkish, Yiddish and English, leapt from every utensil imaginable. At each road junction a band played, the notes shimmering and floating on the heat that washed between the people. We sat in a bar taking our Vitamin B, while the sweat cooled; until outside, a Samba beckoned with insistent finger.

We tried to ignore it but Hilde was as much a slave to the beat as me. We emerged blinking at the bright, and threaded our way to the junction where I watched Hilde take to the road and sway to the rythym, her back impossibly arched, hips swaying, fingerpopping. She returned, glowing, and we moved off up the street to the next delight. She was pressed close behind me in the crowd and I felt her kiss me, a soft cat's paw on my shoulder.

Gaining some breath in the Toxteth pub, a million miles from it's Bristol namesake, the riots started again; this time in the sky. As though irked by the fun that had been dragged out below 'til evening, the sky hit back. It used every trick up it's sleeve to cow the people.

The pub emptied into the street, soaking up the deluge as a treat, whooped and hollered with the bass drum above and *ooohed!* and *aaaghed!* at the electric show that dashed about trying to be menacing. The crowd was tight; ecstatic. But Hilde had to go back to suburbia, school-sock grey and just as uniform. The 'Burbs' though must have cracked, or realised how upset Hilde was, as, after a meal of 'it's only leftovers', they drove us back to the city, cruising Kings Cross to watch the Queens and Johns sauntering and simpering and then dropped us under the Bridge for our goodbye.

We sat on the harbour wall, the full moon crashing through the bitter steel lattice of the bridge and falling in pieces onto the water; facing each other and our fears and hopes. The 'Burbs' took us back to Glebe, where Hilde clung to time and me, tightly.

"Goodbye Hilde" I said, pushing her into the parting we had to do. She lifted her face to me like a newly opened bloom, crying soft, silent tears. Dropping her head back onto my damp shoulder she clung tighter.

"Goodbye Hilde" I said again, and as she released her hold I heard her arms drop heavy. I kissed the top of her head and she staggered like a drunk to the car, which stole her away. I wasn't heartbroken this time, just hopeful, and I had work to get on with the next morning.

*

I TRIED to stave off the nightmare but it wouldn't go; it was my alarm, and it wouldn't leave my wrist. I was out of my bed by 5.20 and walking out into the dawn drizzle at 6.00, wearing a pair of charity shop boots, two sizes too big. I swung them into the cab of the white van that was waiting. 'The Dan Van'. Dan was big; he was wearing the van like a sleeveless pullover. His eyes were slits, his nose - plasticine, and the hair that stuck out beneath his battered cap, was straw.

We rolled through suburbs, cutting corners, mounting kerbs, racing lights. As the next one ahead glared *Red*, Dan, looking up at the sky above, his peak bent against the glass, ignored it, and still watching the plane coming into land, growled -

"Another planeload of fucken' backpackers!" I could hear my sandwiches curling at the corners.

"I don't know why I take on Poms and Micks, I should stick to Asians, they don't spend all day talking about which pub they went to last night or who they're going to shag tonight.!" He turned to me and the lower part of his face cracked into a smile that could freeze a running stream. And I knew instantly what my job description was: whipping post, scapegoat.

But Dan was mostly wind and piss, the proverbial headless chicken, lurching from cock-up to disaster half-hourly. We renovated eight units, eleven hours a day, half hour for lunch.

"How are you with bricks?" he would ask.

"Well I've laid some before." (about six)

"Go round the building and brick up all the holes."

"OK Dan, where's the spirit level or line."

"Aaagghh don't bother with that, just chuck 'em in, haven't you finished yet?"

"How are you with plastering?...render those chasings in."

"OK Dan, where's the float?"

"I'll have to go buy one." Dan went out to buy something ten times a day, and each time he came back he would be panicking -

"What've you been doing, where are you y'slack arse Pom? How are you with electrics? Y've got forty minutes to disconnect all eight main fuse boxes, everyone on site's waiting for you."

"OK Dan, where's the blocks so I can isolate all the wires?"

"Aaagghh just wrap insulation tape round them."

"OK Dan, wher..."

"Oh shit!!! I'll have to go get some; get all the ceilings painted while I'm out." And when he came back - "What've you been doing you sad old backpacker bastard?"

"Painting some ceilings."... "Get that wiring done!!!"

So it rolled on for a month. He threw people off site by the collar, walking them to the bus stop, or by the fist. I took others from my hostel, desperate for work. I warned them,

"You've got to be *desperate* to work for Dan." He sacked them all. Michael the Mick put so much paint on the new door that it ran down in waves. Dave got vertigo going up the ladder - bus stop. I learnt to abuse Dan back, although a playful punch to my stomach that left me breathless for five minutes, almost put paid to that. We rubbed his nose in his mistakes -

"What colour y'painting that fucken ceiling y'bludger?"

"White.".... "That's not fucken white!!"

176

"Yes it is."

"IIITTTSSSS NOOOOTTTT!!!!!"

"That *is* white" said the kitchen fitter.

"Aaaagghh I'm colour blind" said Dan, a nice shade of puce.

Graham, an Englishman, had been in my room for a week. Ears like a wingnut, he only left the room once a day; to get the bread roll and cheese that he ate *every* day. He stayed in the kitchen all day reading books, and sat in front of the fridge so I had to get him to move *every* time I wanted to get to it. I wondered why people like him bothered to come away, and why he didn't do something about his atrocious breath. Similarly there were the Brits that had come over, some getting no further than Sydney, and had simply transplanted their life. They watched the Simpsons every evening, went up the pub, followed the rugby and cricket, kept to themselves, did dead-end jobs.

I heard through my window one evening..."There's no point getting to know the back-packers, they always move on."

It was *their* hostel, they thought they were 'Big Fish'. In reality, they were minnows hiding under a pebble in an ocean.

But Glebe Hostel was good place to stay. It had a rapid turnover of travellers, great for meeting people. Monday night was Welcome night, with free wine and cheese; Sunday - barbecue, with free wine; and any other time could be a trip to the beach, to a pub, club.

I had a new room-mate, an English boy. Although he looked relaxed I could see something was up.

"How long have you been here?" I asked.

"Eight hours." he replied.   "What in the hostel?"

"No, Australia...I flew from England this morning; I want to go back, I miss my mates. I don't know anybody, or what todo."

His lip was quivering and I suddenly saw myself standing in the reception of Chungking Mansions....alone.

"What would you be doing if you were at home with your mates? Down the pub, talking about the same things you did last week, and the week before?"   "Yeh...probably."

"I'll make you a promise. Go down the bottle shop, and buy a slab of beer, take it out to the front of the hostel, find a table with a seat free, and say 'Hello, do you mind if I sit here?'...and I guarantee that by Friday, you won't want to go home."

I swung my old boots out of the Dan-Van, shambled into the hostel forecourt, paint-spattered, filthy, and sat down at the table.

"Have a cold beer Howie, I think you have earned it" said Anders, who'd turned up the previous week, and did this every evening.

"Cheers old mate" I said tipping it up, and a group rushed past. One of them turned back and said...

"Howie, we're going up the Tockie for a few beers and then onto a club, d'you fancy coming?"

"No thanks," I said "I'm too knackered."

"By the way, I don't want to go home now, I'm having a blast. I've met loads of people. Thanks".. and rushed after his new friends.

"*You* did it!" I shouted after him.

"Still helping us beginners Howie... ay?"

"No, I'm still learning myself Anders."

*

Then it was the *last* Friday and I was the only one to have lasted the course. The carpet fitters were coming early Monday.

"Didya finish painting the last unit Howard?"

"Yeah" I said "...all locked up." and threw him the keys.

As we arrived back at the hostel, he squeezed his head out the open van window and shouted -

"Thanks Howard, you were the only one I could trust, y'done a really good job, call me if y'ever back in Sydney." As he sped off into the distance, scattering pedestrians, the other Pom who'd finished the job with me opened his pay packet and asked,

"Have you seen Dan's company letterhead? it was in my pay." There it was in black and white...'Panic-O' General Builders.

Still laughing, I swung my big, smelly, painful boots in the dustbin, and with a can of Vitamin B, soaked in the bath while the rain fell outside to clean the day, looking forward to my bed with no alarm at the end.

I had a thousand dollars in my pocket and rejoiced in the fact that when Dan got to work on Monday, he'd see that the two rooms I told him were finished, still needed a lot of painting; while the carpet fitters hung around waiting. And then he'd see the note I'd pinned to the wall, with a pot of paint and brush below.

"Paint it y'self y'slack arse bastard!!!"   Ho, ho, ho.

*

I woke uneasily, trying to think what was missing. It was the alarm: I wasn't working and had two days to enjoy, so I hunkered down into my bed drifting in and out of sleep. The hostel intercom awoke and floated 'What's up?' by Miles Davis through the dorms. My smile was wide as the pillow. Miles was cut off by Colin, who was manning the intercom that morning, and still had the peaty soil of County Cork clinging to his boots

"Would de tree cleenin burds com to reception please. That's moy burd, the one oy shag sometoimes and de udder one from Noo Zealand. It's noin tirty - check out toim. If youse wanning t'leave dis dump t'day you've got foive minutes t'get yer leezy fockin arses out of y'fockin beds. Udderwoise yer stuck wid yer man here anudder night and youse all have to listen to dose crappy Canadians a brayin and hollerin orl day. Boy the way...if yer wannin ter go to the ciddy, the hostile bus leaves in foive minutes...where's dose cleenin burds?"

I lazed the sunny morning away, at the front of the hostel, chomping down coffee and chatting to three girls. Matt came jogging past, a Pom who was working at a boatyard in the harbour. He was from Devon, a sailor, with oak growing in his bones and shooting from his head in a shock of dark hair. His eyes still narrowed from the winds that had striven to scrape them out like a hoor in a bitchfight.

"I'm shooting over to Bondi in the car, you want to come?"

I looked at my watch. **1.58.** Sigrid, the Swedish girl, looked up with an engaging smile and said "I'll wash your cup for you, go and enjoy yourself, I may see you later, yes?"

"Probably" I said, hopping in the passenger seat.

"Tart!" Matt said, and it rhymed with the door shutting.

"She's alright" I said. "No, you" said Matt "She's been giving you the glad-eye for days, now you've run off for the day and left her to do your crockery!"

"I don't think so Matt, anyway, I'm leaving Monday."

"So's she, but I think she wanted a souvenir to take home and not show her folks, you know, sail your skin boat into tuna harbour!"

"Set sail for Bondi Matt, before I jump overboard."

We took a walk along the Big-Top that was Bondi. We were passed by four shapely brown buttocks, one pair chewing toffees, the other trying to spit out a piece of dayglo string. They passed a gang of Italian Ozzies who were lounging on, around and against the railings like 'The Wanderers'. They were too busy watching other Italian Ozzies to notice the girls; comparing their own muscles, tans and trunks. Bologna, Brooklyn, Bondi, same-same.

Skateboarders grabbed air in the halfpipe, padded and helmeted against hamburger knee and cabbage head. A Brazilian drum band beat their skins to the left, and swinging his arms like an ecstatic soldier, came a man with full moustache and shaved head, on the back of which sat a fur hat. He had on a slingback lycra top, pleated green skirt, black tights and nurse's shoes. His name was Crystal - apparently, and had a new outfit every Saturday. He waved cheekily at the little dog that passed him sporting a sun visor. We sat on the wall with a bag of 'Herbies' watching the bodies that were there with the sole intention of being watched. We didn't want to disappoint. Strains of Forest of Dene, Donegal and Gravesend floated across the sand, hopping over tits and bums, the noise rising up like a host of locusts.

The Bondi Hotel was full but we found some space outside to watch the show. A platoon of 'the Barmy Army' shuffled past, Union Jack trunks, hats and towels; a day off from the test match at the Oval; a practice session for Christmas Day when there would be 20,000 other deadheads on the beach waving their jingoistic cloth. Two 'braves' broke away from the mob to get into the hotel. They were twins, carroty topped, the colour of sunburned Spam, strong as cowslips. The bouncers were trembling.

"What's wrong with ar money y'fuckin Penguin eh?"

"Run along now Sir, there's a good boy."

"What'choo looking at mate?!"

"Nothing" said Matt and turning to the twin "...and nothing."

The irony was lost on the Brothers Dim, as was the second step that they stumbled down, drunk, and dumb as a box of hammers.

"Do run along now Sir."

"We'll be back." "Yeah we'll will back we will...yeah!"

"Those two girls over there are checking us out Howie."

"The only girls that check me out are hotel receptionists."

"No, they are! shall I ask them over?" I didn't really care.

"OYYYYHHH!! would you like to join us?" I nearly choked on my beer and looked at Matt who was smiling. The whole verandah was laughing. They shimmied their little butts, shook their hair and joined us. The verandah stopped laughing. The girl with eyes like a solar system bracketed me and told me she was a Czech, living in Bondi with refugee relations. The afternoon passed in a blur as we were sailing on a sea of empties, both unfazed by our catch. He was an old salt; I was an old bastard.

We quit the hotel when the dark had driven the exhibitionists home, leaving a bitter-lemon sunset on the horizon, and crossing the city, beached the car at 'the Rocks', the original and restored Sydney. We hopped from pub to pub, band to band, eating here and there. The girls wanted to go back to the hostel with us.

"Sorry" said Matt "we're not going home tonight, Howie's leaving tomorrow so we're carrying on." They held hands and went to the toilet for a conference, weaving slightly. We met them coming out.

"We're going now." they said stiffly.

"Oh that' shame..." I said, "nice meet you...good luck in Check-inslonvarkiang, and wherever *you* come from."

"Australia!" she spat at me. And left.

Ordinarily I'd have been embarrassed at my behaviour, but this time I was chuffed. We hadn't played their game you see.

We rolled down to the harbour and sat on the wall, giggling like village idiots. The bridge and the moon, however, took my smile away and snuffed it in the water, leaving me quiet. We sailed our thoughts in different dinghies for a while.

"Hey Howie, what're you thinking about?"

"I'm thinking about Hilde."

"I thought so...I know how you feel." And I wondered what secret thoughts Matt had hidden away in his bilges.

"You're a strange one Howie, you've seen off a Swede and a Czech today, haven't you heard of a girl in every port?"

"Yeah...but the port's only a refuge from the storms."

"Ah bollocks...let's mutiny the Bounty!" said Matt, jumping down off the wall onto now steady feet.

The Bounty was a replica of the original, faithful apart from the restaurant below, where the Japanese 'ah-soh'd around the harbour stuffing canapes and potato-salad every lunchtime. Matt knew the crew, so we were 'halloed' aboard and invited to join in with the crew bar, and potato-salad. I leaned against the bulwark, trying to imagine this little tub, dwarfed by the harbour ferries, sailing seas and storms. We spent the night on the deck, talking and supping. The moon threaded it's way through the upper rigging, arced across the planetarium sky, played peek-a-boo amongst the office buildings of the city, mirrored in the glass side of one; and then settled itself snug into the folds of the Sydney skyline, roughly where Glebe lay sleeping. The black between The Heads was fading to grey as Matt and I rowed back to the hostel in his battered Holdsworth. I fell into a deep sleep, my bed floating over the waves of halitosis issuing from the bunk below.

The sun, the Sex Pistols and a tongue like a furry seat-cover woke me before checkout time and I staggered to the front of the hostel, where Sigrid nursed me for an hour with coffee, orange juice and smiles. When I could see through my eyeballs I noticed that Sigrid had a very fetching outfit on. It was set off by honey brown limbs, hair the colour of honey, lips like bee stings and a smile as warm as toast. Apart from the ice-blue eyes, I could have eaten her for breakfast. I'd choose her once every day and twice on Sundays.

"Would you like to come around Sydney with me as it's my last day?" How did a washed-up wreck like me deserve a day with a piece of loveliness like this? I didn't. "Yes please" I said.

We went to the city to confirm her tickets to someplace else: this had seemed to become a habit of mine. We rounded Circular Quay and watched the wash from the ferries lapping the pylons like thirsty dogs. Shapeless, stinking humans in countless layers stirred into another day of hell; hot dogs leapt down tourists throats, barking mad with mustard; the Opera House bared it's cute side to the Japanese cameras, which flashed, although a hundred yards away and in bright sunlight. The jugglers juggled; the didgeridoos did; the businessmen were busy. The harbour shone. So did Sigrid.

A tractor and trailer passed us in the Botanical gardens and we jumped on the back like kids on a haywagon, the driver pretending he hadn't seen us. We watched the gardens pass on all sides: bushes, flowers and parts of Sigrid blurring with the jigging up and down of the trailer. He slowed when me moved to jump off, and waved. We chatted on, through clumps of Formosa, Gardenia and Honeysuckle that cuddled up to each other and climbed sun-burnt walls; and painted pictures for each other with words.

We spent time in Sweden, in Sigrid's home and on the family skiing trip, where the air reeked of pine resin, the trees were sugar-iced and the skis ran with a *swissshh* along the railway tracks of previous skiers. I joined them for mulled wine and pickled herrings on Christmas morning.

I took her walking around Hydons Ball with Bumble, kicking layers of parchment leaves; along Putsborough sands where above on the hills the trees grew sideways from the winter winds, like a rockabilly's quiff: skiing under the same indigo sky, but a different range of mountains, carving righteous turns down a wide open run, then battling down a black, the turns ragged and urgent; thighs screaming.

She talked of a life ahead, hopes, unmarked paths; asked which roads to take. "There's no map." I answered, and explained the wrong turns, slippery and bumpy roads, dangerous bends and dead ends, that I'd taken.

Holding hands, we Fred and Gingered down the steps of the Opera House. At the bottom she twirled her Doctor Martens on air and kissed me. "Thank you," she said, her iceberg eyes melted to hot pools, "You have given me a lot of hope, I know now I don't have to worry which way to go, just do it." I wish I'd known that when I was her age.

We were passing the open-air restaurants of The Rocks. The 'suits' were lunching on Italian, Thai and French cuisine, their Armani and Versaces decorating the seatbacks as they grazed through salads dressed with sun. We looked at each other, both thinking, 'It would be nice, wouldn't it?' but carried on looking for a cheaper cafe to match our budgets. A road back from the water, we passed a small Italian restaurant with three wrought iron tables outside, on the sunny side of the street. The chairs flung out their legs and barred our way, so to keep the peace we sat down, and before we'd thought once about it the table grew a platter of calamari rings, roundels of saute-potato and an organised jumble of crisp salad, shining in virgin oil and speckled with mustard seeds. The golden carafe of chilled wine shone like a beacon in the centre of the table as if announcing our extravagance to passing travellers. We sauntered through the meal with naughty smiles and finally, leaning back quiet, replete with the food and company, I looked at my watch and waited for the display to flick over to **1.58.** and laughed. "What are you laughing at Howie" puzzled Sigrid.

"24 hours of bliss!" I answered. "I don't understand."

I explained, and then she did. We didn't exchange 'souvenirs' only addresses, and Sigrid left for Perth at dawn.

I was leaving in the afternoon for Melbourne so, deciding to revisit my old home - Manly, hid my bags in someone else's room in case Dan came a-looking for me. As the ferry came in I saw the shark enclosure to the left that used to have a gangplank around it and a diving board and, in our imagination, sharks nosing up to the net while we swam inside. Now it looked like a children's paddling pool, and there was a new shark-enclosure...to keep them in; Marineworld, an architect's aquarium. I walked through the Corso, which could have been a Croydon shooping mall, except that it led onto Manly Beach. I remembered it shaped like a longbow, lined with pine trees; Shelly beach and Fairy Bower at one end, the sea pool at the other, into which the waves washed on rough days and big boys (stupid boys my Dad called them) dived to show off. Aside from a few less trees and a few more buildings, it was the same.

I took the long, long walk adjacent to the river to get to my old house. It was only two hundred yards! And there was the pine tree that had hoisted me up in it's arms to watch the circus unfold, like a pop-up card, in the field: the circus I wouldn't go to as the elephant looked sad and tired, and the tiger as though it had been scraped from some dusty floorboards. The midgets scared me. I never went to a circus.

I looked for my school and found a building where it should have been, but it rang no bells. Then I remembered that at the back there used to be a cloakroom in a lean-to, painted in crayon blue, where we each had a peg to hang our satchels; holding black gym shoes and sandwiches wrapped in paper. Tupperware was still awaiting it's visa to enter from the USA, so each day, by breaktime, a line of ants would file under the door, up the slatted bench, and choose a satchel. There was no rhyme or reason for the choice, as we all had Vegemite, but for some reason they never picked on the same one on consecutive days. I went round the back of the school, being careful not to tread on the lines in case the bears got me, and there was a lean-to. Cupping my hands to the side of my face I looked in like a burglar: the pegs were still there above the slatted bench, now in crayon yellow. Before teacher could catch me, I padded on down to the beach and mingled with the Manly surf.

I jumped over the waves salmon-like until the water was too deep, then duckdived out to the unbroken waves. I bobbed over the plundering green hills until a snow-capped peak came thundering towards me in ten-league waders. Stroking hard for Ayers rock, I felt the elevator carry me up to the heights and as the door opened I planed down the face like a skimming stone, slashing up and down on the palms of my hands, until the washing machine behind me caught up and put me through full wash and spin cycle. I went back out, again and again, hollering with delight and fright. In a lull between sets I heard a shout and saw another bodysurfer heading out fast, so I followed. He was holding a body and I saw it was a Jap, mouth open, eyes closed, body senseless, and then the wave hit us - the first of the set. We came up seperate and lunged for an arm each. I knew the next wave would be bigger and as it hit, we pushed him up above us to keep his head near the surface. As we broke through the spume, we were pulling him up by the fingertips from below and hauling him skywards like a prize catch. His eyes were open but the body was on early closing. Kicking for shore, each wave snatched him from us, and we dragged him back,

184

like a ping-pong game. It was 18-17 and service to Manly, and I felt fear spreading through my limbs. I shouted to my companion -

"Are you Okay?" "N0" he mouthed as the next wave hit and washed away his reply. And then fighting in the sworl for air, it hit me for the first time, I was going to have to leave a man to die if I wanted to live. 19-17. I decided to leave him after the next wave. I kicked hard for shore hoping it would take us further in or the lifeguards would arrive like the cavalry. 20-17 and match point, I'd made my mind up, I was drowning. "We're in!" my partner shouted and my foot touched sand, the fear washing away into shore around the ankles of the paddlers. We hauled him, now flapping like a fresh mackerel, onto the sand where his friends reclaimed him like lost baggage, bowed courteously and took him away. We sat at the top of the beach, shivering, and my stomach was full of dead butterflies.

The tannoy burst out *"All swimmers in front of the Corso move between the flags, you are in a dangerous area....move between the flags...please!!!"* My Australian comrade asked me

"Were you going to leave him?"

"Yes." I said""

"So was I."

And we sat and looked, feeling sick, at the spot where we'd been - dead centre between the flags. On my boyhood beach.

*

MELBOURNE

MELBOURNE wanted a big thing. It had a lot of money to spend. Sydney had it's bridge, opera house and a tower. Melbourne wanted to build the tallest building in the world to put itself on the map, but how long would it remain the tallest?

Melbourne was selling itself short, it was very big on one thing - style. It had oodles of style; coffee bars hissed, steamed and frothed with it; trams rattled, banged and clanged with it. Girls wearing precious little, were swathed in folds of it. Sydney girls knew how to take off their clothes and look like sex; the girls on Bourne and Spence St, put clothes *on*, to look damn sexy. They looked past you, but if you caught their eye, they smiled, Sydney girls looked straight through you as if you weren't there. The two cities bickered daily across the fence, trying to better each other, but were if fact the same, just different. Their botanical gardens, lakes, parks, street-art and monuments would grace any city in the world and improve most. They shame London with it's filth and laziness, whose only saving grace comes with the night, when it twinkles, the crap hidden by the dark.

Melbourne was a monopoly board, set in a square; the City tram clanking round the board, passing Go every twenty minutes; a station in the middle of each side; a gaol in the top right corner with a picture of Ned Kelly peering out. It's savoir-faire came from the bloodline, a heady cocktail of Australia, Greece, Italy and coffee, and a trickle was allowed to flow intravenously out to the suburbs, where I stayed at St.Kilda and later in the city at The Nunnery.

Despite the drinking games (Toss the Barman - heads the drink's free, tails you pay for it), rollerblading along the front in the summer sun, and 'choice' bands at the big hotel on the front, St Kilda seemed isolated and it was tiring, dodging the dope-dealers and dossers from the homeless hostels. The Nunnery, although in the city, also seemed isolated, a solitary and tiny island of travellers amongst a city busy doing it's own thing.

Olembia, Enfield House and The Nunnery all seemed a bit too cosy for me: stain glass windows, petrified flowers arched over doors, room sized mirrors were held in by cupids and cornucopia, strands of ivy and doves. Reading rooms *shusshhhed!* at the comings and goings of the backpacks; the clinking of cutlery and bubbling of snackpots in the kitchen. They seemed to subdue, with their quiet flock wallpaper, soft mossy carpets, massed folds of curtain: clocks ticked slow and loud in the scent of old books. The travelers, like so many Aspidistras, bent their heads to books or sent streams of *zzzzz's* to the ceiling. The thought of spending Christmas here, in front of the fire and twinkling tree, with ho! ho! ho's and pulling crackers - just like home, was terrifying. I wanted to spend it in the 'real' Australia.

Whilst travelling down the East Coast, that old chestnut kept cropping up..."This is not the 'real' Australia."

I would just say..."Really?" because that's the same as saying... "Manchester? Bognor Regis? they're not real England...go to The Lake District, Mortsbury-on-Swale."

Of course they're real piggin' England!!

Brighton baking on a Bank Holiday Monday, Walsall - Friday night on the town, a football match Sunday morning in Gravesend- the ball sticking to the mud. My stomping ground is as average as 1.8 children, but at the same time, as beautiful as anywhere...if you look.

Hambledon - famous for nothing, is one of the villages that orbit Godalming, one of the towns that slowly circle Guildford, which in turn sattelites London. Narrowly missed by a busy motorway, Hambledon is thirty minutes down the line from where the sodium glare of London fades to night; the night of owls hooting, of rustlings, and dark comes in shades of soot, jet, lamp, velvet and any other colour as long as it's black. When the moon hangs full, and the poachers wriggle, it's said that the parish lantern is out.

At a cricket match, played out like English theatre in the lush folds of green, I asked two Australians and a Kiwi why they'd come to the other side of the world, and spent a year in Hambledon. "Why?"

"Look around you mate! it's a beautiful place, the locals are friendly - and interesting, the pub's great. This is 'real' England, this is what we came to find." And they were right. It was time for me to repay the compliment. I was off to Caramut. Of all the Victorians I'd asked in Melbourne, not one of them had heard of it, or knew where it was. Perfect.

*

HOPKINS HILL, CARAMUT, VICTORIA

I'D MET Calvo when he and his friend Duffy were working around Hambledon; drank with them in my local, The Merry Harriers - or the Hairy Mariner, as we called it.

Three months after my first night in Chungking Mansions he'd flown home to the family farm. His father had been unwell and Calvo thought it was time. I was going to stay with them at Hopkins Hill. It was the legacy of generations, a huge spread of 20,000 acres which had now been parcelled, leaving the Calverts 2,000 acres and 'the Big House'.

The red dust drive shuffled past the verandah, it's slender columns marching in true colonial style, holding up the roof, which jutted out like the peak of a Yorkshireman's cap. It crept round the box hedges, dodged past the thorny roses and, fading to brown, tumbled into the paddock, mingling with the beat grass that just burned for water.

The sky above most of Australia played a hard game with the ground below, bullying, teasing, sucking up the water into it's cheeks and holding it there while it fanned the flames below by flapping it's hands. Whilst they moved water around the farm in tankers and chased across country after anything that even looked like smoke, rainclouds sat pregnant in the distance. I eventually gave up asking the boys "Is that rain on the way?"

"No," they'd reply without bitterness, "That's rain over the coast, it won't come inland."

Mrs Calvo - Jane, managed to keep the veggies growing, the box hedges in shape, and the roses still flourished. As was the case in the day, their anscestor had pioneered his way here in Victorian times and created a little bit of England in the middle of bone-dry Australia, to make life more bearable for the later arrival of the wife. It had once taken a small army of workers to keep the estate in trim. Jane, Calvo and his father... Don, worked the whole farm now, helped by Calv's sister and younger brother Jack'son' when he was on holiday from boarding school as he was during my visit.

Jackson, stocky, napheaded, had a sewer for a mouth which often prompted a - "Moderate your language Jack...pleeeease!" from Jane, but 'F's and 'C's and 'B's flew in all directions. He came from the same mould as his father, ample and rounded, as were their sense of humour and fun. Both had stare-eyes that twinkled with barely concealed glee. I was also to see those eyes burn with a dangerous light when challenged. In the whole time I was at Hopkins Hill, Don was a complete gentleman and treated me as a friend. Calvo thought it was because I was writing, and that was something beyond his realm. I think it was because he was a top bloke.

Don didn't drink stubbies. He didn't pour them down his neck. He sucked them dry in one long pull, with the schlluuurp and gurgle of water going down a plughole, until the sides of the can caved in. Then whilst replenishing his lungs, the next would be cracked and on it's way to his mouth. Such is the way for a farmer toiling in the heat, but quantity never dulled his senses or humour.

A knock at the door at 1.00am had Jack and I leaping from our chairs, as this normally meant a fire that needed attending. Rattling the flyscreen open, we saw a bugeyed Don leaning forward on his toes, peering in, the pickup running behind.

"Where's the fire Don?" asked Jack, worried, as we'd been on the beers all evening..."Fire?" and louder, "FIRE?...we're going possum hunting!" Don was shakier than us.

"I'll get the rifles" said Jack turning to me and grimacing.

"Rifles?" and louder "RIFLES?...get the bastard shotguns, this is fucken' war!" he growled into the darkness. Jack, shouted into the dark, "I'll throw a couple of bales in the back of the Ute to sit on."

"BALES?" and quieter, as he crossed the yard, "Bales?...put some deckchairs in there, we'll wage this fucken' war in style!" as the Ute door thundered shut. It cranked open again, "And bring along a slab of beer... shit yeh!" Jack looked at me, "You grab the beer, we're in the army now. Don's army...the old bastard."

I made it clear when I arrived that I was there to help out with anything and not for pay. There was always something to be done but it always seemed to be just enough for the two or threei of them. After a week of resting and writing I was beginning to feel in the way. I suggested to Calvo that it was a shame the homestead was showing signs of wear and tear, and I could do something about it.

"That'd be great" he said, "but it'd be a hoor of a thing; last time it took a team of five a month just to paint the fucken' outside. I'll mention it to Don though."

It was three more days before I got an answer. No. But if I could paint the house we were living in, that would be great, if I was sure, and really had the time and just write down the hours it takes and we'll pay you. Basically, the sun was shining, positively beaming - blindingly out my arse. I would have done it for free; I was working for Don this time, not Dan. "Don't start 'til after Christmas though Howie, enjoy y'self for a while!"

We'd already started the Christmas decoration in 'our house', above the fireplace; a pyramid of alternate green VB, and red Tooheys tins. It waxed as Christmas waned and by New Year's eve had hit the ceiling, six cans wide. "Half those empties are yours Fliptop" they accused me, and were right; *they* were still working you see. That's my excuse.

The young cousin had the body of a siren and dressed - barely. Across the Christmas dinner, between mouthfuls, she pushed out her chest, which looked like two plum puddings in a flimsy muslim bag. Cousin Hugh, sitting next to me with a Christmas Eve hangover, looked at me with each thrust, and groaned. After dinner, walking in the yard - tipsy, she pulled Jackson's cracker by bending over straight legged to pat the dog, crooning "What a lovely boy" and displaying her tiny white knickers that had all but disappeared between two butterball cheeks. Later, as we walked back into the kitchen, Jackson stumbled, as she sat, legs akimbo by the demonic Aga, demonstrating that the front of her knickers had followed the same course as the back.

"Too much drink Jack?" asked his mum.

"That'd be right Jane."

I'd pinned my sock, one of the three pairs I was making do with, to the mantelpiece and put in my note to Santa.

"Please could I have Sheryl Crow, thank you. The Pom"

On Christmas day I woke to a head full of crows, a mouth like a sock and a Christmas sock bulging with VB.

"Happy Christmas Howie" I said, from my mattress on the floor.

"Happy Christmas mate!" I said to my backpack, that lay in the corner, licking it's wounds.

Outside, the sun shone brightly and the dust and gum leaves lay deep and crisp and even. I'd never felt less like Christmas in my life, but at least I was with a family; the raggle-taggle family in 'our house' and the whole Calvert clan over in the homestead.

Don and Jane gave me a great present; they told me to use the telephone all I liked. I phoned home and spoke the Christmas garbage that you do to the family. And I was chuffed to hear my mum say

"I've just had a long chat with Jane and she say's that you've been behaving." just as though they were old friends and I was just around the corner and ten years old. I rang Hilde who was at her parent's house, and spoke the things that two people that are close, but seperated do. Yes she missed me, and she couldn't wait 'til I got home.

The Grandfather had pegged it during the year, his chair at the head of the table to be taken this year by George, the eldest of the three brothers and one sister - Jane.

The 'Leashman' brothers had been 'shockers' when younger. They'd played Ozzie rules football with the sole intention of fighting with a member of the other team. Failing this, they would 'blue' with anybody offering opinions on the touchline, or if the post match drinks failed to produce a scrap, would fight each other. It was in this atmosphere that 'the clan' had gathered to 'sort out the estate' and four hours into Boxing Day the bell rang. "Andrew (Calvo) you were born a ****, you grew up a ****, and you're still a ****" said a Leashman. Only the referee, in the shape of Don's glare, Calvo's cool head and Jane's sobriety stopped the bout before Christmas was on the ropes.

On another hungover morning between before New Year, nursing roaring heads round the demonic Aga, feeding them with kedgeree, Jane entered her kingdom and looking daggers at Hugh, announced-

"I've got a bone to pick with you Hughie!"

"Oh!" groaned Hughie "I didn't make Jack climb the watertower, we all did, didn't we Howie?" We had, all eight of us, rolling and staggering, sliding round the top, shouting at the stars and the booming Peterborough surf and philosophising in the way only eight drunks on the top of a watertower can.

"You're digging y'self in Hugh." said Jane.

"Ohhh! I'm sorry Jane, whatever I done...what did I do?"

"You were in my kitchen last night when I came in with my bridge club...d'ya remember?" "Nooooaahh!"

"You were talking to the dog, eating all the ham..." "Sorry Jane"

"....naked!"

"Ohhhhh!"

"It's alright Hugh" said Don, his eyes sparkling, cheeks bright red, "They didn't see y'dick."

"Ahh, that's a relief Don...how come?"

"Y'had it hidden up the dog's arse!"

Calvo and I lived in the small house across the paddock, it's walls stained by the wrath of the sun, the smoke from barbecues and the russet borewater flung out from the sprinklers, when there was any to spare. It was roomy. The dining room was empty, apart from the beer fridge that hummed to itself in the corner. I called it the ballroom.

I slept in the old office, which shared a glass wall with the sofa-ridden lounge, feed-store calendars, landmaps and flies decorating the remaining walls. The kitchen, with it's endless supply of meat, nachos and smalltown gossip led through to the bathroom with it's brown -stained iron bath that couldn't be used due to lack of water. Four toothpastes and brushes sunbathed round the sink. Then, through the flyscreen, was the Dunny, where the flies hung out playing craps.

The two shearers who shared the house were Azza and Johnny. Big Johnny. Johnny was not quite as tall as a gum tree, and bending down under a corrugated tin roof barbering stupid sheep all day, put a great strain on his trunk. And the heat and the boredom, borne stoically by previous generations, hung heavy on his frame. He also liked to party.

This led to Johnny invariably lying supine on the sofa or on his bed. When awake, he gave a good impression of being a big dumb ox and before any reply to a question, would let out a *"Aaaaaauughh..."* But I knew that there was a lot of thinking going on in that big tired head and my presence had stirred him up. He was a hugely friendly man and I had all the time in the world for him. Eventually, he spoke to me in spits and spurts and I learned that he wasn't content to spend the next thirty years shearing 'til his back bent double. He wanted to travel, and listening to me on the fringes, I'd shown him that he could do it. I hope so.

Azza; short as Johnny was tall. He was dark, front teeth of a cheeky rat, just as quick, and nuggety like a Welsh miner. Azza was a trot-jockey, a junior champion who was now struggling hard against the big-boys. The second day I was there Azza made his first appearance, in a brake sliding dust cloud that overtook the now stationary car, and barreled through the flyscreen door into the lounge. Out of the cloud that was now settling on every surface, popped Azza.

"Hev y'seen a K'wala yet mate?" "No, not outside of a park."

"Hop in the car then!" We slammed off down the drive, squealed onto the metalled road, and stopped a mere hundred yards away.

"There's the bastard" he said, pointing up the tree with his teeth. I'd seen Koalas before, always doing the same thing. Nothing. This was a bull Koala, standing on hind legs, hanging onto the trunk with one hand. He was bellowing, honking, barking, rasping like a camel.

"What's he doing, is there something wrong with him?" I asked.

"Naa mate, that's what K'walas do. He's looking for a scruff."

It shinned down the tree, Azza scuttling back, "He's a big bastard, look at him go!" and the koala ran across the road, bellowing, and into the bush, scattering gum bark, tinder leaves and dust.

"How's it going mate..."Y'must be the pom! d'ya like nachos?"

The working day started early at the house, the three of them up before six, pottering round the kitchen like old maids.

"Hev y'seen m'fucken boots?" Azza would bellow on each circuit round the house. We knew they were laying where he left them the night before, in the lounge, as he did every night. But every morning he did his circuits, late for work, doors banging.

"Anyone seen m'fucken boots?" On about the third or fourth circuit, passing them each time, he'd spot them and put them on.

"Where's m'singlet?...Calv, hev y'seen m'singlet?"

"Azza y' useless bastard , it's on the bed where you took it off last night!"

"Well y'don't have to get dirty on me, I'm only trying t'get to work."

"But y'do this every fucken morning, 'where's m'boots?'"

"What y'hanging shit on me for?" A blue was brewing. "Y'want a blue with me Calv?"

"I just want you to shut up every morning...and do some cooking."

"I cooked last Tuesday...chops."

"You always cook fucken chops, *no*, you burn the chops!"

"That's how me mum cooks 'em, you liked 'em didn't you Howie?"

"And you cremated the fucken chook!"

"That was perfect that chook...ah bollocks to ya"

"What y'getting shitty for y'nuggety little runt?"

"Right," Azza said, whiskers twitching, y'want a shot at the title, come on, in the ballroom." And they would wrestle, bouncing round the room, slamming and heaving, cursing on the bare boards. They'd get up with floor burns, bruises and gouges, panting.

"Right, I'm off, hard day's yakker ahead, where's m'keys?, Calv hev y'seen m'keys?"

"Aaaaaaauughh fuck off Azza, before *I* take a shot." rumbled Johnny.

"What you getting shitty for Johnny.....?"

But on other mornings I'd wake up to the CD blasting Sheryl Crow - *"All I wanna do is have some fun"* pulling on my shorts and walking through the lounge, *"I've got a feeling I'm not the only one"* barefoot through the corner of the ballroom, *"I love a beer buzz, early in the morning"* entering the kitchen I'd see the three dancing, thumbs hooked in the waistbands of their moleskins, chins stuck out, bow-legged, shuffling round the table, making snag sandwiches for their lunch, swilling tea and joining in together on the last line *"Til the sun comes up on the San...ner...mon...ica...boule...vard"*

"Catch y'later Howie!"

Tuesday night was shopping night, and at such a distance that travellers (VB's) were required to help the journey there, and we'd stock up on VB, Nachos and other groceries. As it took the whole evening, food was essential. I'd managed to avoid eating the Australian national fayre, until now, and standing in the takeaway, looking at the menu, I said to Calv, "I don't recognise any of that, apart from 'meat pie'; you'll have to translate."

"Dippy Dogs - they're hotdogs on a stick coated with crap."

"Chiko roll - that's some shit that tastes a bit like chicken, with carpet underlay wrapped round it."

"Yeero - that's Kebab, you know them."

"Yes...but Kebabs made with chicken!!?"

"Dim Sim - they're soggy pancake rolls...."

"I think I'll stick to the meat pie." I said.

"You have to ask for a maggot-bag then." he replied.

"There's a letter for you in the postbox Howie!"

It was from Chantal, long and glorious, painting pictures of places I wished I was sharing with her. It had been forwarded from England and with it a note from my mum. *"Uncle Peter's in Melbourne on the 28th, Park Royal Hotel, if you want to go and see him."*

My Uncle and family were from Connecticut. Uncle Peter had left the family home a fifteen, unable to poke up with his father anymore.

Grandad used to frighten me; a headmaster; a disciplinarian. He took us to Bristol cathedral, and leaving my brother and I in the pews, holding hands for bravery, reappeared in the form of the organ he was playing. Blasting. Trumpeting. Echoing. I was terrified. I've hated organs since.

Of Uncle Peter there was no trace. In the sixties someone sent my mum a clipping from a backwoods Canadian newspaper.

A Peter Gwilym had been involved in a barfight where a man died.

In 1984 he rang my mum up and said "It's Peter, hi Margaret." There followed trips back and forth from England after, and I became great friends with the family. They'd come to Australia to see the brother who'd emigrated, the only one left he hadn't seen; since he was fifteen. It seemed stupid not to go and visit, so I did.

THE PARK ROYAL HOTEL, MELBOURNE

I WALKED into the foyer of the Park Royal, grubby backpack, shorts and boots - the inside of the heels rubbed shiny from rushing past each other to find the next thrill, laces hanging limp, the stitching suffering from a frayed temper.

I looked up at the glass lift shining up into the hanging gardens of Babylon that were the hotel atrium.

"Can I help you Sir?" asked the uniformed concierge, I guessed about eighteen years old.

"Uh...yes, can I have the keys to room 806 please...Gwilym." And as I said it, it sounded like the stupidest question I'd ever asked. Why would they give a key to a scarecrow?

"Certainly Sir, we've been expecting you. Would you take this gentleman's bag to room 806."

"Oh that's okay" I said, "I've carried it quite a long way."

There was nobody in the room, so I retired to the bar.

"Could I help you Sir?" said the barman "Yes, I'd like a cold VB please" and surprisingly it was no more expensive than anywhere else.

"Enjoy your drink Sir." he said.

"Listen, you don't have to call me sir, I'm just a backpacker, you saw me come in."

"You may be a backpacker, but until you check out from this hotel, you are... Sir."

I was cossetted for days. We went out and ate Malayan, French, Italian, barred from paying by Peter's generosity. We cruised the botanical gardens, the whole clan, a flock of uncles, aunties and cousins.

Hilmar, a cousin I hadn't seen since I was four, had strangely mirrored my work and personal career, on the other side of the world.

Morgan, Peter's son had expressed an interest in backpacking, and was asking the same questions we all do.."How do you? what do you? where?" I took him out to show him the ropes, and we strolled straight into the Nunnery.

"That's the reception where you check in, only for one night until you've figured whether it's any good. That's the notice board where everything you need is sold, hired or shared. The kitchen where you cook what you like, treat it with respect though. Dorm room - eight beds, fairly tidy *'hey didn't I meet you in Sydney?'* Television or reading room, *'Hi, this is Morgan he's thinking of going backpacking, yeah that's what I told him.'* Patio- for evening socialising. Front door." And we were out; about eight minutes all told.

I decided to call Hilde in Belgium. "Hi Hilde, how are you? Do you miss me? No?" There was something wrong. She had a problem that she couldn't tell me about. She was really sorry, perhaps it would have been better if we hadn't......I'd heard this one before Hilde.

"I'll ring you in a few days when I get back to the farm."

Shit! shit! shit!

Returning to the hotel on the last night, the family retired to bed and I hit the bar. "A glass of cold beer Sir?...or shall I just bring a bucket?"

The bar was empty, but I had some thinking to do. Three men came in; one of whom I thought I recognised, and sat behind me.

"Shall I move the table over for you Mr Boon?" the barman asked, behind. But it didn't click. Two more came in, younger, with caps back to front. "Hey Boony! how's it goin mate?"

"Alright Warney; it's your shout, three of the same."

I asked the barman, "are these Australian cricketers?"

"Yea, this is their Melbourne base, the Poms beat them today." Not long after, I was surrounded by the whole team.

"Mr Boon, there's a Pommie backpacker here wants to buy you a drink, he thinks you may need it after today." I looked at him in horror.

"It's alright" he whispered, "the hotel's buying."

"I was more worried about staying alive!" I said.

But they chatted to me; asked me about travelling, where I'd been, where was I going? why was I in this hotel?

As we spoke, I noticed a group of midgets, jumping up and down at the window to see their heroes, and then they came in. Seeing my puzzled expression, Boony said "They're doing the pantomime, Snow White."

When I went up to the room, Peter was sitting, checking the three foot long bill. "Have a good time in the bar Howie? was it quiet?"

"No" I said, "I had drink with the Australian cricket team and the Seven Dwarves."

"We're leaving early in the morning, so don't get up. I've told reception you can leave when you like" he said smiling, not quite sure.

They'd spent more in ten days than my whole trip so far. But each to their own, and all I've got to say on is...' Good on yer Peter.'

*

196

I arrived back at the farm just at the right time.

"Y'goin to a 'B and S' Ball Howie." said Calv. "What's that Johnny? I asked. "A batchelor and spinster ball." he replied.

"Beer and sex ball!" Calv threw in, "Sixty dollars for the whole weekend, free beer and food, band and music. They shout the Bundy, there'll be loads of Ute work, if y'can still stand, you'll get a scruff, Sunday's recovery day. We'll have to kit you out in battle dress." And as the weekend unfolded, it all became clear.

After a trip to the bottle shop and the chemist, we set off on the several hour journey; breaking it at a little one-eyed town. There was already a row of Utes parked in front of the milkbar, bullbars snarling, aerials stabbing ten feet into the air, tarpaulins stretched tight bracing themselves for the weekend. They were 'Scotty Tucker', 'Johnno', and 'Angus' and while they tucked into Chiko rolls, dim-sims, dippy dogs, they fell to talk of "four point five litre fully-worked V8 engines and 'working' and 'yea..listen to the note on that engine!!'"

And soon we were off in convoy, and the heat from the sun through the windscreen had me dozing off, until a NASA space shuttle hammered past - ***"gggggggrrrrraaaaaannnnggg!!!!!!"***

"Jesus wept!" I said jumping, what was that Calv?"

"That was just Scotty overtaking mate, there, in the distance. You should see him work it."

"What is 'working' the Ute Calv?" I asked.

"Well y'get on some sand or dust, put the fucken pedal to the floor and spin it around on it's front wheel."

There could be up to four thousand people at a B and S, all farm-owners, stock agents, shearers and jackaroos. It was the closest thing they had to the village dance, and came from hundreds of miles to get there. This was a medium size one.

Arriving at the site, amongst hundreds of Utes, we donned the Battle Dress. Off came the moleskins and T shirts, but not the Blunstone boots, and on went evening wear; dress shirt, bowtie, black trousers. Girls threaded through the car park in posh frocks, little black numbers, long dresses. Each and every hand had a bottle, can or glass stuck, or welded to it, and a girl with a broken arm had a stubby holder cast into her plaster.

Between us and the music tent hung a dustcloud, that bulged at the edges and barrelled this way and that, into the bar, over the car park; a Ute, invisible inside, spinning in manic circles, the scream of it's engine muted by the cloud, a queue of others waiting their turn. Another raced in, and the crowd waited for the scream of twisted metal and broken glass. A madman, arms above his head, walked slowly into the nightmare and it seemed forever before he emerged the other side, dust-brown, arms still aloft, unharmed, and the two Utes could be heard, gunning round and around, oblivious of the other.

The evening grew, and people wrestled on the ground, sleeves torn off, the colour of mud; fell from high places; disappeared into the bushes, threw up theatrically, to applause, danced like one-legged cats burying turds on ice.

"Bundy's on!!" came the shout.

"What's going on Scotty? I shouted, moving with the crowd.

"The Bundaberg rum's been opened, stay with me mate, just drink it 'til it's finished." They were six deep at the bar but the Bundy came back over the heads in cups and glasses, cupped hands, even by mouth.

"You the Pom that's staying at Calv's?" asked a girl. "Yep."

"D'ya wanna scruff?"

"No, not now, the Bundy's on!"

"Catch y'later eh?"

"Didya get a root yet?" asked a bloke I didn't even know.

"No, they all look like sheep or blokes to me."

"So, what!" he replied and poured his beer over my head. I repayed the compliment.

I retired to the back of the Ute just before dawn, people still dancing despite the fact the music had finished, and woke a few hours later. As I looked over the tailgate I saw bodies scattered, in swags, almost in tents, in the road, some crawling along caked in mud.

"D'ya wannna beer Fliptop? " Calv asked, pissing in the hedge.

"Be madness not to." I said. And he threw me one.

We raced across the country into South Australia, "Indian Country" said Calv, or 'Recovery day'. They moved the whole shebang a hundred odd miles to the beach at Robe, and partied on. I saw no signs of recovery, I did see the drunkest man I've ever seen in my life and I wondered how he was still alive.

From over the top of the beer lorry came the dead sheep, landing amongst the crowd, where it danced and drank beer for a while. But when it was slam-danced even I was shocked. It was low, sick; and others seemed to think the same, as, after a short row, it was buried in the dunes.

Wrestling with Calv, I was hit from behind by two shearers.

"Sorry mate," he said "y'glasses are bent." as I spat out sand.

"You the pom that's sleeping on the office floor at Calv's?"

"Yep." I said, and this man came from over two hundred miles away. "Hey Howie!" said Angus, helping me up, "There's a girl over here wants to talk to you."

There were two of them, and I'd seen them earlier walking along the beach. They hadn't been to the B & S, but were on a break from Melbourne University.

She looked French, with anthracite eyes, very attractive, despite the de'Gaulle nose. She was nineteen, and fascinated by my accent.

"Just say something!" As I worked my way round Scouse, Geordie, Cockney, she repeated after me, like a lesson, and she particularly liked West Country.

Much later, after Calv had run a mate's Ute up the back of another and flattened the occupant who objected, after the pub had been cleared - long after closing, we were standing on the roof of The Bank House, an historic building where Angus lived.

"I could listen to you all night." she said.

"You could if you slept here with me."

"I would like that very much indeed." she said, in a perfect 'Home Counties' accent.

As I banged the flyscreen door, heading for my sleeping bag on the floor of the office, Azza shouted from the kitchen,

"Didya get a root Howie?" It was his most important question.

"No, Azza" I said, and he started cackling, "I got scruffed."

I carried on with the painting 'til the end, which coincided with Jack going back to school; So, saying my goodbyes to Calv and Don at the farm gate, I hitched a lift down with Jane, took the short walk across the city, and into the Nunnery. I left Oz the next day.

*

199

AUCKLAND, NEW ZEALAND

FROM the air, New Zealand resembled a green baize snooker table attacked from below by hammers of all sizes. Pressing my nose against the window, I watched the white specks grow into sheep as we descended, and they seemed to graze right into Auckland.

As usual, I took the first hostel bus offering a decent price and found myself in a suburb on the fringes of the city. It wasn't a good hostel; full of deadbeats and wasters, and speaking to as many as I could, found that they seemed to have no aim; the last thing I wanted at the moment, as my own aim was running cock-eyed. On the flight from Oz, I'd sat blank, an automaton. I rang Brian Harding, who lived at Dargaville, at the north of the island. He'd lived and worked at Hambledon for a couple of years and had probably fitted in best of all the travellers; loud, funny, messy; stories are still bandied around the area, even today.

"Hey Howie!, good to hear from y'mate, hard case! No, go and stay at our flat in Mount Eden. The key's under the pot by the backdoor, help y'self to anything, there should be some beers in the fridge, just leave ten dollars in there when you leave. I'll get my niece Melissa to pick you up after work on Friday and bring you up here. Spot y'soon mate."

I conned the hostel into taking me over there in the bus, and let myself in. It was like the little houses they give to old folk in England when they can't manage a whole one, or their partner has died; in a row of others the same. It was a haven. I could lock the door, take a long bath. I phoned Hilde, Coronation Street whining away in the background on the telly.

No, I hadn't heard wrong back in Melbourne, everything had been wonderful, but if I knew about her problem I would hate her. Sorry, but that was that.

"That's alright Hilde," I said, "perhaps we can talk about it when I get home, I may be able to help. Take care, and keep in touch eh!"

I wandered back into the lounge and stared at the screen, the actors mathering away, and suddenly I wanted to smash Mike Baldwin's face in, play baseball with Bet Lynch's head and set fire to the Rovers Return.

Dear Mum and Dad,

How y'all going?- well, I hope. As you can see, I made it to NZ. The thing is, I write this letter very guiltily but I can't help it. You see, when I left Oz, it was in the frame of mind of - "New Zealand tomorrow, so what?" I should have arrived here buzzing, people at home dream of coming to NZ, I used to dream of it too. I'm sure you would have loved to yourselves; I know Dad, you always said that if we'd emigrated to NZ instead of Oz, we'd probably still be there. I think I'm just tired, stuffed to the gills like a child in a sweet factory. It's been ten months now and I'm grinding to a halt. The irony is, I'm only half way round the world. I stayed at the flat in Auckland, had a little break, a bit of a retreat, before going up to Brian's for Bank Holiday weekend.

It was odd. Brian looked very different, and was. He was so distant the first evening, I wondered if I'd got the right person, and he'd become so serious. But then he's working hard on the crops and of course they're his now and not someone else's. It was a good weekend though, and Brian loosened up as time went on, in fact he got very loose. Anyway, his Kumara crop isn't ready for picking yet, no point me hanging around there at the moment. So I'm back in Auckland, looking for a way to spend a week or two before the picking (bearing in mind I don't have much money) Will write soon, I'm having a job writing anything for the book - stuck I suppose! and letters are about all I can stomach.

Cheers now. Howie.

*

It was the kind of morning where mushrooms jumped up with a *booh!* and you had to use a chainsaw to cut down the biggest. The air was aquamarine. Cresting a hill, I walked through a breeze that tasted of bread dough, smelled sweet and warm, and fell out of the Tip-Top bakery windows in bucketfuls.

AEOTOREA - the land of the long white cloud. Looking up at the sky, it could be empty, perhaps an impish cotton wool cloud peeping over One Tree Hill. Then looking down for a second and up again you'll find clouds dancing across hills, running over the sea, and not just one type; wisps, vapours, cauliflowers, blankets; white, grey, bruised purple; as though the weatherman had gone mad and thrown his box of symbols into the sky. Closing your eyes for a second, they all swopped places like naughty schoolchildren.

Auckland City was pocket sized, and I soon found the hostels, on the same road as the stripclubs of course. These were the biggest I'd come across since Chungking Mansions, albeit a lot cleaner. They were seriously well run hostels, they had to be, the turnover was frightening. All nations were represented here in seemingly equal proportions, but these travellers had their packs stacked with money - thrill seeking. I spent an hour in the travel shop on the ground floor, trying to take in the huge selection of activities, in countless destinations. I swear if you wanted to bugger a chicken whilst trampolining in some rapids, a thousand miles away, you could have booked it here if you handed the money over. I looked through the comments book, of which there were many, and tried to assimilate the opinions:

"Go on the Kiwi Experience, not the West Coast Express"

"The Kiwi Experience drivers are tossers, West Coast is much better, unless you're a bloke who likes dressing up as women, and you want to spend a whole week pissed and miss New Zealand."

I was looking for a fairly budget way to spend a couple of weeks, to stretch out the time until the Kumaras were ready, and I saw a comment that made me chuckle. It had me rolling on the floor. My old friends the Israelis, had sent their emissary to New Zealand, one of the most staggeringly beautiful countries in the world, where every adventure you could possibly imagine waits on a plate, and he'd commented:

"New Zealand is okay, but I really miss the great adventures that we have back in my great country, Israel. We didn't really want to visit NZ, but we did even though I would rather have been back home in the best place in the world." Abok, Israel

It's funny, but all desires that I ever had to visit Israeli had disappeared since travelling. Strange that isn't it?

THE COROMANDEL: a peninsula off Auckland, easy to reach, beautiful, quiet, and the possibility of surfing. I took the round-Coromandel bus pass, which was cheap and allowed you to move on at will. Stopping at Thames, Coromandel and Whitianga, I realised that although the hostels were more than pleasant, the travellers were all 'trampers', serious walkers; 'anoraks' we'd call them at home. None had been to Asia or had any desire to, other than to climb Everest, and I had little in common with them. At this stage I didn't actually have much in common with the rest of the world or my head for that matter. Nobody was going onto Whangamata; it was 'off the circuit' and didn't have a 'walk' that had to be done. I went to Whangamata.

Using my fingers and thumb to form an oblong, I framed the scene in front of me. It had more things in it than is possible, apart from perhaps in a child's painting. The sky was still bright midday blue, but also had a sunset glowing, a moon hanging, a forest, an island, waves crashing, a sand beach - but with plants growing, a river estuary - boats at rest, surfers shredding waves, families collecting mussels, storm clouds, cotton bud clouds. You could even see the wind, by the spray from the sea and the swaying trees. I painted the scene, sitting in my shorts, the saltwater still clinging to the surfboard beside me, with a children's painting set from the toy shop.

Whanagamata,

N.Island.

Dear Martin,

Hey broh! how's it going mate? hope Ness and the kids are okay. Found it at last!! Came into town on a bus, (the only passenger) and gave the driver the address. He was sure it was still open. It looked like an 'ex-hostel'. It was, but when I found the owner on the third floor he said I could stay. My room was a whole unit - normally for six. His mates were like something out of 'Surf Nazis must die', stoned as pebbles, and I spent the first night with a chair against the door. When I went up in the morning to checkout though, both him and the Maori with the half-face tattoo were really friendly. It takes a while to get used to the Maoris, they can be fucken frightening at times.

The sandbar was working, right in front of the hostel, about eight foot, a solid lefthander but messy. They were paddling out with the river, dodging between the fishing boats coming in, a long hard paddle, but ending behind the line-up. I left it 'til the morning when it had cleaned up and around six feet, and asked where I could hire a board.

"Nah y'can use mine mate, I don't surf much now, its on the balcony." So I went out , shorts and Saigon T shirt, but through the break to the right. I hung in close, picking off the ones that were missed by the pack, because believe me they still had a hundred metres to go when they got to me. A bloke paddling back out after a long ride, shouted "Yer too far in mate!"

"Yeh" I shouted back "I'm a visitor, I'm trying to keep out the way of the pack."

"Agghh fuck that mate come out and join us, you'll catch more waves." I think I held my own Martin, didn't make a twat of myself,

but what an attitude ay! There were a lot of girls out too. A Jap girl moved into the unit next door, a bodyboarder who told me her name was Risa, so I had some company when I needed it. However, all I did was surf, read, paint, eat and sleep.

'D' Bar - Whangamata. Top place. Hard case.

I've been here for ten days, but Brian's crop still not ready for a couple of weeks so I'm going back to Auckland and then hope to do the South Island on what money I've got left. Write to y'soon. By the way, I said goodbye to the Jap.

"Risa, Risa," she said "My name is Risa!" and then it clicked. Her name was Lisa.

Catch y'later. Howie.

Standing in the queue at the food stall for bratwurst with saurkraut and mustard, $3 with a coffee, a schoolgirl asked where I'd come from.

"Ooorrggh isn't Oz choice ay?" Above, a backpacker was rapjumping (forward abseiling) down the front of the Novotel.

Walking towards us as though on a catwalk, came a six foot Maori, stunningly beautiful, ramrod back; her chin tattooed black like a goatee beard. Seeing my stare, the schoolgirl said, "She's probably royalty."

I decided to go to the cinema to see "Once were Warriors" the new film about Maoris trying to come to terms with modern life. I thought it might shed a bit of light on the people.

The cinema was Art-Deco, and entering the foyer I could have been on a Cunard liner. Hidden lighting in red, blue and green, crept out of alcoves and smothered itself across buddah, frieze and chandelier, and was mopped up by the thick, swirling carpet. Sunk back into the studded leather chairs that shouted *horsehair!* I imagined a Yank, in crisp GI threads, swirling down the stairs with an Auckland girl, floral dress flapping round her North Island tan. There was enough curtain in the auditorium to sail a velvet armada.

Holding on to the past seemed to be something the Kiwis were particularly good at. But they didn't let it bog them down. The whole of New Zealand was a museum to Art-Deco: the roads choked with the history of British motoring. Minis, Bedfords, Cortinas, shared the road with Corsairs, Snipes, Hunters and Gazelles, Oxfords and Cambridges.

But the Kiwis balanced this with modern, eco-friendly Japanese motors. New buildings were built to fit in with old; harmonise. At a club, I knew all the seventies soul records they were playing.

"Is this the sort of music you *have* to play" I asked.

"Yes mate, Rave and Techno's old hat now, even Acid-Jazz is jaded. This is the latest, it's huge." They were way up there with London.

Driving through a small village...somewhere, I saw a sign that snapped my head round.

'This week's cinema presentation is...A Clockwork Orange, by Stanley Kubrick.' I'd wanted to see this film forever, but not allowed in prim and proper England.

Back in the Auckland cinema, two old biddies were watching the most violent film showing in New Zealand, and after being *shussshhed!* by neighbours for chatting, fell to gasps of shock, tut-tuts at nasty bits and "Do they have to say that all the time?" I had a feeling that they'd come in, in 1939, and never left the cinema, unaware that a world like that could exist. It was a shocker of a film, but I felt that you could substitute the Maoris with Scousers, Geordies or Glaswegians: same story.

I went into the travel shop, got a half price bus ticket to Wellington and booked up for the West Coast Express, out of Nelson. It would finish off my money, but at least I'd be able to see some of the South Island, even if I couldn't join in with all the activities. I was along for the ride.

On the public bus down, after a short stop at smelly Rotorua, we pulled into a refreshment stop. The driver annnounced -

"Here, you can get tea or coffee, a snack or meal: there are handicrafts for sale; if you'd like a jetboat ride they're round the back or if you'd prefer a flight round Mt Ruapahue, the airplane takes off over the road there, see them waiting? We'll pick you up about half an hour up the road. !!!

As we slipped past Ruapahue on the main road I saw snow hiding in the folds of the mountain , whilst summer covered it's eyes and counted to a hundred; and I smiled quietly at the thought:

"Tea or coffee?"

"No, a flight around a mountain please."

The bus was scheduled to arrive in Wellington at 6.40pm. It arrived at 6.40pm, and Wellington had it's boots on.

The semicircle glow from the windows of the News Building was working overtime, as the rain lashed them like rice on a drum. Walking round the city I felt I was in a Horlicks advert; people rushing here and there, collars of their overcoats up to their hats against the cold and wet; past the chip-shop, The Rialto, Woolworths and the coffee-bar. I steamed into the harsh glow of a take-away, and took a maggot-bag and coffee - 99 cents; ate it in a doorway of a closed shop, while the flames of the Olympic torches decorating the balcony of the wine-bar opposite, hissed and cowered from the rain.

The clothes and packs in the dorm room sat steaming on radiators or dejected in corners. I tied my 'old' sarong to the balcony outside the window for a spin in the 'Wellington Washing machine', where it waved frantically at the heads of the buildings below.

It had gone without me in the morning I noticed, as I packed my bag and rolled down to the quay; but I resolved not to use Chantal's for anything but sleeping.

The weather changed as soon as the ferry pulled itself away from Wellington. A childish yellow sun shone down, and picked out the whites of the ropes, the deck, and people's smiles. As we crossed Cook Strait on a peaceful sea, the merest suggestion of white horses on the swell, I was staggered to see a long queue of people paying to go into the dark to watch a film.

Outside, a fledgling wind swept into our faces, gulls chased us into the Marlborough Sounds, where dolphins piloted us through the inlets and islands, past coves and bays full of secrets and surprises: Verdant canopies covered the heads of the islands and dipped into the water, land-plant...then sea-weed as the sea rose up and down.

I hadn't bothered with a Lonely Planet for New Zealand, it seemed a bit unnecessary. It would have been a good idea. Unaware of what was at Picton, the ferry harbour, or the route to Nelson, I ambled off the boat after the rush had gone. I'd figured that as I had a whole day to waste on a the eighty kilometre mile trip, I could enjoy it; and save precious dollars of course.

What I should have done was organise a ride on the boat as, by the time I got off, most of the cars were gone. There was only one road out and the traffic all came from arriving ferries. Ahead, on the way out of town were a string of solitary hitchers. The bus that I could have caught, for only 5 dollars, stopped alongside, the doors opening.

"You sure you don't want to get onboard? "

"No thanks," I replied, thinking twice, "I've got plenty of time."

"Ah well, I'll be back for the next ferry in two hours, I'll keep my eye out for you." I saw him stop at each person ahead.

Several cars stopped to tell me they couldn't pick me up, and that the rest of the traffic would be turning off left further ahead. I walked the first five K's until I got my first lift. A dung lorry. There was room for me in the cab but not the backpack.

"Throw it in the back mate, it's clean shit!"

He took me ten K's until his turn-off. I sat on the roadside, thumb out for nearly an hour until, bored and doubting the Kiwis famous hospitality to hitchers, walked on; another five K's. The next ride got me a whole ten down the road until a right fork in the road.

"You need to go down that road." she said dropping me off.

Crossing over and dumping my pack, I watched the traffic sail on down the first road. Nobody came down mine except a rabid Plymouth with the family from hell inside. They came past three times, 'eyeing me up for dinner' I thought, and kept my thumb in my pocket, praying they wouldn't stop. Armed with a can of coke from the shop opposite, I settled down on the verge, getting up for the three cars that passed. The shop closed an hour later and the owner called me over.

"I'm going your way." She did. All three K's of it, and dropped me off outside a closed Winery. She lived in the house over the road. The road stretched as far as I could see in each direction, empty. Cars came past; sometimes; so fast they shifted the verge three inches towards Nelson. I was the only thing that what wasn't getting nearer Nelson.

And then, as the sun was thinking of calling it a day, a car stopped. It was occupied by three Japanese, two boys and a girl, who didn't look old enough to drive a peddle-car. The boys in front admired their new mirrored sunglasses, lighting and relighting their Marlboro with new lighters, for the sake of it, driving round bends like old grannies. The girl in the back, next to me, seemed overcome and blushed, but pressed herself as close to me as she could get. She gave a running commentary as we drove...Tree!....River!....Lake!...Sheep! We had to stop at each thing and take their photograph with it, on each of their three cameras. They explained that this was their big holiday after school and before they started their careers. They had two weeks! Once working they would get three days a year if they were lucky.

They dropped me in Nelson, and after courteous handshakes, drove away in kangaroo hops, the girl waving out the back window, and I rang the hostel, Pete's place. "We were expecting you earlier," Pete's missus said, "I'll come down and pick you up."

By the time I arrived, and sat down in their kitchen to sign in, a red-purple glow hung outside the window. It had taken seven hours. But the Japanese girls, here learning English, cookery and etiquette, put freshly-baked scones and raspberry jam, with fresh-sweet coffee in front of me. "Would you like me to sign-in....Pete's missus?"

"Ah, you already have love, you've eaten your scones."

THE WEST COAST EXPRESS

PETE gave us a lift across Nelson in the morning to the YHA, from where the West Coast Express departed.

And there it stood. A 1961 coach, charabanc, bus; dolphins dancing, whales wailing, trees swaying all over and around it's body like the Illustrated Man. It would have been at home smoking down the A303 to Stonehenge or Glastonbury, a family of new age travellers pressing their studded noses to the windows.

The weasley Englishman and I were the first on the bus, and I watched, heart sinking, as our new companions trooped aboard. The bus filled with Anoraks, Young Christians, Hitler Youth, Librarians, Young Farmers, Mr Walking Tramping Trekker Scout, two deaf Germans; and they were all blokes. I had to spend a week with these people.

But, stopping at another hostel in the centre of town, the remaining places were filled by women, a tattooed Scouser - "Hi ya people, how's it goin' like?......sound!" and an Englishman wearing my flip-flops, the one's that disappeared from Captain Cook's washing line.

"Welcome to the West Coast Express," said the bug-eyed, bush-bearded driver, "You'll have noticed your customised seats (they each had a sheep-skin cover) and of course there's y'air-conditioning if it gets a bit hot." "How does that work?"

"Well, see the windows just above y'heads?.....y'open them."

Then we were off and managed nearly two hours before, on a steep climb, and near the summit, the bus held it's hands up in surrender. The driver, pronouncing it in a critical condition, hitched down a passing tractor going back to Nelson, shouting: "I'll see you later."

By the time he returned, the crew had gelled, barriers broken down, the bus-fool already established, only the deaf Germans still keeping to themselves and their own private and silent world.

They brought us a new bus, a much newer model,1962; only slightly more modestly decorated than the last, and we rolled down the West Coast - Westport, Greymouth, Blackball:

New-Zealand is like a child on Christmas morning, it's little arms overflowing with presents, dropping to the floor as sun, rain, sights and sounds. And each time the bus came to a halt we rushed out and scooped them up. Blowholes, pancake rocks, mirror-lakes, gargantuan Kauri trees, basking seal colonies, pounding beaches. We climbed Fox glacier with a guide, crampons and wide eyes. One of the only two advancing glaciers left on the planet, it glowed turquoise at us and barked as it trundled forwards at four feet a day. We paddled canoes slowly up a crystal river, skimmed breakneck down another in a jet boat, Ian the scouser hollering loud enough to be heard back in Bootle. Gold was panned, and beer downed; the evenings spent sitting and talking.

We had a core group, Ian, John - the new owner of my flip-flops, Desiree - a Dutch girl that I was getting very fond of, and Gunter and Holger. They were the first really funny Germans I'd ever met. They were two of the funniest men I've *ever* met, and the four of us were now 'signing' with them quite well. "Why don't the other Germans on the bus talk to you?" I asked Gunter.

"Because they are embarrassed by our handicap," he explained, miming their looks of distaste.

"They are the ones that are handicapped," I said, "They were born without compassion or humour." His eyes shone and he hugged me.

Wherever we went, Maoris treated them like long-lost chieftains, and took time out to sit and talk to them with eyes and hands, perhaps feeling an affinity they don't share with native whites.

John and I shared a room with them, and in an early morning half-light Holger was up and packing. He was rustling his plastic supermarket bags, the bane of dormitories, slamming in and out of the door to the toilet, humming to himself. There was no chance of sleeping in the din, that went on and on. Gunter joined in; possibly noisier. Then, at last, they went out, leaving a deafening silence. I was smiling now at their innocence, and hearing John, below, mutter.... "Nice one guys!" burst out laughing. The door opened, the light came on, and they jumped back into the room, hooting with their peculiar deaf laugh....

"Hoy, hoy, hoy...heyheyhey!!" They'd planned it the night before.

The trip rolled to it's finale at Queenstown. If New Zealand was Christmas, Queenstown was Santa. It huddled in a crooked elbow of Lake Wakatipu and looked up at the Remarkables above, a mountain range whose colours changed with the mood of the sun, earning them their title. Yes, it *is* a tourist trap, a ski resort, a summer resort, but unique and exciting, busy but peaceful. An amusement park.

From Queenstown you can fly; in stunt planes, strapped to skydivers, beneath silk canopies; glide under delta wings, buzz around in goggle-eyed helicopters, or fall screaming for a hundred metres with a piece of elastic tied to your leg.

You can float, drift, plummet, ride, splash, down rivers: on kayaks, boogie boards, rafts, jet boats, in the sun or shade of vertical walled canyons and gorges: or below in the hidden streams and caves, with stalactites above in place of clouds.

Personally though, I had no pocket money to go on the rides and had to watch my playmates enjoying themselves. We ripped it up for a couple of evenings, until all but a few of the crew had moved on: just a group photograph left behind. And then there was just Desiree and I. And we were close.

She decided that she'd like to come up to Dargaville with me to pick Kumaras, and ringing Brian, we'd be starting on Monday. If we could get up to Auckland for Friday evening, he'd meet us at the flat and we'd go out on the town for the night. We hitched a lift to Christchurch the first thing next morning.

*

CHRISTCHURCH was a city of two halves. The hostels were, of course, in the rough half of the city, contestants in an ugly building competition, milling around waiting for the start.

Walking into the centre though, I could have been in England as we walked down Worcester and Gloucester street, along Cambridge terrace, beside the river Avon.

The nimble fingers of the willow trees dipped in the stream that ducked under stone bridges and dribbled round green-lawned bends. It chuckled on down to the old university buildings, all weathered stone and arches, now the arts centre; and we sat out for a decidedly English evening, drinking best bitter in a fresh breeze, specks of rain in the air.

I was as far away from England as it's possible to be, but in the most English place possible.

(Slowing down now. So tired. Seen so much. A dozen sunrises. A hundred sunsets. A million trees. Said goodbye to a hundred people. I've been Thomas Cook, Livingstone, Alan Whicker, Shirley friggin' Valentine. Need to go home now. Enjoy some time at Brian's. Earn some dollars to make my way home with.)

DARGAVILLE

WE'D booked a bus ticket up to Auckland; it was too short a time to guarantee hitching there in time; and stood waiting in the hostel lobby at 5.30am. A drunken rugby fan, still looking for a last drink before bed, buzzed us like a horsefly.

"Ah, sweet as! I been t'Queenstown an all, yeh....once"

"Ah, Dargaville, I know that, good as! whatcha goin there for?"

"Kumara pickin'...hard case! Y'can't pick Kumaras, only blacks do that, you'll stick out like dog's nuts!"

*

We stopped overnight in Wellington, which had a Sou'wester on this time to try and keep out the storm that was barrelling through. It rattled and shook the timber hostel that perched up on the hill, the wind trying to fight through the weight of the rain pitching down.

And it seemed only a matter of minutes later, that we'd rocked up to Auckland, rolled around the bars for a night and were bouncing up Brian's drive to the bungalow, on the hill above the Kumara fields; almost the length of New Zealand away from Queenstown.

We started picking on the Monday morning at an outrageous time, work seemed so long ago, but it was freshcool....to start. It was a small team: Brian and Lance, the bosses, and eight pickers, a pick and mix of ages, white and Maori.

The tractors rucked up the earth along the rows, but the only way to extract all the kumaras was to grub into the soil with bare hands, knock off the clinging soil and twist then from their vines.

Straddling the row, there were only two positions with which to pick; bent from the waist down or scrabbling along on the knees. By the end of the first row my back was aching, the backs of my legs pulling. I looked at the endless rows ahead of us, heart sinking, and then across at the other fields waiting their turn, bigger than this. We'd been warned. I bent over, started filling the next bucket.

Then to get through the tedium and the pain, you started giving yourself targets. 'I can get to the end of this row.' 'Only two more rows until smokoe, then I can straighten the back, have a drink.' 'If I pick the last twenty metres fast, I can stand up straight for a minute before the others catch up and we start the next row.' 'I can keep going for another hour and then we can knock it on the head 'til tomorrow.'

For Desiree and I it was a matter of principle; we wanted to keep up with the others who'd done it before, and we got better. I could keep up okay, Desiree was knocking us all into a cocked hat.

I stood up in the middle of a row, bucket full, and saw Kim, a dread-locked Maori ahead of me, watching Des pull away from him. He was shaking his head and turning, asked me "How does she do it!?"

"It's all the tulips she picks at home" I shouted..."Ay Cloggie!"

Between rows and breaks though, we started to get to know our fellow pickers. New ones came along; two lads from Somerset, one baby-pink, a day out of England, the other on his second visit; Billy, an ageing and huge Maori with emphesemia, whose breath wheezed and farted out like an old steam train, and who we expected to keel over at any time; an Englishgirl, all prissy, who lagged behind and found every excuse not to keep up; we called her Dolly Daydream. A team of Maoris fron another farm turned up on their day off. All young, they were rapid, and we called their leader Sam Speed. Even Des trailed in his wake. At times it was like picking with L.L.Cool.J, Cypress Hill and a gang of Yardies from Trenchtown.

But they had time for us and asked questions about our travels. Most hadn't even been to South Island. "Ah it's too cold down there brah!"

"I've heard of Holland" they'd say "That's Amsterdam isn't it...yeh I want to go there man...get some real good smoke.

"So you pick tulips then Des?"

"No, I work at a ski-resort on Mount Edam,"...."Choice!"

"I work on the chair-lifts in the winter...and for a summer job I am employed sticking my finger in Dykes"... "Hard case!"

'Just one more row and then it's the weekend.'

The Hardings had ben at Dargaville from it's conception and there was even a Harding Park which wrapped itself around the base of the hill topped by a Maori 'pa' site, ancient and sacred; and the Dargaville museum. In front of the museum sprung the masts of The Rainbow Warrior, sunk by the French, and they cast their spindly shadows over the family cemetery.

They also had a 'batch' (a beach house) on Bayley's Beach, ten K's to the north, tucked in the lee of a shrubbed bowl above the beach, with a jumble of others.

Brian called in his dog...Sam. Still really a puppy, he was a pig-hunting dog and could clear my head with a leap already. Hunting wild-pigs is still a big thing all over New Zealand, dangerous, and it takes two dogs to pull one down. Sam was still learning to find them, and so, a domestic pig was allowed to roam the farm at will. It's name was 'Practice'. Sam didn't know what to do when he found it, his parents would have show him that. (Brian wrote to me later "Sam got his first pig recently with the help of his father, and then gave his dad a good hiding!")

But we were off to Bayleys, one of the three access points onto a 110 Km beach. Driving there in the ute, Sam on the flatbed like a Pointer, ears flapping in the wind, I watched the countryside roll past, and it seemed so much like Sussex or Shropshire, apart from the houses.

They weren't lichened stone or mellowed-brick, folding themselves into the ground, but stood up straight, in dazzling white ship-lap. They had two eyes and a tall mouth, like a child's painting, and over-fat cows and wooly-bully sheep were scattered around the yo-yo hills, smiling... *mooos* and *baaaahs* floating in speech bubbles above their heads.

Like Fraser Island, the beach was also the road, and we drove along it looking for signs of the fish, brown patches of plankton that they'd be feeding on. But you could see the fish themselves cruising in the waves; mullet, like submarines in a cold-war scramble. It was fishing the way it should be done.

Carrying a pole each, holding a rolled 100 metre net, we pushed out into the waves sometimes bobbing over them, sometimes below, then creeping behind the shoal, unfurled it to full length and *pull pull pulled* it into the beach, closing the net around them like an old lady's drawstring purse. The mullet shouted to his friends 'over here!' and they rushed over and jumped into the net. We pulled them out of the sea in sixes and sevens, until tying them up with rushes, we had a Huckleberry-Finn string of fish. The scales flicked off with a mussel shell, golden roe spilled onto the sand, and we washed them in the sea and took them up to the 'batch'.

Cooked fresh under the grill, we washed then down with cold beers and basked in the sun, watching the sea go about it's business.

A whale cruised across in front, and spying only surfers, gave the signal for the rest of the school to cross. I borrowed a bodyboard from another batch, joined the line-up, and played like a fool in the waves.

I spent the rest of the afternoon drinking in sun and beer and friend-ship and I knew that I wanted to finish my life on a beach, in a hut, and sit facing the sea; watching the sun rise, and the sun set, and every minute in-between. And I'd know that if I dipped my toes in the sea, I'd be joined clear round the world by it, to Manly, Sunset, China, and Padangbai beaches. Looking behind, I'd want to see a familiar road that, turning the corner, becomes a strange road going nowhere, in case the urge to go walkabout came upon me.

Heading back, the dying sun turned the trees blue and purple, the sky green, and then as my eyelids drooped with happy tiredness, the sunset gathered behind and pushed us back to Dargaville with red hands.

*

'Just a couple of more bucketfuls and I'll be at the end of the row.'

'One more row and it's smokoe and I can put my arms in the water-trough.'

The constant pulling at soil and twisting the kumaras from the vines had buggered my arms. From wrist to elbow they looked as though they'd been blown up with a bicycle pump. I had tendinitis and could hardly move my fingers. Soaking them in the cold water kept me going for short periods, but my days were numbered. 'Stop, or do some real damage.' said the Doctor.

So, I had to sit up at the bungalow and watch them in the fields below, crawling up and down the rows, slowly turning green strips brown. And at the end of the day, Desiree would trudge up the hill hot and tired and dirty, and try and make me feel better. But I was doing nothing; earning no money. We were still going out to the pubs, parties, cricket matches, family gatherings and my finances were seriously low.

Then I got a letter one day, brought over from the 'big-house' and I was already confused. I opened it as I watched Sam twitching in his sleep, dreaming of pigs. It was from Chantal, still chundering around India and Nepal. She took me trekking in the Himalayas, showed me things she'd seen, made me feel that I was there as well. And then she turned my world over....again.

"....in the meantime I'm back from the group trek and have spent seven days trekking on my own...It's nice to stop and sit when and where you want....I did a lot of thinking...what I wrote to you before. I really want to see you again. To be honest I wish this moment was right now. I miss you so much. I'm going home at the end of March and will let you know when and where to find me...if you want to!

Take care. Chantal."

214

She was already home. Things were conspiring against me. I wanted to go home. I felt guilty, as Desiree and I were very close, but we'd made no promises together, no plans.

It was another weekend. Brian, Des and I took a trip up to the far north, to Cape Reinga. We left early, and with Sam and some bags of kumaras in the back, sped out of Dargaville up the Western route, the mist still settled like an eiderdown on the nodding heads of village cottages, and sheep wriggled around the fatback hills, like maggots on a fly-blown sheep..

We stopped off after a few hours in a small town and stocked up with beer from a tin-shack brewery, a most excellent brew, and it fuelled us into Waipoua Forest the home of the mighty Kauri tree.

Brian stopped off to see 'Tanemahuta' the tallest kauri of all. Much of travelling seemed to be concerned with collecting these 'freaks' of nature, or construction. 'The oldest Banyan tree' 'The highest waterfall' 'Largest temple' 'Oldest building'

In Hoi-An I visited the ancient Chinese house, and whilst being guided by a lovely, bashful girl I asked..."How old is it?"

"250 years!!" she exclaimed. "Ah..it's quite new then."

"No!!...Ancient!!" she exclaimed. Teasing, but truthful I told her...

"No, that is quite new. We have houses in England 500 years old, and some older!" I didn't carry on with it as she looked close to tears...

"But they're not as beautiful as this." Her smile returned.

Tanemahuta wasn't the oldest, nor the biggest. For me, better is a clump of smaller, ordinary ones, ringing a crystal pool where ferns fan the ground, birds shoot through the sunrays like exploding fireworks, and moths spiral like catherine-wheels.

We crept up the switchback road over the hills; unmetalled, it reminded me of Vietnam. I was seeing other countries everywhere in New Zealand, it was that sort of place. Unique.

Stopping off in Opononi for a lunchtime drink we were still there at closing time. We'd befriended a gang of Maoris, drank, played pool.

"I know Holland... Amsterdam! I'm going there one day."

Brian gave the kumaras to the landlord.

By the end of the night they were arguing about whose house we were staying in, and we slipped out to save embarrassment. We shot off to the next town to a small motel that Brian knew, as the rain was so heavy it was like being underwater, and all four of us couldn't sleep in the cab. (Sam) We didn't really have the money for it, and they charged per person, so as Brian woke the owner and got her to open a room, we hid in the ute.

"Yeh, s'only me," Brian said "Nobody else....just one" and she went back to bed. We crept in under darkness and sat on the floor for a few more beers. Conked out.

In the morning, the office door opposite, it was impossible to leave without being seen. Des and I strolled out as Brian knocked the office door.

"I thought you said you were on yer own. You were bloody noisy!"

"Ah yeh...I must have been confused." The worst excuse I've ever heard.

"I'll only charge for a couple." she said, and Brian gave her twenty five dollars.

" Here, get y'selves some breakfast.' she said handing ten back.

"Ah, thenks," Brian said through his hangover "Next time I come through I'll bring y'some kumaras."

"Make sure you do!"

We carried on up to Cape Reinga, the Northernmost tip of New Zealand, walked the deserted beach, it's sand blowing across in wisps like the sahara. We stood on the tip looking at the point where the Tasman Sea meets the Pacific Ocean, and there was a straight line where the two blues of the different seas met. It looked as though Moses had just disappeared into the distance.

Tripping down to the perfect little beach at the base, we were met on the way back up by a park ranger.

"I have to shoot your dog." he said. "Pardon?... we said in unison."

"Didn't you see the sign - No Dogs Beyond the fence?" We hadn't.

"That is a 'pa' site down there, you've desecrated it with the dog, and by rights I must shoot it."

By playing ignorant tourists, we persuaded him against it.

I think Brian would probably have shot him if he'd tried.

Later, I asked Brian about the Maori situation. They were occupying a town square to the south at the time, refusing right of entry to any whites. The government were at a total loss as to what to do. It was a 'pa' site, and much like the Aboriginies, they had these everywhere in New Zealand, so in their eyes they owned everything.

"A lot of your friends are Maoris, Brian, and I've heard it from the more militant locals that they'd be up to take your land back when the uprising comes."

"That's probably true, but if they come up, m'brothers and I will be there with our guns. It may have been theirs once but we've been here for a hundred and fifty years, and done something with it. Until it happens though, we'll be mates. Why worry?....dogs worry, and we shoot them."

I managed a couple of more fields when we got back, as my arms had rested, but the time was running out faster than the money. It had been raining steadily for a while so picking kumaras was out. There was however, a 'squash' crop, semi-submerged, that could be rescued.

We spent our last day, tramping down the foliage, cutting the vines and heaving them into the trailer, until the tropical heat faded into a chill evening wind and darkness came down. It was as soul-destroying and tiring as the kumaras and I was beat. And writing this, I realise that I almost ran out of Dargaville at a trot to get away from that bastard picking, and resolve to go back and enjoy it, at a more leisurely pace.

We got a lift down to Auckland with Brian's sister and then we were back in the little flat. Just the two of us. I put my flight back so I could spend another day with Des, and we enjoyed each other, quietly.

Sitting outside on the verandah on the last evening, Des in the bath, I tipped philosophy from my beer bottle.

A trip has a length, starting before you leave - in planning and longing, and runs out before you come home. Oppositely a trip can carry on long after you've stopped moving.

John Steinbeck wrote: *"A man in his middle years travelled to Honolulu and back, and that journey continued for the rest of his life. We would watch him in his rocking chair on his front porch, his eyes squinted, half-closed, endlessly travelling to Honolulu."*

I knew now that I would ride again along the Vietnam dirt-track, often stroll around Hanoi in my somnambulations, rock back and forth on a bristled jumbo head through wet hills, Chantal at my back.

My journey ended right there in Auckland, the city of sails. The wind blown out of the trip, leaving me becalmed, limp. I tried to puff it up, blow some life back in it's lungs. But no, it was dead and gone, and the irony was, I was only half-way round the world.

I heard Des tinkering in the kitchen, fresh from the shower, and I asked myself...What have I learned from this trip?

"Do you want a beer Howie?" Des shouted through the flyscreen.

"Madness not to!" I replied, and thinking of her, decided.

The two most important things I'd learned were to say Hello and Goodbye. I'd learned to approach new things, and places, and people, walk straight up to them, look them in the eye and say 'Hello...what are you? and dare them not to reply. Otherwise you stay ignorant and alone.

And there are no 'Good-byes'. If I watched a boat disappearing over the horizon, there would be people on the other side seeing it appear, and they would be saying hello. So, when Des plonked my beer on the table and put her arms round me, I smiled. I loved her...and Chantal...and Hilde, and I knew we'd be saying hello again...soon.

I left the beer, and we went to bed.

I flew out of Auckland the next morning.

*

NORTH SHORE, HAWAII

HAWAII was the USA, and I'd had a job getting into the land of opportunity before. The immigration official was moon-faced, yellow parchment skin, eyes boring through my papers; bored.

"Do you have a visa?"

"No, I'm English." His eyelids lifted.

"You've been travelling through Asia!"

"Yes." They lifted some more.

"How much money do you have?"

"350 New Zealand dollars."

"But you say here you are staying for a month!" His boring little face was alight. He knew it wasn't enough.

"I'm not staying that long now." His eyelids dropped like a venetian blind with the cord cut, and his voice and head lowered with them.

"Where's your outward ticket?" the top of his threadbare head said.

"It's here." I said, sticking my tongue out and crossing my eyes as I took it from my file. I slapped it on the table and shrugged at the rest of the queue. They had to let me in now, I had an escape route.

"Your flight from New York to london was last Thursday."

My eyes focussed on the little square on the ticket that said 5th April, not...May. My mind went screaming into a foxhole. Although my mind stuttered, my tongue didn't. Taking a leaf from Big Johnny's phrase-book, I let out a long *"aaauuuuuuugghhhh..."* and then "I have to change that while I am here, it's a variable ticket." A what!?

He flipped my papers and tickets, occasionally looking at me with disdain. I effected the face of a jovial English Parson, albeit with sweat blinding my eyes, and my mind registering quietly that I had 350 dollars and no ticket home.

His head sighed with scorn and he dismissed me as a twat, with a hefty stamp in my passport. like a good Englishman, I said thank-you and sauntered through customs blindly and undetained, with a Kumara in my pack: a crime second only to smuggling cocaine, or strolling through JFK airport with John F's head in you hand luggage.

It was 3am, I was three sheets to the wind and I hadn't had a drink. I grabbed the first hostel-tout to the north shore, and smoked four cigarettes while I waited for the minibus to fill; each one only heightening my awareness that I was up shitcreek without a paddle. I went over all the things I wished I'd said to the immigration man, and some of them were incredibly cutting and clever. But you can never think of them at the time ay?

The billowing base of the heavy, low clouds glowed orange from the Waikiki below.

"Thee that glow Brah...path the airport," the driver lisped "thats one of the biggeth tourith traps in the world. It'th chocker. You're then-thibly heading for the North Thore brah!"

"Choith!" I said.

Carried along by disbelief at my stupidity, and the hostel bus, I arrived at plantation village as dawn got up and shook her tousled hair. Even the cockerels' chorus failed to keep me awake, though lord knows they tried hard enough

I woke mid-morning and groaned at my situation. I didn't have enough money to get across America as I'd planned, unless I stopped and worked. I didn't want to stop in America at all. I groaned again.

But there again, I was on North Shore, Oahu, and it would have been unthinkable to fly past the hallowed ground, my mecca, the holy grail. Even as a piss-poor surfer I'd drooled over the photos, shivered over the horror stories of those brave or foolhardy enough to take on the giants that roll in.

Hawaii is like a fat green spider in the middle of it's web. From anywhere on it's spokes, a pressure system can develop like a thrashing fly, the shockwaves travelling into the centre.

These arrive like charging bulls on Oahu, and the biggest and strongest and most frenzied, rage onto the North Shore every winter.

Lying in my bed, 400 metres to my left was Waimea Bay, 800 metres to the right - Sunset pipeline; the two most famous waves in the world. In Peru, is the longest rideable wave in the world.. At Jefferys Bay, South Africa, the waves barrel in with the relentlessness of a Zulu army, but at Waimea they thunder in ten metres high and wipeouts require lungs like hot water bottles, an allegiance with the lord or a helicopter rescue, if the waves allow you to the surface. Sunset, though not always as big, has the added attraction of pushing you into coral caves, never to come out.

Plantation Village was nicknamed Foo's Zoo, after Mark Foo, a local, a world champion and a legend, who spent a lot of time there and was a regular on 'big' Waimea. He died when I was in Australia, surfing Mavericks - a huge Californian wave. A year later, to the day, Donnie Solomon, a Californian, drowned surfing Waimea.

Hawaiians measured their waves from the back, so a five feet wave could have an eight feet face. And to me they would have felt like ten.

"Waimea's flat, it needs a storm to crank it up" they said. "Sunset's flat, or maybe a foot" they said, so I decided to go and sit and try to imagine what it looked like with waves. There were a dozen surfers out, bobbing up and down on a swell as gnarly as Littlehampton. I wondered why.

Rummaging through my pack for a book, I took my eyes off the surf for ten seconds and looking up, a solid six foot wave was peeling left and right, a surfer on each shoulder. Behind it the second of the set was still jacking up, two surfers windmilling their arms to catch the pouting lip, the rest duckdiving to escape to the back. I'd never seen waves appear from nowhere before and now I understood the magic of Hawaii. Sunset could pull rabbits from a hat, and the rabbits had teeth.

Late takeoffs were pitched over the falls and slammed into the sand, late pullouts tumbled onto dry rock as the wash sucked back. I was watching a feeble Pipeline, and it was scary. At least I'd seen it, but I had to go.

I knew that, bad as I was at it, I *was* a surfer. However grungy we look , we are true romantics, looking for perfection, eyes glazing over at the shape or colour of a wave. Surfers are tuned in to the feel of the water, the wind, the rush of the ride. Often I would hear, on the beach after a session, or in a silence round a fire -

"Look at the stars"..."I love sitting in the ocean when the sun goes down"..."the feel of rain when I'm out there"..."being in the surf when dawn arrives"..."the seals in the lineup"

It's hard to get closer to life than to tie a board to your leg and throw yourself into the elements, where all your senses are coaxed and bullied at the same time; and the tiredness you feel after a good session comes in a box marked 'post-orgasm'.

As we drove up to the airport before dawn, we passed Waimea Bay, "It'th going to be huge brah!" said the driver, looking out to the darkness. I knew; I could hear it pumping up. I tried to block the sound out.

Missed it. I was always missing the surf.

*

HOME

As the plane rolled along the tarmac to it's parking space, I could see I was in Los Angeles. The aircraft, in contrast to the sleek silver, white, clean liveries of Europe, were dressed like gaudy circus performers.

Here was one whose logo was a silhouette of Bob Marley, Jamiroquoi or an Eskimo; there - a chocolate and orange design - a flying iced lolly; and Nevada Airways looked like the flier for a Rave club.

The hostel tout was pretending to be one. They didn't have a bus. I was taken way across the car-park to her boyfriend's clapped out wreck of a car. She had to pay him to take me to the hostel.

It was a few rooms above a launderette playing at being a hostel. It was the most crowded since Chungking. I had seventeen in my small room, they were stacked like a wine-rack, and the solitary toilet groaned in the corner.

'Right on the world-famous Venice Beach', the hostel flier said. I took a walk along the beach, passing a film crew filming beach-babes. They put on their false smiles and tans over their false tits, some of them decidedly out of whack, and shivered with cold when the camera turned it's beady eye away. Lines of wannabees took notes on the sidelines, their eyes flitting frequently to the Hollywood sign on the hill.

Venice was a travesty, humans with false muscles, dogs dressed as humans, earthlings on another planet, all ignoring where they really were because the sun was shining .

I went back the next day, a wet Sunday, and saw Venice in all it's glory. A few desperate stallholders had still turned out, in the hope that the sun and a few customers may show. That left me, drug-addicts, pushers and tramps on the strip. Whichever direction I looked, a police patrol car was crawling, four cops in each.

The escape from the squalor was Hollywood or Paramount studios, where you could believe you were somewhere else; the shopping- malls where rubbish is sold at a fairy-tale price; and the homes of the 'Stars' where you can believe there's no justice in the world.

L.A. sucks. I jumped on the first bus I could get down to San Diego.

I'd given up the idea of driving across America long ago and there was no way I was going to work in America. Time to call Uncle Peter.

They were going to send enough for an internal flight across, my ticket had been renewed by the airline for a small fee, I had a couple of days to spare. I wandered the streets, drank some beers, had the worst haircut since leaving home, went to The Blue-Note club.

The hostel did a weekly trip into Mexico...just. It was a night-out in Tijuana, and basically a cheap piss-up, but I thought - one last party before I go home. They gave us all the warnings; stick together; keep your passport safe; if the police hit you, say thank you; don't wander up side-streets.

"So, where is your passport?" asked the officer at the border.
"It was stolen from me in The Red Square club."
"You will have to stay in Mexico and go to your Consulate."

Neither the Aussie nor myself had much money, and now, no passports. He was cursing and stomping, holding his head in his hands, he may as well, he was off his head anyway. 'Great' I thought, I get to spend a few days in Mexico trying to arrange a new passport, with a demented bludger. We sat on the floor and tried to work our way through it, I didn't have the clearest of heads myself.

I went back to the desk; explained again, gave him my passport number which I knew off-by-heart.

"I couldn't let my mother in without papers" he said, "You're here to stay, go and find a hotel."

"We don't have enough money, we'll have to sleep here on the floor."

He shrugged.

We slept against the wall for a while, fitfully, and each time I woke up I tried him again. And then as the faint light of an American dawn crept into the lobby and through the turnstiles, I noticed that there was a new guard. I explained again.

"You are English and he is Australian?"...."Yes." He didn't look very happy, looked down at his papers, and pointing at a small alleyway leading to a door, mumbled "Go through there." I hesitated...

"GO!!!" he shouted, and I grabbed the Aussie.

"Where we going man?" he asked, as we climbed over a barrier...

"I don't know." I replied, looking over to the guard.

"NOWWWW!!!" he screamed.

I pushed the door open, looked out into the open air...of America.

"Move man!" I said, "we're out... in."

"You had your passport stolen in Tijuana Mr Cobb?..."Yes" and I could hear her thinking 'not another one'. In my hand was the group photo of us all in the club, shouting at the camera, one of the waiters, his arm round my shoulders, hand just above my buttoned pocket with the passport in.
"So where are you now?"...."San Diego."
"No, where are you right now?...."San Diego."
"You can't be in America if you lost your passport in Mexico."
"They let us in."
"They don't let *anybody* in without a passport."
"They did!"
"They don't!!...oh just apply for an emergency one when you get to New York, stop bothering me."

So I went out with a bang, but at least it wasn't the banging of prison doors.

I hopped over to New York for a pleasant week with Uncle Peter; skipped across the Atlantic to England, which from the air looked like England; and jumped from the last step of the airplane steps to the tarmac.
Home......Shit yeh!

*